In this book Bradley Klein draws upon recent debates in International Relations theory to raise important questions about the nature of Strategic Studies. He argues that postmodern critiques of realism and neorealism open up opportunities for new ways of thinking about nuclear deterrence. In clear and uncluttered language, he explores the links between modernity, state-building and strategic violence, and argues that American foreign policy, and NATO, undertook a set of dynamic political practices intended to make and remake world order in the image of Western identity. Klein warns against too facile a celebration of the end of the Cold War, concluding that it is even more imperative today to appreciate the scope and power of the Western strategic project. The book will be of interest to students of International Relations theory, Strategic Studies, Peace Studies, and US foreign policy.

STRATEGIC STUDIES AND WORLD ORDER

CAMBRIDGE STUDIES IN INTERNATIONAL RELATIONS

34 BRADLEY S. KLEIN
Strategic Studies and world order

33 T. V. PAUL
Asymmetric conflicts: war initiation by weaker powers

32 CHRISTINE SYLVESTER
Feminist theory and international relations in a postmodern era

31 PETER J. SCHRAEDER
United States foreign policy toward Africa
Incrementalism, crisis and change

30 GRAHAM SPINARDI
From Polaris to Trident: the development of US Fleet ballistic
missile technology

29 DAVID A. WELCH
Justice and the genesis of war

28 RUSSELL J. LENG
Interstate crisis behavior, 1816–1980: realism versus reciprocity

27 JOHN A. VASQUEZ
The war puzzle

26 STEPHEN GILL (ed.)
Gramsci, historical materialism and international relations

25 MIKE BOWKER and ROBIN BROWN (eds.)
From Cold War to collapse: theory and world politics in the 1980s

24 R. B. J. WALKER
Inside/outside: international relations as political theory

23 EDWARD REISS
The Strategic Defense Initiative

22 KEITH KRAUSE
Arms and the state: patterns of military production and trade

21 ROGER BUCKLEY
US–Japan alliance diplomacy 1945–1990

20 JAMES N. ROSENAU and ERNST-OTTO CZEMPIEL (eds.)
Governance without government: order and change in world politics

19 MICHAEL NICHOLSON
Rationality and the analysis of international conflict

Series list continues after index

STRATEGIC STUDIES AND WORLD ORDER

BRADLEY S. KLEIN

Trinity College, Hartford, Connecticut

CAMBRIDGE
UNIVERSITY PRESS

Published by the Press Syndicate of the University of Cambridge
The Pitt Building, Trumpington Street, Cambridge CB2 1RP
40 West 20th Street, New York, NY 10011-4211, USA
10 Stamford Road, Oakleigh, Melbourne 3166, Australia

First published 1994

Printed in Great Britain at the University Press, Cambridge

A catalogue record for this book is available from the British Library

Library of Congress cataloguing in publication data
Klein, Bradley S.
Strategic studies and world order / Bradley S. Klein.
    p.   cm. – (Cambridge studies in international relations)
Includes bibliographical references and index.
ISBN 0 521 37034 5 (hard). – 0 521 46644 X (pbk.)
1. National security.   2. National security – United States.
3. North Atlantic Treaty Organization.
4. World politics – 1989–
I. Title.   II. Series.
UA10.2K58   1994
355'.03–dc20   93–36182   CIP

ISBN 0 521 37034 5 hardback
ISBN 0 521 46644 X paperback

CONTENTS

Preface   *page* ix

1 INTRODUCTION   1

2 THE POLITICS OF STRATEGIC STUDIES   13
Violence and world order   14
The state of Strategic Studies   16
Toward theoretical critique   23
Opportunities   31

3 WHAT NUCLEAR REVOLUTION?   39
From "fortuna" to "friction"   39
Classical principles   47
Total war and the triumph of aerial offense   53
The nuclear revolution   59
The maximalist response   63
The uneasy synthesis   74

4 MILLENNIAL LIBERALISM AND DUAL
  MILITARIZATION   81
American power projection   83
The violence of liberal modernization   89

5 DETERRENCE AS A SOCIAL PRACTICE   106
The promise of technological salvation   109
A text on the world   112
The nuclear alliance   118

6 THE WEST OF ALL POSSIBLE WORLDS   123
The "celebratory" enterprise   124
Gorbachev as a critical strategic theorist   130
What it might really mean to end the Cold War   133

Notes	141
Bibliography	169
Index	189

PREFACE

Thanks are due to my editors, John Haslam, Michael Holdsworth and Steve Smith, for their considerable patience, and to Marcia Carlson for the index. For their help in various incarnations of arguments over the years, I am also grateful to Richard K. Ashley, William Connolly, James Der Derian, Mick Dillon, Jean Elshtain, Jim George, Stephen Gill, Marvin Koff, Allan Krass, Ekkehart Krippendorff, Chris Kruegler, Jane Nadel-Klein, H.L. Nieburg, Stephen J. Rosow, Ahmed Samatar, Michael Shapiro, Christine Sylvester, Frank Unger, R.B.J. Walker, Alex Wendt and Michael Williams. David Campbell's extensive commentary on what I thought was a completed draft proved indispensable.

Institutional support was provided by the German Academic Exchange Service (DAAD), the Peace Research Centre and the Department of International Relations of the Australian National University, and the Program on Nonviolent Sanctions at Harvard University's Center for International Affairs. Trinity College, Hartford, facilitated my getting the manuscript ready for publication.

A section of Chapter 2 was first published in *Millennium*. Chapter 4 incorporates material that first appeared in an article co-authored with Frank Unger in *Militärregime und Entwicklungspolitik*, edited by Reiner Steinweg and published by Suhrkamp, Germany. Chapter 5 combines and elaborates various texts first published in *International Studies Quarterly*, *Alternatives*, and in an occasional paper by the Center on Violence and Human Survival at New York City's John Jay College of Criminal Justice.

A disclaimer is in order. To the extent that the following chapters appear unduly centered on the Western (or Atlantic) community, this is a deliberate analytical tactic rather than the product of some misguided ethnocentrism or Occidentalism. The many divergent strands of strategic thought emanating from regions beyond the centers of global power deserve serious treatment in their own right, as much for their originality and dissidence as for their attempts to coopt or conform to dominant modes of discourse. But such a worthy undertaking has proven impossible here. Instead, I concentrate on an internal exploration of the Western strategic experience, and am especially concerned to see how the realist presentation of Strategic Studies veils the inherent uncertainty and contestability of modernist political–military state practices.

Appreciation goes to Terry and Callie, each of whom at times found a comfortable niche under my desk while I was pounding away at the keyboard; and to Thunder and Misty, for their uncanny ability in positioning themselves so they could keep a watchful eye on just about everything.

This book is dedicated to my wife, Jane, and to Cory-Ellen, our daughter, who have given me all the reason in the world for writing about peace.

1 INTRODUCTION

This book has its origins in the realization some years ago that the two fields in which I was most interested, social theory and strategic policy, seemed, in terms of the prevailing literature administered to graduate students at that time, to have little directly to say to one another.

Social theory was essentially occupied with issues of domestic policy – democracy, economic growth, theories of the state, and political legitimacy. Moreover, the range of concerns was largely confined to the so-called advanced industrial states, usually capitalist, but occasionally, socialist as well. The presumption was that the trajectory of Western culture had delivered most of the interesting questions to be addressed by apologists and critics of modernity. The pathologies usually attributed to these social orders were largely confined to issues seen as "internal," so that domestic concerns were granted priority while international dimensions were relegated to other fields and neglected by social theorists themselves. The tradition of post-Marxist critical theory, from the Frankfurt School to Habermas, and including such French structuralists as Poulantzas and Althusser, was particularly egregious in its neglect of transnational issues. But post-Weberians, following the lead set by Parsons, were equally negligent in their oversight of global, transnational dimensions to problems besetting advanced industrial Western societies. Concerns with international trade and security, to say nothing of imperialism and militarization, were curiously left out of the debate. There was, in particular, no attempt to address the questions of war and peace so central to International Relations.[1]

Strategic Studies, meanwhile, was entirely taken up with questions of military balance and the relations between conventional and nuclear weaponry. Neither contemporary social theory nor the grand narrative tradition of Western political thought was deemed to have much relevance to the enduring concerns of political–military strategy. One could certainly find a selective reading of certain classical thinkers – Thucydides, St. Augustine, Machiavelli, Hobbes, Rousseau, Hegel,

1

Weber – in the works of E.H. Carr and Hans Morgenthau. But much of this appropriation was *ex post facto*, imposed retroactively upon thinkers whose political and philosophical concerns were richer and far more intellectually adventurous than as presented to a postwar American audience in terms of the divide between "idealism" and "realism."

What passed for "theory" among scholars of International Relations was largely a collection of totalizing efforts by postwar behavioralists concerned to isolate various levels of analysis and to reduce political dynamics to static hypotheses and predictions.[2] From the standpoint of sheer style, most of this was clumsily written. Worse yet, it tended to be narrow in terms of the range of its concerns and of the intellectual horizons it embraced. How else to make sense of the claim, so widespread after Hiroshima, of a "nuclear revolution," as if the concept of revolution could be explained in terms of a technological change in weapons systems. To be sure, a European realist tradition was more sensitive to theoretical discourse in a classical idiom than were US practitioners of International Relations. This is precisely what made the likes of Friedrich Meinecke and Raymond Aron so appealing to International Relations students – as contributors to what Robert Gilpin has called "the richness of the tradition."[3]

The philosophical and sociological dimensions of classical *Realpolitik* gradually have imperceptibly given way to narrower, more determined commitments to an abstraction called "The State." Hypostatizing this entity of sovereign authority had been an element of European thought dating back to Bodin. And Hegel's whole philosophical system is given life by the idea of the state as the embodiment, indeed, the apotheosis, of an ethical teleology.

What is interesting in terms of the development of International Relations as a discipline is that postwar thinkers, while consciously eschewing reference to such elusive philosophical constructs, nonetheless retained commitment to a curiously reified entity, the state, which they insisted had some originary existence as the source of all action in world affairs. These thinkers were for the most part wedded to a conception of the state that, while heavily relied upon and reiterated, was annoyingly underspecified in its scope and historical character. Thinking about the state seemed to be stuck in a time-warp, as if a model derived from eighteenth-century mercantilism could render adequate service in an era of globalized armaments and transnational exchange relations.[4] Thus, notions of "the national interest" and "national security" enjoyed a widespread circulation precisely as the welfare of modern societies was thoroughly dependent upon the

2

resources derived from beyond national borders. Yet there was precious little conceptual space for understanding such relationships.

In the 1970s, attempts were made to elaborate the foundational conceptual framework of academic International Relations through a generous appropriation of certain sociological traditions of thought. Functionalist sociology began to inform writings on balance of power politics and the structural character of the international system. Rational-choice theory, micro-economic analysis and the organizational approach to decision-making also contributed to the development of both foreign policy and international political economy as articulated within a reconstructed realist frame. This came to be called, variously, neorealism or structural realism, and there can be no doubt that these insights did much to alter the character of International Relations research.[5]

In refashioning International Relations, however, these "state of the art" debates within International Political Economy relegated classical and enduring questions of strategy, war and peace to a back seat. It seems that military force had for too long enjoyed undue attention at the hands of classical realism, and that modernist perspectives were now needed to overcome that debility by concentrating instead on issues of interdependence, economic bargaining, regimes and liberal hegemony.[6]

Yet questions of war and peace are too important to leave to students of Strategic Studies. Or, to put it another way, insights from social and political theory can help us enhance our appreciation of such crucial constructs as "the balance of power," "the states system," "alliances," "security" and "deterrence." Each of these is, after all, a social practice, not a primordial given, and has a history and a place in the making of the international system. In this sense, the basic point of *Strategic Studies and World Order* is to locate these practices in a generative account of the modern world, to see, in other words, how the organization of violence has helped produce the subject matter that presents itself to scholars of global politics. In this way, recent concerns about nuclear strategy, and contemporary concerns about war and peace, can become historicized and seen as part of ongoing political debates about the nature and evolution of world order.

The impetus for this critique derives from a debate about the basic categories of International Political Economy. For soon after neorealism began incorporating sociological and economic perspectives, a more critical orientation developed challenging the very terms of the discipline. Called the "Third Debate" (as a successor to earlier controversies concerning idealism–realism and realism–neorealism), this literature has raised fundamentaily critical questions concerning the whole discourse of International Relations.[7] And as the following chapters elaborate, such a critical perspective makes it possible to re-examine enduring assumptions about the character of war, peace and political–military strategy.

Chapter 2 explores the strengths and limits of contemporary Strategic Studies. The concern here is to elaborate an influential perspective on world order, according to which a formally anarchic condition of a system of sovereign states provides the ineluctable backdrop for the security dilemmas of its constituent units.

Chapter 3 casts a critical eye at contemporary claims of a "nuclear revolution" and reinterprets deterrence in terms of its place in the dynamics of contemporary world order. Along the way, I historicize the evolution of Strategic Studies. My focus here is on the transition from the pre-nuclear to the nuclear world, and on how modern strategic practices became coupled with the establishment of military representations of global space and political identity.

Chapters 4 and 5 explore the decisive postwar shift from "war" to "deterrence," or from "Strategic Studies" to "International Security." Here I examine in detail the relationship between extended nuclear deterrence and strategies of industrial development and modernization throughout the Western world and throughout much of the Third World – undertaken by the United States and the Western alliance in ways that are obscured when presented through the analytical lens offered by Strategic Studies. Two crucial arguments are made here, the first concerning the link between militarization and modernization, the second examining the nature of deterrence as a globalized social practice.

The final chapter offers as much a summary conclusion as a prospectus on thinking about the future. It is notoriously difficult to speculate on what the coming millennium – or decade, for that matter – will look like. It is more helpful, I believe, to dispatch cautionary notes about the analytical approaches available to those who would address the contours of an emerging world order. Thus the concern here is less with the architecture of global politics than it is with, more simply, the analytical practices by which any world order can be understood. In particular, I distinguish two forms of speaking about "the end of the Cold War:" the one a self-congratulatory account of Western strategy; the other a more critical recasting of the basic categories of International Relations now that certain essential structures have exhausted themselves politically. What is most interesting about "the end of the Cold War," I argue, is that despite the rhetorical excesses of the West having "won," the material infrastructure of armaments and nuclear weapons remains very much in place. Ironically, however, the foreign policy establishment has quickly – all too quickly – moved beyond these issues in its attempts to shape a new global architecture. Having paid too much attention to weapons for decades, there is now the danger of not paying enough attention. And this suggests, as I conclude, that the dynamics of strategy and militarization are far more deeply embedded than conventional accounts acknowledge.

A note here is in order about the politics of what follows. It is, I believe, all too easy to launch into a critical diatribe regarding all that has passed for nuclear deterrence. But just as intellectually irresponsible is the smug celebratory triumphalism found across the spectrum of popular and academic publications dealing with world affairs in the aftermath of 1989. By invoking the relationship between Strategic Studies and world order, I want to praise the genius and the ambition of deterrence strategy in ways that neither its staunchest defenders nor its most ardent critics have been willing to articulate. The point, in effect, is to recognize the power and politics of deterrence strategy. The intent, however, is not to praise its practitioners but to examine it critically for its scope and ambition while recognizing, as well, the unavoidable incompleteness of modern strategic practices. In this sense, following Richard K. Ashley and R.B.J. Walker, the text engages in a "countermemorializing" reading of recent strategic policy.[8]

A key argument in this text is that strategic violence does not merely patrol the frontiers of modern culture. It helps constitute them as well. If Strategic Studies assigns to violence a regulative function in the international system, the argument developed here elaborates the generative nature of that violence – generative of states, of state systems, of world orders, and to some extent, of modern identity as well. In this sense, the ability of strategic violence to reconcile itself with liberal discourse and modern civil society is possible only because that violence draws upon a variety of discursive resources that are themselves widely construed as rational, plausible and acceptable. Chief among these is a series of apparent opposites – contending concepts – such as domestic and foreign, inside and outside, order and anarchy, peace and war, us and them, good and bad, First World and Third World.

What Strategic Studies does, I argue, is provide a map for the negotiating of these dichotomies in such a way that Western society always winds up on the "good," that is, the former – side of the equation. Our putative enemy, whatever the form assumed by its

5

postulated Otherness – variously the Soviet Union, or Communism, guerrilla insurgents, terrorism, Orientals, Fidel Castro, Nicaragua, Qaddafi, Noriega or Saddam Hussein – simultaneously is endowed with all of these dialectically opposed qualities. Strategic violence is then called in to mediate the relationship, patrol the border, surveil the opponent and punish its aggression.

This is not an ameliorative or reformist work. I am not concerned, for instance, with proposing a more workable treaty for regional arms control treaty, or arguing the merits of this or that weapons system. But I am concerned with the terms by which arms control treaties and weapons systems circulate in the economy of representation and discourse that animates – and also forecloses – public debate on security. Thus, my interest is not in arguing for or against a distinct theory of security but, rather, in exploring how the language, referents, and attendant social practices of military strategy and international security have come about in the first place. At the same time, I try to show that each representation of strategy comes, so to speak, at a price, a political and cultural price in terms of what those ways of speaking and doing exclude by way of silence and inaction.

The argument pursues some themes suggested by the works of Michel Foucault regarding the enabling nature of power. In his view, modern power does not delimit or constrain human action and identity; it functions, rather, to enable and make possible a range of specific social identities. Power, in other words, is a constitutive relationship rather than a delimiting one, and modernity is characterized by a diffusion and decentralization of the mechanisms by which power manifests itself on the social body. In this schema, the pre-modern model of the sovereign state becomes anachronistic and assumes a back seat to the subtler, more invasive procedures of specialized, disciplinary intervention by which knowledge affixes its gaze to an object.

Michel Foucault has explored a variety of medical, psychiatric and disciplinary strategies by which contemporary practices of selfhood and self-knowledge have been constructed.[9] Such a perspective can be harnessed to an analysis of contemporary military–strategic practices in an attempt to see the constitutive and enabling character of the modern state's interventionary modes. Such a project might seem to contradict Foucault's understanding of the modern state – as itself a congeries of competing, fragmented discourses of social intervention in the name of civic freedom. Yet Foucault's account of the mechanisms of modern power seem well suited to a study of a field whose interventionary and disciplinary power is, on the surface, all too obvious. For what else is Strategic Studies about but the political–military defense of the state?

The answer, I think, is that rather than understood merely as defining the modern state and delimiting claims upon its sovereignty, modern military practices can be understood as recurrent and always incomplete attempts to constitute and create what from a traditional perspective looks like a self-evident project – the state. In this manner, strategic violence is less a function of the state than an instance of its own assertion. And instead of regulating the territorial and ethno-national boundaries of modern state identity, strategic violence is an ongoing process of defining state boundaries, excluding that which differs from its domain, and punishing those who would challenge it. In other words, Strategic Studies empowers the displacement of difference.

In all of this, there is a strong temptation, one could even say, an expectation, for scholars to declare undying adherence to this or that school of thought. Yet paradigm battles fought from the safety of a particular intellectual redoubt are no longer immune to the theoretical critique that here a privileged position is harbored. One of the defining principles of the age in which we live is that a theoretical stance cannot ultimately be grounded – except, that is, in uneasy and always inconclusive relation to the social world of which it is a part and which it hopes to engage. In this sense, to take a position, to adopt a pose, or to assume an attitude toward a social practice means to engage dialogically with it, to examine it, criticize it, take it seriously and to check continually so that the terms of analysis bear some relationship to it.

If this seems like a refusal that is because my own perspective is informed by a certain reluctance to engage the imaginary questioner on the terms he would so confidently pose: "Well, what is different about your point of view, how is it different from and superior to that which has been said before?"

Posed in this manner, the question cannot be answered on its own terms, for it presumes that a single unifying framework is available. There is little doubt, in my own mind at least, that this text is most heavily influenced by critical reading of a variety of recent schools of thought, among them discourse analysis and poststructural readings of modernity. Yet without an engagement with critical social theory and the traditional Marxist critique of ideology and hegemony, it would be all too simple to succumb to the avoidance of social practice of which postmodernism is (for the most part, wrongly) accused.

The danger can be mitigated by heeding certain principles in the course of analysis.[10] To begin with, a conviction that an appropriate account of International Relations in general and specifically of Strategic Studies needs to stand in a critical relationship to classical realism. It must certainly take seriously the realist tradition's emphasis upon power in world affairs, and there can be no escaping a sustained engagement with the primary texts that demarcate that tradition. But here it is important to see that tradition not as some fixed map of the yellow brick road to modern realism or its "neo" variants. For contemporary articulations of the genre have tended to sever the tradition from its roots in political theory. Realism, as it evolved and has been transmuted in the hands of diverse thinkers over two and a half millennia, after all, did not necessarily recognize a distinction between domestic and international affairs. Nor did it bracket off from its primary concerns an understanding of the possible worlds in which the polity, the republic, or civic virtue could flourish. Indeed, a central characteristic of the realist tradition – if one can speak at all of a singular "tradition" in this regard – is the essential incompleteness and "indefinite" quality of the state which is both the subject and object of its concerns. This quality has to do with countering the sacred realist assumption of a sharply edged, politically sovereign political entity of hierarchic authority which is presented as the center of power and whose units comprise the dominant actors in the world community.

This understanding of the state, which achieved its sharpest articulation in the Absolutist era and which is embodied in the economic doctrine of mercantilism, is countered throughout this text. At the same time, I do not think it helpful to dispense at one stroke with the classical realist's emphasis upon power. Instead, I displace it slightly, from the centers of power to a dispersion throughout civil society. In other words, the perspective relied upon here draws heavily upon certain elements of the tradition, but recasts them dramatically to highlight the explicitly political and process-oriented character of realism.

Secondly, there is also a need to engage in a critical dialogue with the Marxist tradition. The serious study of international life cannot escape certain analytical influences of Marxism, in particular, highlighting the historical and material construction of economic and cultural processes. Moreover, the critique of ideology has exercised an important hold over twentieth century students of international politics. It is impossible to imagine E.H. Carr's critique of utopian universalism, for instance, without the intellectual underpinnings provided by theoretical Marxism.[11] By highlighting the social sources of political institutions and hegemonic ideas, this tradition has supplied rich intellectual capital for peering behind the veil of power. Yet in a curious way, Marxism has lent itself to a kind of structural complementarity with realist conceptions of the state – to be seen in V.I. Lenin, for instance, as well as in the economic dimensions of such apparent realists as Otto Hintze and Captain Alfred Thayer Mahan. Indeed, the ability of certain strands of Marxism to transform themselves into economistic readings of class structure and the social relations of production have enabled them to become depoliticized and to feed an abstract, ossified structuralism. The critical Marxism of the Frankfurt School has not succumbed to this particular paralysis, but it has nonetheless founded itself upon the conceptual totalization of civil society – an element drawn from and indeed animating the core of the Marxist tradition.

It is in the interest of refusing such a totalizing interpretation of modern life that I invoke here the injunction of taking seriously, yet simultaneously going beyond, Marxism. This constitutes a warning not to presume that identifiable expressions of modern life can be exhaustively explained in terms of underlying structural factors, or that manifestation of culture can be traced to an interested party, whose positive and negative account balance can be accordingly identified in the outputs of the policy process. Moreover, materialist accounts of global affairs are woefully neglectful of a whole series of concerns that fall, roughly, within the ambit of identity or meaning. Such cultural contests today over nationalism, regionalism, religion, gender, and environmentalism all are characterized by dimensions that can scarcely be captured within the totalizing discourse of the Marxist idiom. So while there is a need to be sensitive to material forces, this cannot be done at the price of ignoring those more elusive dimensions of life that are part of the politics of culture and interpretation.

Third, this text is guided by a sensitivity toward debates about the "poststructural." The intellectual substance to the various poststructural approaches requires more than the passing backhand dismissal that they normally receive in contemporary surveys of the International Relations literature.[12]

To be sure, some deconstructionist works have invited such a critical reception to the extent that they have limited their domain to the writing and interpretation of literary texts. But the principle informing such a method of criticism can be extended, first of all, to the political documentary record, and secondly, to specific social practices that are not themselves confined to the written word. In other words, documents are amenable to such a reading because they stand as codifi-

9

cations of social practice and linguistically mediated understandings. But because all social practices necessarily rely upon a documented record as well as on repertoires of meaning and interpretation that are always made available through the medium of language, they are also susceptible to critical methods of inquiry that explore the construction of truths. The point of such an extension, from the narrowly textual to the explicitly practical, is to explore how webs of signification, representation and interpretation are spun and put to work.[13] From this standpoint, all practices acquire a "curious literariness" that is not available to narrowly materialist or empiricist explanations.[14]

Thus, such widely circulated constructs as the state, the security dilemma, the nuclear revolution, deterrence and peace need to be explored in terms of their constituent elements. And such an analysis would not rely upon a Marxist or realist account of the interests served and the structures underlying the visible manifestation; rather, the position would be opened up as to how these things came into being and enjoyed their recurrence. The idea would be to open upon a continuing and, in principle, never-ending, succession of questions regarding the mechanisms by which ordering principles of the military–strategic world acquired their shape and staying power. Moreover, the exploration of these practices, and of their linguistic, interpretive, and representational qualities, would need to locate them within a broader cultural and episodic context of the resources upon which the modern world is founded.

Once again, what is required here is less a systematic theory than an attitude of skepticism whenever certain key organizing principles are invoked. Among those organizing principles – sometimes called meta-narratives – which need to be treated gingerly rather than with awe, are "rational man," "the market," "progress," "the working class," "the states system," "the Third World," and "the West." There is a great danger of presuming that these concepts have some unambiguous meaning and are somehow essentials that can be confidently invoked. Yet each of them is a cultural construct made intelligible to social agents through the medium of language. Instead of presuming their existence and meaning, we ought to historicize and relativize them as sets of practices with distinct genealogical trajectories. The issue, in short, is not whether they are true or false but how they have acquired their meaning, and how that meaning has changed to sustain the shape of contemporary political life. That they can also lose their meaning is clear to anyone who has followed the breathless pace of developments in the former Soviet Union, particularly since August 1991, as the totality of institutional and civic life virtually unravelled.

10

This suggests more than the fragility of a particular state formation; it suggests, as well, the multiple forms of political mobilization and participation, at levels that both precede and transcend the modern structures of institutional power. An attention to the poststructural here thus means looking at and listening to the multiple dimensions of political power, so that instead of presuming a fully articulated and delineated character to modern life, a principle of interpretive openness and inherent possibility is made a constituent element of analysis.

A final point, this one regarding the advice to be "post-hegemonic." Hegemony, in a variety of forms, has long served as an ideal guiding approaches to International Relations. In its traditional realist manifestation, hegemony has meant the search for a dominant, organizing state power capable of subduing rivals while practising imperial functions of global regulation. Neorealism, always more linear in its depiction of how power is exercised, has portrayed structures of regimes for the mechanisms of transnational politics. And in its more radical guise, hegemony has involved the search for a class-based form of social coordination achieved by the dominant ruling power blocs. Thus, while the resources of hegemonic power are differentially understood, a common principle informing each of these accounts is the dependence of world politics upon forms of dominance exercised within each of the constituent units of international affairs. The Gramscian modification of the radical tradition suggests a fundamental difference in the nature of hegemony; it sees hegemony as a succession of interlocking cultural and ideological practices which make and remake social integration. In the face of this, political mobilization assumes less the form of a frontal assault on, than an indirect maneuvering over, access to symbolic, cultural and work space, including the arts and education. This questions the centrality of hegemony as a necessary mechanism of social order, and it raises the possibility, without decisively settling the issue, of a post-hegemonic order, of social life as an expression of contending popular, democratic movements.[15]

This idea, developed in terms of state–civil society relations, can be extended to the great academic and intellectual contests by which academic battles are fought in the various disciplines. Competing theories, organized as research agendas or paradigms, vie for control over their respective fields, and with it, control over access to journals, foundation grants, academic appointments, and the mechanisms by which scholarship reduplicates itself over time.[16] It is not clear whether such intellectual dominance – paradigm hegemony, if you will – can be achieved. The reasons have much to do with fundamental transformations in the philosophical foundations of the social sciences. And they have to do, as well, with the de-centering of political and economic life in world affairs today.

The precise details of this are to be worked out in the pages that follow. But it might nonetheless be helpful briefly to indicate here how a concern for "the post-hegemonic" actually achieves expression in research. For the basic issue is that instead of searching for a new form of theoretical dominance, the triumph of this or that theory to the obliteration of all oncomers, we need to ask interesting questions that speak and listen to ongoing social and political struggles. In this sense, the task of social science is to give voice and clarity to the multiple forces and social movements that help constitute international life. Insofar as hegemonic orders have been achieved in the world, it is our academic responsibility to explain them. But is it possible to do so in ways that do not foreclose social processes and political trans-formation? Indeed, the concern that guides this study is to explore areas of modern life – political and military strategy, Strategic Studies, fundamental issues of modern war and peace – that appear to be defined by enduring structures of power and dominance, of domestic hegemonic order counterposed to anarchic international conditions, yet which themselves can always be understood as saturated with language, textual mediation, and representations. This makes them amenable to political inquiry and political change. In so doing, I believe it possible to keep the question open as to the socially consti-tuted nature of practices and to allow continually for the analytical possibility of contestation and political transformation. Such an approach is not wedded to an evolutionary teleology. Nor does it ever presume that articulated structures are homologous and complete. Instead, such an enterprise stands at the intersection of rigorous, theoretically informed scholarship and a commitment to democratic practices, even when it comes to the making and remaking of military strategy and security policy.

2 THE POLITICS OF STRATEGIC STUDIES

... in the conversation among the Powers there is a convention of silence about the place of their human subjects, any interruption of which is a kind of subversion. (Hedley Bull[1])

There are many reasons for being concerned about military-related issues, the existence of vast nuclear arsenals being only one of them. While there is nothing particularly contemporary about questions of war and peace, it is fair to say that in the twentieth century such issues have become paramount to the life and death of whole societies. When examining those weapons of mass destruction and the strategies so crucial to their deployment, attention needs to be focused on the ways of thinking that have guided practitioners of policy. In a world in which such weapons have been widely "used" in a variety of ways short of (though, of course, including) actual detonation in warfare, the communicative, symbolic and interpretive dimensions of strategy assume enormous importance. Moreover, the very processes of militarization, both in terms of domestic armaments infrastructures and a worldwide military order, tell us that military strategy has an importance that transcends the boundaries of the standard battlefield epic.

A significant body of critical peace research has, in the last quarter of a century, contributed to a detailed understanding of how war and armaments accumulation have shaped, and often devastated, Third World affairs.[2] Not surprisingly, such critical undertakings have remained marginal with respect to the main work of the Western strategic community. The overwhelming majority of the work produced by analysts in Strategic Studies has concerned issues of deterrence and security pertaining to the major states and their two respective alliances, NATO and the former Warsaw Pact. Third World regional security issues acquire relevance only insofar as they can be slotted into the overall pattern of major power geopolitical global conflict.[3] When the security problems of the Third World have been addressed by the Strategic Studies community, the dominant intellectual framework has been a regionalized version of the global strategy/security paradigm, so that the dilemmas facing "small" or "less powerful" states are analogized to that of the states system of the major powers. In other words, Third World conflicts have been explained in terms that pit each of the actors against one another, so that the relevant model is of clearly articulated states that stand over their own civil societies and seek to fend off nascent security dilemmas that manifest themselves in the external, anarchic world of potentially hostile neighbors.[4]

In this chapter I raise some basic theoretical questions about the way violence has been handled in the field of Strategic Studies. This discipline, as one way of interpreting world politics, has tended to reduce the drama and openness of international life, subduing it to a plot suffocating in the kind of language that George Orwell railed against.[5] The results are texts that have confined and delimited the political, while reifying an explanatory framework referred to as "the states system." In so doing, they have obscured the central place of strategic practice in the making of the modern West. Whether in the form of outright war, military planning, or the structures of a world military order, violence, including its organization in the form of strategy, has been indispensable to the shaping and preservation of contemporary life.

Violence and world order

Some years ago a (West) German peace researcher, Ekkehart Krippendorff, raised the empirical question of "how many people paid with their lives for the evolution of the international system as we know it today?"[6] The analysis was intended to expose certain hidden dimensions of global economic relations, particularly those overlooked in structural explanations of Third World underdevelopment. The accounting procedures for reckoning the total number of lives lost proved more problematic than Krippendorff had first thought. What looked on the surface to be a quantitative problem quickly became enmeshed in thickets of interpretation. What counts as a war and how to total up the victims were relatively simple questions. Far more challenging was the politically shaped character of the very historical record upon which researchers must rely. After all, many of the deaths came about through punitive raids and "police actions" that bordered on wars of extermination. The determined military resistance of Maoris in the face of settlers and tradesmen in New Zealand was the exception to the rule of massive military domination throughout the colonializing process. Far more deadly than outright military conquest, however, were more indirect forms of depopulation resulting from the aftermath of first contact between explorers, missionaries and entrepreneurs, and those whom Eric Wolf has referred to as "the people without history."[7] Where disease did not obliterate indigenous populations, landlessness, enslavement and the exhaustion of labor power often did. When Cortez began the campaigns of 1520 against the Aztec empire, the Mexican population was anywhere between 9 and 25 million. Thirty years later there were only between 1 and 2 million people left.[8] In North America, the population of indigenous tribal peoples is estimated to have dropped some 94 percent, from pre-contact levels of 7 million to some 390,000 in 1930. In Lowland South America, the corresponding population loss was 95 percent of the indigenous tribal populace, and in Oceania, some 78 percent.[9]

But this is not a question merely for the historical record. It also goes to the heart of contemporary strategic issues. For the overwhelming majority of the world's peoples, global politics since World War II has been anything but peaceful. Peace may be relative, as the saying goes, but it depends where your relatives live. For those with families in Afghanistan, Angola, Bosnia-Herzegovina, Cambodia, Chad, Ethiopia, Iran, Iraq, Kuwait, Namibia, Nicaragua, Northern Ireland, Somalia, Sri Lanka, Sudan and the West Bank, life these past few years has been wracked by war. Short of overt armed conflict, the presence of foreign military forces has been a conspicuous dimension of daily life on both sides of the Korean border. The ubiquitous presence of military forces in Eastern Europe and the former USSR exercised a corrosive effect on the quality of everyday life there and contributed to the region's internal bureaucratic and political stupefaction. An international arms market linking the major industrial powers, both East and West, with many developing countries of the Third World has emerged from its subterranean links to form a globalized military order. Warships patrol the earth's oceans. Otherwise desolate regions of the Northern Hemisphere serve as launching pads and communications centers for intercontinental rockets. Hundreds of thousands of skilled researchers labor away in design laboratories perfecting weapons of mass destruction. Hovering above all this is an electronic network of satellite surveillance and the constant monitoring of phone calls, telegrams and radio messages the world over. And lurking in the minds of airport passengers is the awareness that, at any time, a terrorist bomb packed in the luggage compartment could rip the plane in half. There is, then, no escaping these global relations. Not all of them are as conspicuous as outright "war." In some ways they contribute to what many call "peace."

The state of Strategic Studies

Much of modern social science is predicated upon an analysis of a world that stands on its own, as an externality upon which the researcher gazes. The task of rigorous academic investigation is to devise terms of analysis and understanding that come as close a humanly possible to the logic and reality of that realm. The model of the natural sciences exists in this sense more as a regulative norm to be approximated than as an actually achievable standard. Nonetheless, the intent is clear: to set aside one's own subjective biases and values and to confront the world on its own terms, with the hope of gaining mastery of that world through a clear understanding that transcends the limits of such personal determinants as one's own values, class, gender, race, or emotions. In this sense, International Relations has been shaped decisively by the injunction to be dispassionate, realistic, and above all, practical.

The particular purposes to which such knowledge is supposed to be put vary markedly in this account. Sometimes, it is knowledge for its own sake. On other occasions, it may be the technocratic project of control or adjustment through intellectual mastery. In either case, the realm of action under scrutiny has an existence that is literally and figuratively outside the body of the analyst. Scholars explore this realm, analyze its patterned interactions, and prescribe policies for it.

For the field of Strategic Studies, the dismissal of basic ontological questions has allowed for an interpretation of the world military order as founded upon interactions among major political units, called states. This view posits a knowing man at the center who is in need of order. "Man" here refers to a universal construct of human nature, supposedly abstracted from location in the particular sinews of gender, class, or religion. Yet in the light of recent feminist studies of human nature and political theory,[10] it might be more helpful, rather than reading "man" as a non-gender specific "human being," to take the nominative designation literally as an attempt to impose upon a universal construct what are specifically engendered traits. In this manner, it is possible to read and recapture the tradition of political theory and the realist foundations of modern International Relations while remaining perfectly sensitive to the textual strategies of engendered discourse. Such a being – of man – needs a place in the

16

world which can ensure his ability to use nature – also seen as a separate entity – as an abundant resource. The world thus stands at his disposal.

The task of politics is to create a familiar space and to extend this over time so that man can act upon nature to his own satisfaction. The need for the state thus arises from an uneasiness about the idea of pre-political life. Whether fallen from grace and morally flawed, covetous of his neighbors, or merely looking to protect himself from those few who might well transgress the natural law, man needs some ordering principles and a means of ensuring predominance of these rules in daily life.

The modern state provides this. It effectively creates a sphere of civil society in which orderly, mutually beneficial social relations are for the first time rendered possible under a common political authority. The territorial state provides a spatial representation that coordinates daily life. The late-Medieval collapse of Christian cosmology led to a fundamental rethinking of the bases of human association. The Thomistic hierarchy of divinely inspired terrestrial order gave way to experiments in thought and practice about the new bases of association within a newly forged civil society. Thinkers as diverse as Machiavelli, Luther and Bodin all looked toward the secular state as the arbiter of domestic order. Sociologists of these developments, including Tönnies, Durkheim and Weber, all based their accounts of modernization upon the state's ability to replace naturalistic hierarchy in securing the worldly order of things. The advent of market relationships assumed much of the burden from the modern state for enabling human beings to achieve their personal security.

The state's centrality in making possible the functioning of that market is a staple of liberal thought dating back to Hobbes and Locke.[11] With the emergence of the state as the ordering force among nascent civil societies, realism was able to triumph as a political doctrine for describing and prescribing relations among states. In this manner, Medieval Christendom, with its universe beholden to God, became subject to a displaced representation of its aggregated self in the form of sovereign authority. The mythic prince of Machiavelli's world had become figuratively embodied in the recognizably modern secular state.

The emergence of territorial sovereignty as definitive of the modern state took place gradually. The multiple forms of state that evolved all varied by virtue of local differentiations in landholding, class structure, and imperial ambitions. The literature exploring these dramatic developments is, of course, vast and impossible to cover here.[12] But for the

17

purpose of exploring the nature of Strategic Studies, several definitive characteristics are to be noted.

The first is the radically provisional character of the state that emerged. Contemporary realists like to extol the virtues of the state, as if the construct were self-evident and as if it were unproblematic in its articulation over civil society. Yet in retracing the historic path trod by the epic realists, what emerges is less confirmation of a grand tradition than a series of open interpretations regarding the uncertainties of securing power. Machiavelli, after all, proclaimed the virtue of the prince in trying to master the vicissitudes of history, of what he called "fortuna." The task of mastering political life, he argued, was an impossible necessity. Thus was born a regard for what might be called "the indefinite state" – a polity marked by ambiguity and uncertainty in the heroic but ultimately unsuccessful effort to secure itself against the cyclical plays of power that marked secular history.[13]

Four centuries later in the evolution of realist political thinking, Max Weber extolled the ethic of responsibility inherent in statesmanship. The task of political leadership, he argued, was to use force judiciously as an arbiter of difference in a world where values and interests were inherently in conflict. In this sense, political realism seeks to establish the domain of state power over domestic society while patrolling the frontiers where its own efforts are exhausted. Realism, in other words, seeks to create differentiation between domestic and foreign, inside and outside. And it recognizes its politics as precisely the establishment of that boundary, so that statesmanship resides in the recurrent exercise of power. Sovereignty is thus less a description of a state of political life than a critical resource available to the state in its own political struggles. It thus never has been a simple matter to create the state so dear to the hearts of realist strategists: to create, in Max Weber's terms, that "human community that [successfully] claims the monopoly of the legitimate use of physical force within a given community."[14]

Political history is littered with the remnants of would-be states. Enormous efforts involving social movements, institution building, and the articulation of functioning national economies have all been part of the precarious process of state-building. Postwar strategists of development theory and political modernization understood this clearly in terms of the newly emergent, post-colonial states of the Third World. A massive literature has documented the successes, along with the many false starts, characterizing the history of states.[15] Yet such "internalist" accounts covering the making of various state structures are bypassed in the realist tradition, and no more so than in

Strategic Studies. For what counts from the standpoint of the strategist is less the constitutive processes of states and states systems than their existence in fully functioning form. Transformational processes, either at the level of the state or at the larger level of the system itself, are subordinated to a regulative model by which power, military force and strategic practice are used to police and to delimit the internal boundaries of a system whose existence is not rendered problematic. One recent example can be seen in John Mearsheimer's claim that a post-Cold War Europe would be stabilized through Germany's acquisition of nuclear weapons. The argument overlooks domestic politics completely, articulating instead a wholly externalist account based on a formal balance-of-politics model. Such concerns are part of a long and abiding tradition that is coterminous with Continental security politics. "Since the inception of the modern state system in 1648, politics among European states has revolved around the competition for power."[16]

The claim about the appearance of a recognizable state system has been projected backwards by many other students of strategy. The Italian states system created by the Peace of Lodi in 1454 is one example used by historians. Others point to the Greek world of the Peloponnesian Wars as the first exemplar of coherent relations among states.[17] Michael Howard, one of the most distinguished students of political–military history, says, for instance, that the kind of stability to which nuclear weapons have contributed is structurally identical to the stability and order which realist strategic analysts since Thucydides have valorized.[18] There is no problem in International Relations in finding the "eternal recurrence and repetition" of that global drama in which states have sought to preserve their own survival by recourse to defense through self-help.[19] "We would be blind therefore," concedes Howard, "if we did not recognize that the causes which have produced war in the past are operating in our own day as powerfully as at any time in history."[20] Thus, in analyzing twentieth century world war, the strategist is counseled to consult the lessons of the classics. Howard crystalizes this view:

> The causes of the Great War are thus in essence no more complex or profound than those of any previous European war, or indeed than those described by Thucydides as underlying the Peloponnesian War: "What made war inevitable was the growth of Athenian power and the fear this caused in Sparta."[21]

In positing the historical continuity of balance of power politics and security concerns, Howard is relying upon a tradition of *Realpolitik*, though shifting it in a subtle, decisive way. The classical realist concern

19

for power politics in securing the state is furtively transformed into a transcendent architectonic of strategic violence which is necessary to secure one's own survival against the threats posed by all other states.

In the postwar era, these claims about the political nature of strategic violence as a tragically creative force became transformed and embedded into a structure of global relations which came to be known as "the security dilemma."[22] By so designating the problem of political difference into formalized distinctions represented by various states, the concept of "anarchy" becomes the definitive characteristic of International Relations.

The invocation of anarchy, however, has carried a huge burden in terms of the politics of strategy. For the concept emphasizes the radical separation of states from one another, as well as the separation of strategy from political economy within those states. The argument of Strategic Studies, in short, is that security considerations and the need to pursue security from other states are driving forces of world politics.

In *People, States and Fear*, Barry Buzan contests the elegance of the term "security" and argues that it often functions at cross purposes, depending on whether it is invoked at the individual, state or international levels.[23] What for International Relations analysts, following Kenneth Waltz, presents itself as a relatively straightforward trichotomy among levels of analysis – the individual, the state, and world order defined as a states system – becomes under Buzan's critical gaze a more fluid realm wherein practices of security on behalf of local units contribute to conflicts and rivalries in other geopolitical dimensions.[24] Thus the basic unit of security becomes inherently problematic: individual security? national security? international security? or something more elusive, like regional or alliance security? In other words, questions of "whose security?" and of "what domain?" become important. More importantly, what "security" means is far from clear. There is no need to resolve these questions: merely, for Buzan, to raise them so that at least one foundational concept of Strategic Studies is inherently contestable and susceptible to plausible contestation as part of any political conflict.

Yet in an accompanying textbook on the field, *An Introduction to Strategic Studies*, Buzan abandoned claims about the "essential contestability" of key concepts and concerned himself instead with fashioning a more integrative view of the field.[25] That this runs contrary to the deeper philosophical meaning of "essential contestability" does not keep Buzan from his task.[26] And so he conveys the basics of the whole of Strategic Studies *sans* a politicized dimension.

Buzan demonstrates that, as a subdiscipline of International Relations, Strategic Studies is a product of the nuclear age. Its intellectual traditions are derived from classical realism and the balance of power among distinct, sovereign states co-existing (uneasily) in an anarchic states system. The military–technical means available to statesmen provide the tools for the rational control and management of policy. The goals of that policy are defined as the pursuit of political–military security in an age of unavoidable vulnerability.

It turns out, however, that this version of the states system has no history – except as that of states, fully formed, acting strategically. The state itself presides confidently over civil society and appears to be entirely immune from all social forces. Domestic order stands absolutely cut off from the international security dilemma posed by international anarchy.

So rigid is the ensuing global order that at one point Buzan reverts to a most revealing verbal locution, according to which "the anarchic structure reigns."[27] To be sure, this reign is presented in the conditional mode, as if a transition from it to a world state were at least in principle possible. But by posing a futuristic, singular world state as the only imaginable alternative, Buzan can defend the viability of nuclear deterrence as the sole feasible guarantor of world order – a world order, it must be noted, which is then equated with justice. Measured against the abstract ideal of a distant visionary peace, a modicum of contemporary order assumes, by contrast, the force of a moral imperative. For Buzan, then, and, to be fair, the whole tradition of Strategic Studies, an anarchic states system has provided the unquestioned backdrop for the rationality of deterrence.

The argument is thoroughly state-centered. The security dilemmas of all states are cast into the mould set by sovereign states confronting each other across the nuclear divide. Once the states system is so tightly structured, it becomes possible to account for military technology as an exogenous variable which affects strategic thinking. The political economy of the armaments industry thereby becomes construed as a realm of private activity which neutrally provides technology for either civil or military purposes and which contributes to an important phenomenon, which Buzan calls "the technological imperative," of progressive developments in the quality of industrial productivity. This creates incentives for ever-mounting research and development efforts in the field of military technology. Buzan hopes that if the security interdependence of all modern states is sufficiently recognized, then rationality will prevail and states will desist from a

21

full-scale arms race and opt instead for the normal background condition of what he terms "an arms dynamic."

The problem here is Buzan's limited conceptualization of contemporary power relations. He deflates the scope of global conflicts. There is no world military order of arms sales, military regimes and security alliances tying peoples of the world in to global relations of political economy. Whatever differences might exist in the world – capitalist/socialist, developed/underdeveloped, economic rivalry, intra-Alliance friction, revolution/counter-insurgency – are subsumed under the sanitized concept of "the political." So conflict emanates from political factors, and Strategic Studies must deal with the military manifestations of essentially political conflicts.

We have, then, two separate realms: the strategic and the political. Strategy is not part of state-building or empire-building. Strategy, by contrast, is conducted outside of those (unexamined) state–civil society relations which give rise to global conflict.

The point here is not that Buzan is wrong but, rather, that his work is based upon an unreflective, common-sense version of realism that is divorced from a convincing sociological or philosophical point of view. There is no rendering problematic of "the state" or "the states system," no attempt to historicize its production. Nor is there any evidence of a philosophical claim being made for the particular criteria used so back-handedly to dismiss alternative conceptualizations. In short, there is no sense that one is confronting a particular representation of world politics, a point of view which both includes and excludes, which selectively views one dimension of international life while discursively excluding, sometimes ruling out, other representational practices that might challenge the dual hegemony of Strategic Studies and of the states that practice it.

In this sense, the limits reside as much with Strategic Studies as with Buzan's account. An alternative account, or at least a more self-consciously critical one, would not so much argue that deterrence has been untenable but rather, that the very terms of Strategic Studies – the state, anarchy, world order, the revolution in military technology and the security dilemmas facing states – have themselves been the product of historical forces and social relations of power. Without understanding these social forces in the making and remaking of world order today we are ill-equipped to understand the cultural biases and contending historical forces that have made the world military order. Only with such accounts can we appreciate how a thoroughly Western (more precisely, North Atlantic) mode of analysis constituted itself as the savior of politics on a global scale.

Toward theoretical critique

Perhaps all of this is unfair. After all, the dilemmas faced by Strategic Studies are not unique to this one field of thought. All modern theories are problematic in so far as they impose an analytic order upon the world. That, after all, is why academic fields of thought are construed as "disciplines." In the literal sense, the disciplining achieved by formalized modes of intellectual representation imposes necessary boundaries. Great intellectual "discipline" is required in order to gather evidence, sift through contending explanations, and organize political and social life along the lines suggested by various key principles such as those that animate Strategic Studies: the balance of power, the states system, conflict resolution, bargaining, arms control, alliance systems and coalition warfare. But the disciplinary character also extends to a variety of other practices having to do with principles of inclusion – and exclusion – of relevant variables.[28]

Within Strategic Studies, the foundational concepts of the state, state sovereignty, of state–civil society relations, of the distinction between war and peace, and the ideas of national interest and state power, are accorded peculiar spatial and temporal configurations that continue to exercise a decisive hold over the terms of global political discourse today. We can discern the particular shaping of global space and time from within the tradition of historicist realism. For it is this tradition, a precursor to contemporary structural realism and International Relations theory proper, that deliberately sought to build an identifiable states system from its European core out to the margins and peripheries of the world's lands.[29]

It is no simple matter to presume the completeness of the constituent categories of political–military strategy and then to read them backwards into history as if they had always been there. This has been the textual strategy of postwar realists, who have reached back into the grab-bag of history and pulled out examples attesting to the veracity of universal claims.

> The texture of international politics remains highly constant, patterns recur, and events repeat themselves endlessly. The relations that prevail internationally seldom shift rapidly in type or quality ...
>
> The enduring anarchic character of international politics accounts for the striking sameness in the quality of international life through the millennia ...[30]

Waltz is the most uncompromising exemplar of this strategic reading, and his structural realism enables one confidently to conclude

23

that the future will be very much like the past because the structure has always been present.

"Structural" here refers to accounts of a particular system of states that at any historical moment exhaust the significant relations among political units which students of world politics deem interesting and relevant. Within that given arrangement of units, the important issue for Strategic Studies has been the distribution of military force, the relative shares of military capabilities and intentions, that characterizes interactions among those units of analysis. The systemic nature of the object of inquiry consists in the pattern of relationships governing the external policies among the constitutive units. Those units are states. The structure is a states system. External interactions among the units either directly involve individual states or are mediated via an alliance of states. In International Relations, this has come to be known as structural realism. It remains the dominant mode of analysis in the field and has animated most mainstream policy analysis.

On this account, the sovereign state is presented in Newtonian terms of a culturally and socially undifferentiated space existing in precarious relationship with – and amongst – other homogeneously constructed states. A crucial distinction is made between the coherence of life internal to these states and the flux of fortune and incoherence external to them. Domestic unity is counterposed to foreign plurality; the one inside, the many beyond.[31] Familiarity and identity flourish within the protective confines of the frontiers. But just beyond, in the netherworld outside the sovereign's domain, otherness and difference well up as immanent forces which by sheer virtue of their existence threaten the security of states. As Waltz explains it,

> The parts of domestic political systems stand in relations of super- and subordination. Some are entitled to command; others are required to obey. Domestic systems are centralized and hierarchic. The parts of international-political systems stand in relations of coordination.
> Formally, each is the equal of all the others. None is entitled to command; none is required to obey.[32]

Within this framework, strategic violence has a regulative function. Domestically, as Weber reminds us, the monopoly of the legitimate uses of violence which characterizes the modern state enables it to enforce public law and to punish transgressors. The authority for deployment of force is specifically granted by the sovereign power. International life, however, lacks such a centralized coordination of legitimate violence. There is no sovereign center, no transcendent public law to uphold, and no overarching mechanism of enforcement. There is only "self help."[33]

Military power therefore has the function internationally of patrolling states and of imposing a modicum of equivalence in the distribution of their ability to harm or conquer one another. This balance of power is the prerogative of great states. The basic idea, so decisive to centuries of Western strategic practice, has been to prevent any single power from transforming the anarchic structure of the international states system into one that would render it like domestic politics – with hierarchy and super/sub-ordination. So long as no singular hegemonic power achieves this ability, a measure of peace prevails among the world's states, as no one state can impose its will upon any other.

Yet the history of warfare and of strategic violence cannot be exhausted by this "regulative mode." From the standpoint of structural realism, violence preserves a precarious balance among (potentially) contending forces. But such a synchronic, "balancing act" view of violence and war overlooks the diachronic or constitutive nature of violence in modern global life. For violence, or military strategy, has served to impose and maintain integration beyond the boundaries of any single state. In large measure, for instance, structures of military power have enabled the European world to extend itself and to absorb the cultures and resources of vast stretches of land the world over.[34] The result has been a world order in its own image, in the form of the modern state system. But while structural realism emphasizes how violence preserves order, the question remains how that violence helps generate order.

The formal representation of a states system in the guise of structural realism is also problematic in presuming the completion of this modern Western totality. The conspicuous and often terrifying appearance of Western military power – what W.W. Rostow subsumes within the anodyne term of "demonstration effect" – has never sufficed to homogenize global life.[35]

The aura of material certitude when it comes to the strategic enterprise is part of larger political attempt to encode and normalize a world military order of violence. Yet the strategic enterprise, despite what its most devoted celebrants proclaim, is a practice fraught with ambiguity, uncertainty, interpretation, ritual and symbolism. One need only examine the whole procedure of "intelligence gathering" to appreciate how provisional and contestable is the empirical foundation of what would otherwise seem to be the most empirical and realistic of enterprises. To take one example, the entire process of making national intelligence estimates about the Soviet strategic threat has been characterized by institutional and interpretive difficulties that reduced accounts of Soviet power to a thoroughly politicized guessing game.[36] In the absence of satellite surveillance or electronic eaves-dropping capabilities in the immediate postwar period, the process of gaining accurate information was an especially precarious enterprise. Two subsequent assessments of what American analysts would have found had they had full access to actual figures on troop deployments and weapons readiness in the late 1940s reveal levels of Soviet arma-ments that were woefully inadequate for offensive, Western-directed operations.[37]

The absolute distinction between appropriate and inappropriate forms of political violence in the international system further exempli-fies this normalization process. Just as nuclear deterrence, for instance, has been seen to preserve international order, strategies of flexible response, including conventional counter-insurgency operations under the guise of "low-intensity warfare," are considered part of the normal panoply of means available to leading states. Meanwhile, terrorism is relegated to a dark and murky status of the political netherworld, which civilized states have an obligation to fend off. In the words of one influential analyst, "the problem today for most Western governments, with their vast nuclear and conventional arse-nals, is dealing out small doses of force" against terrorism.[38] This patrolling of analytical borders is particularly profound in Strategic Studies, since the great difficulty of the enterprise lies is delineating the difference between legitimate and illicit forms of political violence.

The resolution of this problem comes in the form, and in the mainte-nance, of modern state boundaries. The classical European balance of power system elevated this to a foundational principle of world order. The essentially conservative nature of diplomacy and strategy was to preserve the existing states that constituted world politics. The formula, hammered out in the aftermath of the Treaties of Westphalia of 1648, was convenient for preserving dynastic power, but had to be continually upgraded during subsequent domestic transformations in the basis of political legitimacy. Various stages of national state build-ing, whether in the form of Frederican Prussia, revolutionary France, or the Second German Reich, raised the stakes and the social basis of national military power but did not fundamentally transform the underlying principles of balance of power conservatism. In seeking to defend the status quo against revisionist powers, balance of power politics became an avowedly conservative enterprise that, as with Metternich, readily revealed itself as reactionary. When faced with social upheaval or with a state that might expand its power and gain

26

hegemony, balance of power considerations counselled wars of intervention and restoration.[39]

As the policy arm of classical balance of power realism, Strategic Studies has been particularly interesting because it has identified itself with power and with the modern state. It has chosen, as the saying goes, to "whisper into the ear of the prince." As Waltz says of his own work, "A general theory of international politics is necessarily based on the great powers."[40]

Strategic Studies, the predominant way of thinking today about political–military affairs, is a historical achievement – specific to the post-Renaissance era, and rooted in the social structures of the early modern state. While the strategic literature is able to go back in history and identify all sorts of evidence about prior "strategists" and national strategies, this suggests less the universality of the basic categories of Strategic Studies than it does the ability to reinterpret history in light of present points of view. This might be called "the strategicalization of global politics" – the rendering of events as subject to human mastery at the hands of statesman and to the logic of a peculiarly contemporary, i.e. postwar strategic discourse.

The term "strategicalization" is far more powerful a term than, say, "strategizing." For "strategizing" requires the invocation of an already existing set of rules for strategic thinking that is merely to be applied. It entails a matching of means to ends in the pursuit of various geopolitical interests. But as an act of policy, it is dependent upon the articulation of a world view in which regions and peoples are parceled out, divided up, and presumed to be subsumed under a master narrative of instrumental control.

By talking of "strategicalization," we identify processes by which political domain is extended beyond realms of immediate sovereignty. It becomes thereby possible to unmask practices as themselves embedded in a logic of expansion and control. There is, then a need to appreciate the genesis, or genealogy, of strategizing as but one of many possible ways of thinking about and doing politics. How is it possible, for instance, to construe the Caribbean region exclusively in terms of potential sea lane vulnerability should the US Navy have to provision NATO forces engaged in a European land war against the Warsaw Pact?[41]

In its academic guise as the foundation of security policy, the field of Strategic Studies has become somewhat winnowed down to a narrower, more technocratic enterprise that has armored against critical reflection. To a great extent, highly technical modes of study such as game theory and systems analysis have come to predominate. But

27

THE POLITICS OF STRATEGIC STUDIES

these behavioral modes of analysis have not fundamentally transformed the foundational concepts of Strategic Studies.

Contemporary social and political theorizing, however, has tended to stop at the water's edge. The nature of the state, legitimation crises, relations between the state and civil society and the future of industrial society: all of these theoretical debates have been conducted in terms of a domestic politics divorced from international relations.

Similarly, International Relations theory is often divorced from social theory. A succession of great debates regarding realism/idealism, traditionalism/behaviouralism, and realism/neorealism have all been predicated on a set of categories that have themselves remained unexamined: subject/object, inside/outside, domestic/international. These debates thereby suffer, for they lead to a foreclosure of reflection upon the basic concepts that inform international practices.[42]

Strategic Studies has celebrated or memorialized a master narrative of institutional order. It has effectively demarcated the boundaries of modern Western cultural identity, and relegated those peoples and practices which do not fit to marginal, alien status. Within the familiar confines of the West lives civilized man, a part of international society. Beyond exists the terrorist, the anarchist, or the "madman" aggressor such as Qaddafi or Saddam Hussein. The unity and consensus which have marked Western political society might occasionally be interrupted by shouts from such "peripheral voices" as those of peace activists, feminists or ecologists. But when it comes to exercising leadership in a tough, threatening world, the responsibilities of citizenship delimit how far such criticism can legitimately go.[43]

Critical approaches to international studies, by contrast, engage in the "countermemorializing" of those whose lives and voices have been variously silenced in the process of strategic practices.[44] To insist, for example, on raising questions about lost lives and social body counts serves as a reminder of the brutal social practices relied upon in achieving the power to proclaim "peace" and "order." In this sense, liberal order may be seen to rest upon a sanitized veneer that is especially susceptible to interrogation. For the celebration of "modern man," "modern institutions" and the globalizing practices of "modernization" in the world economy all are animated by the claim of being cleaner, more civilized, less violent than the savagery of the pre-modern world. In such a representation of modern culture, the raw unmediated world of the primitive becomes subordinated to a status only marginally higher than that of the undomesticated animal on the evolutionary ladder. Meanwhile, it is modern man who has built such an enduring index for earthly progress, and it is modern

28

man who sets the standard. The violences that may have occurred are thus regrettable and relegated to a distant and primordial past. Contemporary modern man suffers no guilt. Having washed his hands of blood, he abandons the gun and attends to his affairs with briefcase in tow. Those who raise unruly questions about the silences of the past – or silences of the present – can be more or less dismissed or marginalized for their stance.

That world politics has been a violent affair comes as no surprise to strategic analysts. Their job, after all, as both academic and practitioner, is to reckon with the sources of that violence and to reduce, if not stop their spread. In this sense, strategists see themselves as the hand-maidens of peace. Despite the somewhat unconventional, militant means at their disposal, they have recourse to organized violence in order, over the long run, to reduce human suffering.

The same is said about strategies of nuclear deterrence. However unfortunate they may be in terms of threatening the destruction of humanity, they served the important purpose of presiding over, policing and punishing violators of global order. In this sense, the genius of "deterrence" over earlier strategies of active military defense and outright fighting has been that its legitimacy derives from its not being actually called upon. In other words, the strategy has remained in place and has derived its support only so long as it has not been used as an instrument of actual war. The precarious balance of terror has been psychologically unsettling, but obviously, this has proven preferable to the centuries of war preceding the postwar era.

It is, however, no easy matter in the social sciences to determine why something did not happen. In this case, that "something" was another world war, or more specifically, a direct confrontation between the US and the USSR over the fate of Europe. One of the great ironies of contemporary strategic relations is that a field which champions its own "realist" heritage should find itself, in the postwar era, so devoid of observable and empirically verifiable material regarding the operational utility of nuclear deterrence as an instrument of stable world order.[45] Thus it is important, even within the terms of reference championed by the strategic community, to regard with scepticism triumphal claims of strategic analysts regarding a "long peace" that has characterized postwar world politics and that owes its existence to the various strategies of nuclear deterrence.[46]

The argument, it must be noted, borrows from previous claims about "the Hundred Years' Peace" said to have existed across the European Continent from 1815 to 1914, though in that case owing to the conventional balance of power.[47] This time, however, the classical instruments of statecraft, replete with their limited wars of maneuver, have been supplanted by the delicate balance of terror and the prospects of imminent annihilation should one of the nuclear powers have initiated aggression upon another. The peace we have enjoyed in recent years, goes the argument, has been largely due to the sensibility of statesmen, who, in the face of overwhelming nuclear threats, wisely desisted from aggression since no gains were apparent given the escalatory threats of retaliation.

But upon close inspection, this claim of "peace" and a stable postwar order pertains, like its predecessor a century ago, not to global affairs, but merely to a few dimensions of International Relations involving the major powers. The peace that has prevailed, it turns out, has involved only restricted dimensions of global life and has left largely untouched – or perhaps, more accurately, it has left embattled – vast "peripheral" stretches of the globe. Here, after all, where, the majority of the world's people live, none of the world's interesting historical events seems to originate. In asking about "the implications of the end of history for international relations," Francis Fukuyama admits that "[c]learly, the vast bulk of the Third World remains very much mired in history, and will be a terrain of conflict for many years to come. But let us focus for the time being on the larger and more developed states of the world who after all account for the greater part of world politics."[48]

But there never was a compelling reason for Strategic Studies to have monopolized the terms of debate regarding the meanings of "security" and "peace." That its norms have been commonly understood and taken for granted as the starting point of analysis suggest not the veracity of its analytical categories but that these, instead, have simply become adopted as part of the conventional wisdom. To challenge Strategic Studies, then, might mean to challenge common sense. But there is nothing sacrosanct in common sense. Indeed, the more common the conceptional framework, the more necessary it is to undo its historical reification.[49] In this way, we can see how a distinctive social practice for the organization of violence and the coordination of life on a global scale becomes established as a singularly powerful ritual, an ethos of globalized public policy.

The distinction between war and peace has always been a problematic one. When the shape of "war" is configured in accordance with Continental balance of power politics and warfare, then many of the forms assumed by organized violence do not reach the analytical threshold of war. Only when the operative understanding of war is confined to national armies taking to the field against one another can "peace" become an enormously large residual category. Strategies such as nuclear deterrence, which miraculously contributed to that happy state of peaceful affairs, can be celebrated as among the greatest success stories.

Opportunities

The difficulties entailed in interpreting world military order are evident in the most cursory survey of recent political developments. In the last decade, for instance, the West has witnessed challenges to several dimensions of prevailing postwar strategic practice. Years of strategic decision-making that used to be made quietly behind closed doors were gradually but irrevocably dragged out into the streets for mass scrutiny. This played no small role, though by no means the most powerful one, in removing the spell of secrecy that had frozen politics across – and within – the respective blocs for decades. The democratization of security policy was part of the democratization of politics, and with it the power of those who masterminded the (inter)national security apparatuses were exposed, like the Wizard of Oz, for the facade of power which insulated them.

Politically, strategists, both East and West, had to confront a renewed wave of European peace movements throughout the early 1980s. These various challenges did not by themselves alter Alliance strategy, but they did legitimize critical efforts and forced strategic planners, for the first time in postwar history, to reorient their policies and to take into account issues of political legitimacy. NATO's Pershing II and Cruise Missile deployments went ahead as originally scheduled, but the public was increasingly skeptical of their value. Strategists and politicians were forced to pay attention to criticism.[50]

This heightened sensitivity of strategic officials can be understood as a specific historical response to the demands of a suspicious and critical social movement – a phase that seemed to pass when the peace movements, as they had earlier, receded from the political forefront after vociferous years. By the late 1980s, the widespread view was that the Western Alliance, having weathered the Euromissile deployment crisis, and having proceeded on its own terms to have subsequently negotiated away the Intermediate Nuclear Forces, could thereby reclaim its former self-confidence as the architect of a stable, rational, and peaceful world order. In such a view, the basic analytical tenets of Strategic Studies could validate themselves as realistic categories of policy analysis and prescription.

Intra-alliance squabbles there would continue to be – over NATO

31

strategy, over negotiations with the Soviet Union, and over burden sharing of military expenditures. But all of these issues, which had characterized Western strategic politics since the immediate postwar days, could nonetheless be contained and managed within the comforting rhetorical ambit ensured by Strategic Studies.

It seemed that the ensuing strategic stalemate functioned as a pacifying force. Within each of the alliance systems, however, there was turbulence and unrest. In the West, the unease could be mediated via an appeal to a common cause, a shared enterprise which legitimately affirmed the express purpose of deterrence. But in the east, there was no such consensus, and it became evident early on – from the days of the first uprisings in East Germany in 1953, down through Budapest in 1956, Prague in 1968 and Danzig in 1980 – that the effective purpose of Warsaw Pact troop deployments was to facilitate internal occupation and to provide against popular uprisings. The presence of an enemy, if not a potential aggressor, on the western border provided the much-needed patina of credibility, without which such a policy of (ersatz) military occupation would have been much more difficult to implement. Small wonder, then, that the first crumblings of the facade quickly turned into a dramatic collapse from the core.

Globally, the ideological opposition between the First and Second Worlds, between the leading capitalist powers and the leading socialist powers, has been altered at breakneck speed. Nominally, the geopolitical map of the postwar world, and with it, the chessboard of global strategic relations, has been dramatically redrawn. In a stunning series of developments, frantically pursued by the major television networks in their ritual attempt to be "on the spot," the political and social boundaries of Europe were reconfigured. Suddenly, East and West were effectively dissolved and Central Europe was reborn. The Berlin Wall has literally been dismantled, a degree of democratic reform has come to a great number of countries where no change could have been predicted a year or two earlier. And the great bipolar conflict between two hegemonic superpowers finally – or so it seemed – has played itself out. To be sure, the changes vary markedly. In Romania, what looked like a social revolution turned out to be a palace coup. In Poland, the socialist world's first genuine democratic working-class movement inherited a bankrupt industrial infrastructure. In Czechoslovakia, an unlikely alliance of writers and workers transformed the dream of the Prague Spring into the region's most boldly democratic experiment – for a while, until that country succumbed to deep-seated internal tensions and eventually split into two republics. The German Democratic Republic was simply erased from the map, united (not "reunited") with its western neighbor in a process so palpably undemocratic that by the time of the merger on October 3, 1990, a majority of (former) West Germans opposed it and the majority of (former) East Germans were beginning to regret it since it would cost many of them their jobs.[51]

These dramatic changes in the social and political landscape have been accompanied by a series of analytical developments regarding the nature of social inquiry. There is no need to make any argument of causal connection here between practical politics and the philosophy of the social sciences. Structures of intellectual mediation are so diffuse that no one can confidently claim anything more than the most tenuous relationship between broad-based social movements for change and ferment regarding social analysis. Nevertheless, an important connection can be pointed to, however fortuitously it developed. For the basic issue is that a critical perspective has emerged within International Relations that focuses less on institutionalized politics within and between states, and far more on those social and cultural practices that transcend such boundaries as "man," "the state," and the "states system."

It is not clear, however, and it remains very much an open question, whether something will replace the old familiarities – whether something called a New World Order, or a new economic order centered around Japan and the European Community, or perhaps a revived *Pax Americana*. Nor is it necessarily something to celebrate. A few years ago, all the talk was optimistically about "the end of history."[52] It was not long, however, before newspapers and popularizing journals began to muse, in the words of political scientist John Mearsheimer, whether we would all soon miss the Cold War.[53] In the Soviet Union and Yugoslavia, the promise of democratic renewal fragmented and crossed over into various forms of outright civil war. Gorbachev's attempt to control the pace of liberalization broke down as long-suppressed religious and nationalities conflicts began to implode the Soviet state. No sooner did the United States begin to discuss allocating a post-Cold War "peace dividend" than war erupted yet again in the Persian Gulf, bringing with it a whole spate of questions concerning nuclear proliferation, regional arms races, the agony of military regimes, and the specter of renewed cultural and social conflict.

Moreover, for vast stretches of the globe, the breakdown of the older world order offers no visible hope for the future. The talk of building a New International Economic Order has subsided as the Western world, politely referred to as the "multilateral trading system," refused to acquiesce in a series of structural reforms. The result is that many

33

national economies are stagnating, mired in growing debt. With the collapse of primary commodity prices on the world market, some of these countries now find it more attractive to turn themselves into tourist outposts or to export drugs to the industrialized world.

All of this has meant something of a crisis for the teaching of International Relations. To put it mildly, major chunks of the old reliable war-horse textbooks in International Relations and Comparative Politics are no longer usable in the classroom. And this is symptomatic of a deeper dilemma. The fundamental issue is that like the Cold War and all the other formulas for organizing world politics, the prevailing discourses no longer seem flexible enough to accommodate the extraordinary changes that are taking place throughout the world.

If we are expected today to continue in the empiricist tradition of discovering observable and verifiable truths about a world and encasing them in a single dominant approach to world politics, then we will be disappointed. Philosophies of language and of social inquiry have continually eroded away a set of distinctions that were previously part of the social sciences enterprise. The distinctions, for instance, between objective and subjective, real and ideal, reason and passion, and most importantly, between the knowing subject and the object under consideration. Another way to put it is that the old goal of the social sciences was to test our knowledge of the world. A different task, by contrast, might be to look at how the choice of paradigms enables us to include – and exclude – certain variables as relevant. To take one example from the field of Strategic Studies, the very meaning of the concept "security" is being subjected to questioning. Where once the term referred to freedom from external military aggression, at least on some accounts the concept of "security" has now been expanded to include issues of human rights, economic sufficiency, and environmental balance. Thus armaments policies may contribute to national security understood in terms of a classical security paradigm; but when measured by the criteria of new security paradigms, the same policies contribute to widespread insecurity and immiseration.[54]

In this sense, a paradigm does not gaze at an external world, but rather, it contributes to its representation in various ways and selects for us appropriate avenues of political action and public policy.[55] Instead of measuring and testing the world, then, we need to consider how our various forms of thought help give particular form and meaning to what we are examining. From the realist standpoint, for instance, the dominant unit of analysis in world politics is the state. The state is construed to preside over civil society, and the world

34

consists in a formal structure of anarchy in which each state is entirely responsible for its own welfare and security. This realist, state-centered perspective might help us appreciate – and promote – strategies of mercantilism and of national defense, but from such a perspective, issues such as transnational trade, ecological fragility, and the fate of non-market economies will appear marginal. We are unlikely to appreciate such phenomena, and are likely to misconstrue their dynamics as we impose our own modes of explanation upon them.

What is interesting about the once-dominant International Relations discourse of realism is not that it was in some sense an accurate account of the world, but that it helped contribute to the legitimacy and persistence of a world dominated by major powers. It is not that realism is wrong, only that realism is one of many possible representations of global space and global practices. Its truth, so to speak, derives only from its compatibility with dominant powers in the world system.

A generation ago there was a great debate in International Relations, a search, in effect, for a new International Relations paradigm. A massive intellectual effort yielded much dissension and the emergence, among other things, of a rival paradigm – what came to be known as pluralism.[56] It was based on neoclassical economic theory and sought to look at interdependence and the politics of global economic relations. It was a much-needed corrective to classical realism's emphasis upon the balance of military power, but no sooner did the pluralists win their paradigmatic hegemony than along came the first of many volumes by Immanuel Wallerstein and with them, the emergence of world systems theory.[57] And this, in turn, conflicted with a variety of neoclassical and critical approaches to transnational relations.

There is no need to rehearse the details of these debates. The point, instead, is that there has been a continual march of pretenders for the throne – realism, pluralism, world systems theory, dependencia, world order thinking, followed by realism in the technocratic guise of something called structural realism.

There has also been a critical turn in the discipline, an attempt to draw upon the insights of Marx, the Frankfurt School, and scholars ranging from Jürgen Habermas to Robert Cox in what has come to be called critical theory. This is an attractive alternative, because it contains an explicitly politicizing approach that seeks to democratize international practices and to link up issues of world relations with social processes, social movements and transformations in class and economic relations.

There is a growing recognition among scholars of International Relations that theoretical developments informed by a range of critical sentiments are increasingly important to the discipline. Indeed, Robert Keohane has attempted to corral many of these approaches into a framework which he calls "reflectivist." Yet many of those whom he herds under this inclusive umbrella – Durkheimians, Gramscians, hermeneuticists, deconstructionists, intertextualists – repudiate such claims of sharing a common epistemology and prefer to elaborate positions at odds with sovereign claims of providing a new theory for International Studies.[58] But regardless of attempts to locate diverse schools of disruptive thought within recognizable frontiers, the analytical power of these emergent unconventional, marginal approaches is clear. The social sciences, among them International Relations and Strategic Studies, are being recast. Memorializing accounts that celebrate Strategic Studies as the arbiter of world order can now be seen less as the wisdom of cool analytical realism than as the highly politicized exercise of power through a discourse that itself violently inscribes the world. A critical look at the discipline of strategy thus reveals it to be concerned with demarcating political space and establishing boundaries of inclusivity and exclusivity at the margins or frontiers of sovereignty.

But of course "critical" can mean many things. It can, for example, mean the application of formal logic to explanatory chains or statements. Ever since Marx, "critical" has (also) been understood as showing the hidden connection between the ideological, superstructural realm of appearances and the underlying, substructural realm of reality. And in the hands of the Frankfurt School, this style of immanent critique was harnessed not only to traditional philosophy, but to a variety of cultural forms as well, including the family, the arts, the media and popular lifestyles.

In recent years, another mode of criticism has emerged to exercise a decisive hold over the social sciences. Drawn from neo-Wittgensteinian language philosophy, and sometimes heralded as the linguistic turn, the kinds of critical methods I have in mind here share as a common concern the over-turning of foundationalism.[59] While there are diverse strands and methods at play, some more explicitly literary and others more rooted in classical Continental sociology, there can be little doubt that the various schools of thought concerned to move beyond a commitment to structures of knowledge and practice are influencing contemporary research. And while there is always a danger in announcing oneself as the bearer of this or that perspective, there can be little doubt that genealogical and discourse-analytic modes of inquiry have much to say of interest in social science in general, and International Relations in particular.

Thus drawing on a tradition of thought which can be traced through Marxian philosophy, Nietzsche's critique of ethics, the critique of ideology, the sociology of knowledge, and debates about representation and the intertextuality of forms of life, this body of thought can be brought to bear on strategy, war and peace. The result may not be the confident, reconstructive alternative account of strategic arrangements that both traditionalists and their critics may want. But that may be less the failure of this argument than an example of the common commitment to foundationalism and totality that such analysts furtively share. It is no abdication of intellectual responsibility today that the account here is exploratory rather than conclusive – an attempt to open up new dimensions of international life and to think critically about them.

We are now ready to explore a dimension of military force and warfare not currently emphasized in prevailing accounts of Strategic Studies: the constitutive nature of organized violence in the making of modern political identity and global politics. Strategic Studies needs to be historicized. Such a conceptual opening up cannot be confined to narrating the history of war and of succeeding hegemonic states. Strategic Studies already does this, and does this in a manner which recapitulates a grand narrative of "there has always been war, there always will be war." What escapes critical analysis in this tradition is the question of how states capable of conducting warfare emerge in the first place. The ability to coordinate material resources, personnel, and industrial technology and to bring them to bear against other political units presupposes dimensions of political economy that elide strategic analysis. Strategists examine the war-making capability of states, but the analytic categories deployed in such a policy-making enterprise merely presuppose the existence of these capabilities and then take account of how much has been achieved and how much is achievable in the near future.

War as organized violence, however, requires more than the marshalling of material resources. It requires human resources and forms of political identity. Such practices are presupposed, but not explained, in prevailing modes of strategic analysis. Strategic Studies relies uncritically on what most needs explanation – the development of political units capable of relying upon force to distinguish at the frontier their internal and external identities. In exploring how sovereign states use violence to defend and advance their interests amidst a hostile, anarchic world, Strategic Studies overlooks the extent to which

37

Hasn't
been
shown

states rely upon violence to constitute themselves *as* states and to impose differentiations between the internal and the external. A major point of this study, then, is that a critical account of war and military strategy requires analysis of the constitutive role of violence in the making of states that act strategically upon the world. This is not simply a question of military capabilities, nor even one of the political economy of militarization. It involves, rather, discourses of violence by which military practices are embedded and legitimated within the texture of modern life. It is, after all, in this sense that nuclear deterrence has assumed importance – as a most sublime expression of the violence done by liberal states to the world in the name of maintaining an order that in fact is being continually established in the first place.

3 WHAT NUCLEAR REVOLUTION?

A wall was erected between the civil and the military, a wall which cut off all relations between them and shut them away from each other's view. And because the people on the inside of the wall were engaged in something which seemed mysterious to profane eyes, those on the outside considered that something beyond their comprehension and bowed to it with a respect almost religious. (Giulio Douhet[1])

The last chapter explored the political nature of strategic thought. In this chapter, attention focuses on nuclear deterrence. Arguments about the character of nuclear strategy have been decisively shaped by claims made nearly a half a century ago regarding a "revolution" in the nature of political–military strategy that was ushered in with the advent of the overwhelming offensive power of atomic and thermonuclear weaponry. This has been called the nuclear revolution, the absolute triumph of offense over defense, and with it a transformation of the nature of military force, from war-winning to war-prevention through deterrence. But such arguments are founded on technical understandings of military force abstracted from social purpose and cultural processes. In this chapter, I elaborate the Clausewitzian foundations of arguments about a nuclear revolution and criticize the "thin" accounts of politics, force, technology and revolution which animate such views in the first place. The result is an awareness of the rhetorical or representational practices by which Strategic Studies removes questions of organized violence from social practices.

To undertake that, I begin with a short account of realism, followed by a detailed account of the terms of nuclear "revolution."

From "fortuna" to "friction"

Contemporary Strategic Studies emerges from a peculiar historical and intellectual achievement. It is coterminous, both temporally and spatially, with the rise of the West as the dominant subject of world politics. By "the West" I refer here not (just) to a geographically bounded North Atlantic space; nor simply to the legally sovereign states comprising the Western Alliance. Rather, the referent is broader still: to that diffuse cultural and political formation which defines itself in terms of values and practices of a specifically modern orientation. The subject of security in this sense is not limited to the member states of various alliance systems. For the field of Strategic Studies codifies the very practices by which modern statesmen, working with their coteries of technologists, architects, scribes, bureaucrats, warriors, businessmen, academics and explorers, have shaped a contemporary world system which it is now their job to "secure."

In formal terms of constituent units, the practices encoded through Strategic Studies involve a fully articulated system of states – a phenomenon that is not in itself exclusively Western, nor necessarily modern. Versions of such a states system are discernible in the Hellenic city-states of Thucydides' era, and scholars can rightly point to *The Peloponnesian War* as an early, dramatic statement of power politics, balance-of-power considerations, and strategic thinking.[2] Contemporaneously, but at another end of the world, Sun Tzu's political–military writings in the Chinese era of The Warring States attests to something akin to a states system. And the Indian commentator Kautilya is heralded as having articulated a version of statesmanship with remarkable similarities to what much later became known as realism. That such commentators have found analogous rules of relationship within a states system provides much of the persuasive force underlying the claims of modern realism to universal validity. On these terms, the power of power politics derives from the truth of its claims regarding the foundational behavior of man and the state.

But despite the apparent similarity of these many traditional writings, the claims to universality are suspect. For what is one to make of those realms where no formal states system is discernible? And what of the great interregna within the so-called Western tradition itself when formal state structures gave way to overlapping and multi-dimensional forms of political and cosmological association. The absence of an identifiable strategic literature in the early Medieval era, for example, suggests that claims to the universality of the strategic approach are questionable if not simply invalid.

The affinity that can be sustained, however, is not that between the strategic approach and universal truth, but, in more limited terms, to strategy and a states system of global dimensions.

This may seem to be an unexceptional claim, and surely one that will

40

not draw refutation by defenders of the tradition. But in such matters it often pays to illuminate precisely those truths that form the unreflective, background conditions of an activity. As we shall now see, to problematize this affinity between strategy and the state is to see the mutually constituting and enabling role each plays. Strategic Studies is a fundamental means by which the modern states system sustains and reproduces itself. Its heritage is linearly derived from the Greco-Roman world, and after having lain fallow during the interregnum of the Dark Ages it emerged in the Renaissance, was absorbed within the modernist vision of the Enlightenment, accumulated most of its intellectual capital during the era of British hegemony, and achieved worldwide apotheosis in the heady postwar era of the American quarter-century. Strange as it may seem, Strategic Studies today is part of the West's intellectual capital. It is an essential component in the articulation of world order in terms that create and perpetuate a global political vision in which Western values, institutions and political economies are valorized in sublimated form. In this sense, Strategic Studies celebrates the construction and preservation of the West.

The great German historian Otto Hintze wrote in 1906 of the basic affinity of military organization with the structure of the state. For him, the modern state has its origins in the need of peoples to demarcate and secure an economically viable political space. "All state organization was originally military organization, organization for war."[3] Subsequent to the modern, sovereign territorial state, there were less-structured, less bureaucratically organized states with correspondingly less structured armed forces: clans, for instance, or feudal allegiances, each closely related to a particular political form that, in retrospect, is distinguishable from the modern state and its virtual absorption of purely military institutions. The standing army, and its successor, the citizen army, are peculiarly modern sociological phenomena that are coterminous with the modern nation–state.[4] Distinctive here is not the disappearance of the military but its subjection to a specific state apparatus. To study the state was to study its military structure: "the form and spirit of the state's organization will not be determined solely by economic and social relations and clashes of interests, but primarily by the necessities of defense and offense, that is, by the organization of the army and warfare."[5]

In outlining his military sociology, Hintze draws upon a conception of the state that was self-consciously steeped in the tradition of German historicism. This was a tradition that grew explicitly out of the historical experience of the European state and the European states system in the post-Westphalian era. It was a tradition that emphasized

41

the role of political organization in marshalling various resources of economic and military power so as to strengthen the sovereign's hand. In ways that contemporary realists have scarcely acknowledged, the tradition of historicism has found its way into contemporary thinking by a peculiar genealogy that can be said to have been founded by Machiavelli, was politically institutionalized by the absolutist statesmen of early modern Europe and that was philosophically mediated by the political sociology of Max Weber. Indeed, it was only by way of Weber's peculiar sociology of the state that German historicism, in its nineteenth-century guise, was rendered acceptable and transmittable to modern scholars of International Relations. But what became the Americanized version of realism, as seen particularly in the works of Hans Morgenthau and in a structural variant by Kenneth Waltz, dispensed with much of "the dirty hands" that had shaped the classical tradition. Classical realism is embedded in institutional arrangements and forms of legitimacy that are anything but liberal and anything but consistent with an orderly system of international affairs. It is important to reclaim this side of realism – and of Strategic Studies – for the simple reason that only by studying the genesis and transformations of the classical tradition can we appreciate how in contemporary world politics, longstanding practices of militarism and militarization have not disappeared but rather, become insinuated into the quotidian fabric of life.

Historically speaking, in Hintze's pithy formulation, "power politics, mercantilism, and militarism are all related."[6] Yet he also observed a shift within the modern state from "military" to "industrial" principles. Here, following Herbert Spencer,[7] Hintze observes how a dominant bourgeois social class was able to wrest control of the military from a longstanding aristocratic corps and embed it within a state apparatus.

That relation had been foreseen somewhat earlier. It was, after all, Thucydides who first analyzed a recognizable version of power politics. He saw the origins of the Peloponnesian War in terms of Corinth allying itself with Sparta in order to thwart the growing power of Athens. In the narrative of war, and in the many dialogues which report either what orators actually said or what Thucydides believes was called for by each situation,[8] we can discern the origins of an intellectual tradition which sees the states system as subject to no central authority, as the product of each polity's interests competing against the interests of other polities, as a realm in which good will or professions of intent are irrelevant if not misleading, and as a realm in which war stands as an acceptable arbiter of political disputes. It is a world in which citizens, rather than being appalled by recourse to violence, are actually supposed to be ennobled by the state's willingness to resort to warfare when its leaders believe it is threatened or that vital interests are at stake.

We see evidence here of realist considerations and of a states system based upon them. Realism is more than "a theory" of International Relations. It is a discourse on the management of force in politics among states that relies upon the threat and use of military power to establish a modicum of peace. It sees world politics in terms of a given immutable structure to which states have to orient their policies. It attributes to that system an objective, unyielding character over which no unifying sovereign reigns.

Such statesmanship entails a peculiar responsibility for the fate of a polity: a responsibility construed in the realist tradition as requiring political leaders to accept the risks of war in the name of restraining other states.

In the centuries after Thucydides, the realist tradition repeatedly addressed the anguish, the moral anguish, of a statesmanship whose means involved recourse to force. St. Augustine agonized over the legitimacy of violence in the "civitas terrena," the city of man. His work focused upon the politics by which fallen man must order his world. Only with power can the public peace be assured. It is a peace based upon the just uses of force and not upon justice itself.

With Machiavelli, this moral dilemma of realist statesmanship was made all the more vexing because of the secular conditions in which politics had to take place. Shorn of gods, unable to appeal to purer forms of knowledge and the good, struggling with the vicissitudes of "Fortuna" in its always incomplete attempts to secure a political space, the strategies of power advanced by realist statesmanship have been of central concern to Western thought and practice.

The claim that violence and power characterize an emergent state system finds its warrant in the Machiavellian tradition. "Realpolitik," "Staatsräson," are two views of international relations that have emerged in the wake of, and that first found support in, the writings of this Florentine diplomat. No one in the history of political thought has written so passionately of power. The prince or legislator seeking to found and maintain a polity must not shy away from the uses of violence in securing a political space.

Machiavelli's work, of course, especially *The Prince*, abounds in counsel to the manipulative political leader who is impelled by ambition and who searches for glory by becoming the head of state. But though a would-be tyrant may find license in Machiavelli's work, he will only do so at the price of misconstruing the larger purpose of those writings. For Machiavelli's realism is considerably more complicated than one finds by pulling out this or that quotation from his most-read work.

In its entirety, Machiavelli's work displays a remarkable ambiguity about the use and propriety of violence in founding and maintaining a state. While having no doubts that a well-run principality or republic had to be founded by the use of force, Machiavelli repeatedly stresses that without good laws and respected institutions, sufficient arms and resolute leaders are to no avail. The language of political virtue that informs a well-run state is not that of military conquest but of a people's willingness to defend when necessary the land and laws they respect. To found such a state the forceful prince must not shy away from eliminating corruption and greed. But Machiavelli repeatedly makes clear that a state based exclusively on violence is tyrannical and unworthy of merit. In short, the Machiavellian leader, whether prince or republican, must always agonize about the political nature and consequences of the force he uses in securing and maintaining a polity.

To recast this slightly in terms more familiar to modern statesmanship, the Machiavellian leader is compelled by the nature of the secular state to balance the quest for legitimate policies with the need to establish the credibility of his willingness to resort to arms should the polity's security be threatened. The "virtù" of which Machiavelli speaks so often stems from the knowledge among a polity's citizens that a state is able to preserve the liberties of its institutions should an attack – whether by domestic conspirators or foreigners – ever be launched upon them. Such virtue is political insofar as it pertains to the recognition that a set of political values exists, are widely acknowledged, and are cherished dearly by a populace. And that virtue is paramilitary insofar as adherence to those values entails an obligation, indeed, a willingness, of a people to fight for and defend their own country when necessary.

This should not be mistaken for militarism. It is rather patriotism on constant guard. A republic or principality unable to raise a citizen-army, that must in its stead rely upon mercenaries paid by and contracted through *condottieri* of dubious allegiance who merely seek commercial gain, is a state neither legitimate nor likely to preserve for very long what few liberties it may have. Foreign powers and potential rival claimants to power will be dissuaded from launching attacks on republics or principalities only when these are imbued with virtue.

In *The Prince*, *The Art of War* and *The History of Florence*, Machiavelli views strategy as an essentially politically practice, as part of the attempt by the virtuous prince to tame the vicissitudes of "fortuna" through the sagacious deployment of force and public violence – through what Machiavelli calls the acumen afforded by "necessita." An open-textured quality of public life is preserved in terms of the inescapable vortex known as "fortuna," but the need to domesticate political life is reserved unto the prince as the embodiment of the state. There is, however, no transcendent structure accorded life beyond the principality or republic, no architectonic "state of war." That only comes in subsequent centuries with the development of the modern state apparatus and the consolidation, under the Treaties of Westphalia of 1648, of a more formalized balance of power state system.

The psychological bonds of patriotism, and the political relationships of civic virtue, were repeatedly represented by Machiavelli in terms of a citizen-army. The willingness to fight for one's state, in fact, is construed in his account of statesmanship as an obligation entailed by citizenship. For Machiavelli, this characterizes a virtuous state: one dependent upon an infantry force of local volunteers and conscripts. The symbol of Machiavelli's respect for infantry was the disdain he expressed for cannon. Machiavelli's Luddite dismissal of artillery, his preference instead for Roman column formations and the tactics of Swiss pikemen, embodies in stark terms his concern for building into his military strategy a place for the patriotism and political zeal which he thought should underpin the virtuous polity.

This balance of power was built upon the imminent recourse to warfare as a means of intervening in the affairs of ambitious or emboldened states and as a means of preventing them from becoming too powerful. In effect, many wars of the balance of power were pre-emptive, much like the allied intervention of Corinth and Sparta in the Potidean revolt which sparked the Peloponnesian War. In 1756, for instance, Prussia seized Saxony in the face of a new alliance between Austria and France that Frederick the Great feared would threaten his hold over Silesia. Even offensive wars, such as Prussia's seizure of Silesia in 1740, or earlier, recurrent attempts by Sweden to capture lands along the south coast of the Baltic Sea, were undertaken for specific objectives – though without annihilating opposing armies, and without warring upon homelands and civilians. Wars, to recast Clausewitz's famous dictum, were the continuation of political intercourse, with the addition of other, though limited, means.

Gradually, of course, the firepower of states grew, as did the size of their armies. War increasingly became a matter of national mobilization and professional effort. It began to approach – asymptotically – the total integration of a country's resources. The mercenary armies of

Machiavelli's Italy became the standing citizen forces of Frederick the Great's Prussia. During this entire period of development, the armies of Europe retained their classical role: to win wars by compelling the enemy's retreat or surrender, cutting off its supply lines, and preventing it from besieging fortresses or walled-in cities. The armies of the Continental balance of power, particularly before Napoleon and after Metternich, were instruments of political policy, but that policy had limited aims. Armies sought neither to destroy the enemy completely, nor to engage an adversary's whole land and people in battle. Popular and courtly outrage over the destruction wrought upon Germany by the various Protestant and Catholic, French, Swedish, and Imperial armies during the Thirty Years' War led the statesmen of Europe, after the Peace of Westphalia in 1648, to restrict the movements of armies. Mercantile considerations combined with technological limits and widely shared Christian sentiments to shape and confine the aims of warfare.[9]

In the 300 years separating Machiavelli's armed civic virtue from Clausewitz's articulation of total national warfare, the terrain of political relationships expanded, and with it, the scope of warfare. The nascent urban republicanism of Renaissance Italy gave way to the obligatory military service of conscript armies within a Continent-wide balance of power political system. Within this new state system that characterized Europe after the era of religious wars, from the Thirty Years' War to the French Revolution, citizenship and allegiance to the state evolved dramatically from Machiavelli's seminal formulations of the emergent indefinite state.

In this new state system, a more ordered hierarchy of public power developed. The dynamism of competing urban factions gave way to centralized mercantile economy and to the "statism" of bureaucratically organized, aristocratically led, standing armies. The "animo" and "ambizione" of private citizens were absorbed by state-controlled monopolies, the primary concern of which was the expansion of state fiscal and military strength. The balance of trade and the balance of power occupied the courts of Europe. The glory of military leadership in the muster of feudal chivalry increasingly became the domain of war cabinets and professionally trained career staffmen. The commercial military system of Italian Renaissance warfare gave way to standing armies with their coterie of technologists, metallurgists and manufacturers entirely occupied in the development of mass firepower, military engineering, artillery and naval science. These bureaucratic military institutions only drew upon mercenaries to supplement the

46

manpower requirements of warfare in the service of the balance of power.

The economic constraints of mercantilism expressed themselves in elaborate battlefield tactics designed to avoid costly expenditures of men, provisions and armaments. But eventually, this, too, gave way to the intensification of firepower afforded by technical improvements and by the ability of some states, pre-eminently Prussia, to train and discipline their growing number of soldiers. This gradual expansion in the scope and intensity of war found its apotheosis in the French Revolutionary Army. The rules of absolutist warfare, assiduously followed by the Continental powers throughout the shift from dynastic to national politics, demanded that citizenship be construed in terms of supplying the manpower necessary for political competition. The open public space of Machiavelli's city–state became narrowed, structured and firmly institutionalized within the stultifying ministries and bureaucracies of the modern nation–state. The flux and challenge of overcoming "fortuna" became the mechanics of managing "friction."

Classical principles

Writing in the aftermath of Napoleonic warfare, the Prussian military educator Carl von Clausewitz (1780–1831) believed himself to have discerned the limits of military force in the form of the French revolutionary *Grande Armée*. Its reliance upon the "levée en masse," its stunning deployment of mobile field guns, and its unremitting Continental ambitions, combined to endow it with a scope unparalleled in all of political–military history. Clausewitz, writing as both a student of military history and as an advisor to the Prussian Reformers, witnessed with both military awe and nationalist fervor how this powerful force had been unleashed upon the European powers. His analytic efforts by way of response codified the nature of contemporary warfare in terms that have decisively shaped all subsequent debates about the nature of force.[10]

Like so many of his contemporaries, Clausewitz wrote under the influence – in his case, without acknowledgement – of a Kantian epistemology that posited a distinction between the real and the knowable, between the "noumenon" in its philosophical form and its "phenomenal" presentation to human perception in everyday life.[11] The distinction between the noumenal and the phenomenal is paralleled in Clausewitz's representation of war. Clausewitz poses a distinction between "absolute war," the ideal as it can be understood in all its

47

purity, and "real war," or its various embodiments as encountered on mankind's battlefields.

The opening pages of Clausewitz's posthumously published volume, *On War* (1831), focus on the analytically separable content of "absolute war." In its unmediated form, the pure philosophical ideal of absolute war can be understood in terms of a duel between two forces, each of which strives to escalate the use of violence in order literally to disarm the adversary. In every violent struggle, in every act of war, there exists metaphysically a filament of this "absolute war." That, after all, is what distinguishes violence from disagreement or conventional politics. The resort to violence entails a principle of struggle that logically culminates in the triumph of one party and the exhaustion and elimination of the other. In its absolute form, war escalates toward the annihilation of one party to the battle.

Clausewitz then introduces modifications. This is his way of shifting from the "absolute" to the "real." Here, however, he is actually betraying the Kantian heritage, since on logical terms it is impossible to move from the noumenal (absolute) to the phenomenal (real) as if shifting from one end of a continuum to another. In arguing that real war is but a modification, a compromise, of absolute war, Clausewitz wants to argue that the relation between the absolute and the real is one of degrees rather than of kind. From a technical standpoint, much of the rest of the opening section is redundant since there is no need to belabor why "real war" is something less than "absolute war." The deficit is inherent in the conceptual relationship. Yet by not remaining true to his analytical heritage, Clausewitz gave generations of strategists to come much to argue about. For the issue raised by Napoleonic warfare is, according to Clausewitz, whether real war, in its full or total form, can so closely approximate unconstrained annihilatory violence as to be, in effect, absolute war.

From the standpoint of Kantian logic, the question is grievously misplaced, akin to asking how close one can come to infinity by counting forever. But Clausewitz's awkwardly introduced modifications of the pure concept nonetheless have their utility. They enable him to characterize modern warfare in relation to, or as relaxed versions of, something uncompromised and absolute. Indeed, the tension which Clausewitz sets up between "absolute war" and "real war" was to stimulate debates that took place 150 years later when deterrence theorists argued whether nuclear warfare only approaches, or does actually achieve, the status of "absolute war." In other words, does the much proclaimed "nuclear revolution" mean the transcendence of all classical principles of real war and the actual advent of the possibility of conducting absolute war, or is nuclear warfare, however total and destructive in form, merely an extension of classical principles that uphold for all forms of real war? If nuclear war is, indeed, the realization of what Clausewitz referred to as absolute war, then the only principles that can obtain are those that seek to prevent war. This is the argument of deterrence theorists such as Bernard Brodie and Robert Jervis.[12] The counter-argument, that nuclear war is but a continuation, "in extremis," of real war, is a position adhered to by such "warfighters" as Herman Kahn, Paul Nitze, and Colin Gray.[13]

For Clausewitz, three principles ensure that all real wars will be less than absolute. First, he declares, "War is never an isolated act." By this he means that as a political act, as "the continuation of political intercourse, with the addition of other means," war always involves a set of relations involving not merely the armed forces but the state and the populace as well. These three he called "the holy trinity." As if to foreshadow the warnings of classically trained, postwar realist strategists against their narrow-minded, techno-strategic brethren who often considered war in the abstract, as a mere "exchange" or "spasm" of weapons-systems removed from social processes and purposes, Clausewitz warns of the dangers in removing war from politics.

> As a total phenomenon its dominant tendencies always make war a remarkable trinity – composed of primordial violence, hatred, and enmity, which are to be regarded as a blind natural force; of the play of chance and probability within which the creative spirit is free to roam; and of its element of subordination, as an instrument of policy, which makes it subject to reason.
>
> The first of these three aspects mainly concerns the people; the second the commander and his army; the third the government ... A theory that ignores any one of them or seeks to fix an arbitrary relationship between them would conflict with reality to such an extent that for this reason alone it would be useless.[14]

It must be remembered here that Clausewitz was exclusively a theorist of land warfare. He never wrote a telling word about naval operations, and of course aerial warfare was unimaginable to him. But his argument about war never being an isolated act comes out of his understanding that land armies required long periods of time to put in the field – time to recruit, train, march. There had to be a reason for dispatching men to battle. The rhythms of diplomacy alone ensured that wars were part of inter-state relations. The very nature of war as a human activity entailed that it serve state purposes. Here and elsewhere, Clausewitz argued not merely from the logical category of war as a human activity. He was also doing his own bit of pleading against what he perceived as a tendency within Napoleonic warfare to fight "outrance," what the German military historian Hans Delbrück was later to call "eine Niederwerfungsstrategie," a war of annihilation through mobility, overwhelming numerical superiority, and the taking of the offense.[15] In other words, Clausewitz's modifying principle suggests the need to maintain war within rational purposes of state policy. Thus the logician and the military analyst conspire to formulate first principles that articulate war as an inherently – and unavoidably – limited "real" human enterprise.

The second modifying principle makes less a philosophical point than a strictly military–analytical one. In war, the tendency toward maximal exertion is always and unavoidably constrained by the limits of knowledge, of space and time, and of human character. Clausewitz condenses whole worlds into a single terse phrase: "War does not consist of a single short blow."[16]

In other words, war is protracted through space and over time. There is a given structure to that space, demarcated by frontiers, battlefields, and the distances between national capitals. The battlefield itself lies sprawled out over a definite space, which the sagacious military commander can apprehend through his keen eye, the "coup d'oeil." But even in the era of total national warfare, the constraints posed by communications, terrain, and sheer human exertion limited the extent of war. "The abstract world is ousted by the real one and the trend to the extreme is thereby moderated."[17] A whole range of resources basic to warfare "cannot all be deployed at the same moment."[18] The "fighting forces proper, the country with its physical features and population, and its allies"[19] all comprise relationships which bind statesmen in their pursuit of war. The frequency of periods in which no direct combat takes place, the suspension of action in war, means that violence in battle is not of one piece. The natural hesitancy resulting from inescapably faulty intelligence further impedes the war effort.

Here Clausewitz introduces two principles of political–military strategy to explain how war cannot consist of a single blow. The first is the inherent strength of the defensive position; the second is that of "friction." It pays to explain these at some length because debates about nuclear strategy have turned on the contemporary relevance of these two seminal concepts.

Clausewitz repeatedly emphasizes that the defender enjoys a familiarity with the terrain, secure lines of communication, established supply lines, a clear line of retreat, and – usually – support of the populace.[20] Such strategic advantages are only overcome with extraordinary difficulty, and with overwhelming numerical superiority, on the part of attacking armies. Battle drags on, it ceases at night, and it grinds to a halt in winter. Much of an army's time consists of gathering supplies, securing billets, waiting for word from convoys, marching for days, weeks, on end without ever confronting an enemy. War thus consists of a whole series of disparate engagements, each of which involves battles but which rarely call upon whole armies. "The very nature of war," concludes Clausewitz, "impedes the simultaneous concentration of all forces."[21]

Clausewitz understood that warfare entailed obstacles to success in the field: that there existed a fundamental difference between the plan of war on paper and battle as it actually unfolded. He expresses this difference as one of "friction," a concept which enables one to appreciate how plans and strategems will often go awry because of accidents, misinformation, the fog of battle, exhaustion, faulty equipment, or untimely weather. In this military equivalent of Murphy's Law in engineering, Clausewitz makes the reader aware that war involves reducing this factor to a minimum, but that unforeseen, indeed, unforeseeable, difficulties are bound to arise.

No military strategist before Clausewitz had developed a systematic account of why things are destined to go wrong. A general whose plans depend on the perfect coordination of all his troops and equipment is likely to face military disaster.[22] Through practice an army learns, at best, to minimize friction and to accommodate itself to the vicissitudes of chance inherent in warfare.

The concept of friction is far narrower than the flux of civic history which Machiavelli had accounted for in terms of "fortuna." The cyclical nature of success and failure, the ephemeral nature of good fortune and wealth: these Machiavelli had incorporated into a concept of history that confronted the most virtuous of princes. But what 300 years earlier had codified the destiny of whole polities is with Clausewitz, in the era of conscript national armies, reduced to a range of technical problems in managing total warfare. Friction, after all, "is the only concept that more or less corresponds to the factors that distinguish real war from war on paper."[23] Thus "friction" serves in Clausewitz's work to mediate the transition from "absolute war" to "real war." But this leaves open the question of might happen if friction were reduced to, say, infinitesimal proportions. Would this not open up the possibility of "absolute war?"

The final modification introduced by Clausewitz is that whatever the course of battle, "in war, the result is never final."[24] Even defeated armies are never totally obliterated, and victorious nations must still

51

face the postwar tasks of resettlement, reconstruction, and establishing control. When nations are not totally defeated, when wars stop short of annihilating the enemy – and this is always the case, because there remains land to be tended, an economy to be re-started, and a civilian population – negotiations and peace settlements take over the tasks once carried out by weapons. War in its real form, not in its absolute embodiment, entails a range of responsibilities that neither victor nor the defeated can overlook.

To sum up, "the art of war deals with living and with moral forces," wrote Clausewitz. "Consequently, it cannot attain the absolute, or certainty."[25] This would seem to follow from the terms of the Kantian distinction between absolute and real war with which *On War* opens. Yet in this text, and in his essays and studies of Bonapartist generalship,[26] Clausewitz slides over to the view that with Napoleon, for the first time in military history, war achieved its absolute form.

The ambivalence of Clausewitz's formulation is not merely a matter of historical curiosity, nor simple testimony to Clausewitz's philosophical clumsiness. It goes to the heart of what modern warfare has – or can – become: whether through the advance of technology and the political mobilization of the democratic state one could actually conduct warfare at the absolute extreme.

Clausewitz's condensed sociology of military history in Book 8 of *On War* presents a teleology of war's development into its fullest, total form.[27] What he repeatedly refers to in *On War* as "the natural course" of battle achieved apotheosis under Bonaparte. The era of national warfare ushered in after the French Revolution brought the scope and intensity of warfare to its highest point since the beginning of military history. The "element of war itself, stirred up by great national interests, has become dominant and is pursuing its natural course."[28] The French campaigns of 1805–6 against the Third Coalition "are the ones that make it easier for us to grasp the concept of modern absolute war in all its devastating power."[29] "[W]ith our own eyes we have seen warfare achieve this state of absolute perfection . . . Bonaparte brought it swiftly and ruthlessly to that point."[30]

Clausewitz equivocates on this issue. Within Book 8 of *On War*, he shifts terms and qualifies his claim of modern French warfare's absolute character. "Since Bonaparte, then, war . . . closely approached its true character, its absolute perfection."[31] His account of the 1812 Russian Campaign is also ambiguous. "This was not, observes Clausewitz, "the kind of campaign that drags feebly on to its conclusion, but the first plan ever made by an attacker bent on the complete destruction of the Russian Army and the occupation of her country."[32]

Despite Bonaparte's attempt at such an absolute conquest, a strategy of annihilation ("Niederwerfungsstrategie"), he failed for having underestimated the enormity of the enterprise.

Clausewitz, however, leaves open the question whether with more forces, Bonaparte could have succeeded. And this is part of Clausewitz's larger ambiguity, left unresolved, whether in fact absolute war is really possible. For Clausewitz equates the philosophical distinction between the two concepts of war, absolute and real, with the practical distinction between two kinds of real war, total and limited.[33] War in its greatest possible form is total, but nonetheless real, not absolute. The subsequent history of strategic debates was to side with this question of categories: whether, following Kant, absolute war was severed by definition from real war; or whether, following the Hegelian transition from quantity to quality, the undisputed expansion of the technical forces of warfare available to statesmen could indeed make feasible something like absolute warfare. Those who argued after 1945 that this was, indeed, the case, made the argument for a nuclear revolution. In such a world, the Clausewitzian modifications of war were rendered obsolete, and with it, the use of war as an instrument of national policy. Such a view contrasted with those who, citing Clausewitz on their side, attempted to assimilate nuclear weaponry within the rubric of conventional warfare. On such an account, nuclear weaponry was but the latest stage in an evolution of real war whose basic principles Clausewitz had, indeed, discerned and whose fundamental truths still obtained. Thus did Clausewitz's ambiguous legacy deed the terms of debate regarding nuclear deterrence.

Total war and the triumph of aerial offense

The argument about a fundamental shift from the pre-nuclear to the nuclear in political–military strategy emerges from the claim that Clausewitz's three modifications of real war no longer upheld in the nuclear world. If conventional military conflict was characterized as protracted over space and time, fraught with limitation, and as never ultimate in its consequences, warfare in the nuclear age is claimed to be instantaneous, unlimited, and irreversible in its overwhelming consequences.

Clausewitz effectively condensed his argument about war as protracted into the straightforward observation that the defensive position enjoys inherent advantages over the offensive. But gradually, the development of military power, itself pushed onwards by the unfold-

53

ing of advanced industrialization and the mechanization of warfare, would lead to the twentieth-century phenomenon of total warfare. And this, in turn, began to press the limits of Clausewitz's understanding of all war as limited. While theoretically, total war, too, should be subjected to the constraints of friction and protraction, it began to seem, even to Clausewitz himself, that this might not be the case.

Clausewitz had been greatly impressed by Bonaparte's ability to mobilize and command an army, and he discerned in the French general's maneuvers the limits achievable in real warfare. In 1816, he observed that since the rise of Bonaparte, "the most daring of gamblers ... all campaigns have gained such a cometlike swiftness that a higher degree of military intensity is scarcely imaginable."[34] These comments were written before industrialization began to take hold on the Continent. Armies then consisted of mobile cavalry infantry with muskets, and horse-drawn field cannon that could shoot 100-pound balls up to half a mile accurately. Clausewitz's confessed inability to anticipate great changes in the technology and scope of battle may strike us today as somewhat naïve, the more so because Clausewitz was himself a skilled military historian. But we can now see that the armies of Napoleonic Europe stood far closer to those of the Renaissance some 300 hundred years earlier than to those that fought the Great War less than a century after Clausewitz.

In the era of mechanized warfare, an era ushered in by the rapid advance of technology accompanying the industrialization of Europe, the face of battle underwent a stunning transformation. Warfare went from the clash of men in battle to a struggle between machines and technologies of destruction.[35] Behind this new iron veil of firepower stood nations in arms not capable of a decisive victory in the field but intent instead upon mere survival through attrition ("Ermattungs-strategie").

When war broke out in early August 1914, the young men of Berlin and Paris marched off eagerly to the railroad stations expecting to return by Christmas. Visions of yet another charge of the Light Brigade, the cavalry that had inspired Britain's efforts in the Crimean War of 1855–6, filled the air of Europe. Men and women celebrated the outbreak of the war that August with an enthusiasm normally reserved for sports rallies. The decisive breakthrough achieved so stunningly by Germany in the Franco-Prussian War: surely this could be managed once again. The Schlieffen Plan, the bold German strategy of sweeping through Belgium in an enormous move to encircle Paris, was born out of this vision of another Sedan. If the last man on the German right flank brushed his sleeve against the English Channel, victory would be Germany's in a matter of weeks. The last words uttered by Schlieffen on his deathbed were reported to have been "make the right wing strong."[36]

Two years later the land of Verdun was covered by rotting bodies. In the forests and mud of a valley eight miles long and half that distance across, 700,000 men of France and Germany lost their lives. Further north, in Flanders Field, flamethrowers enfiladed rat-infested trenches in which the young men of three countries ended their lives. Phosgene gas filled the air. Land minds laid waste the once-arable soil, and flares lit up the night time sky. Machine guns rendered cavalry simply obsolete, and long-range artillery heaved half-ton chunks of metal across twenty miles of no-man's land. Front-line soldiers fought not to win but merely to survive. Home fronts, now fully mobilized, worked overtime as national economies were transformed in a year's time into full-scale economies of death. In mid nineteenth century, the citizenry of Paris and Vienna would occasionally venture out for a picnic astride the battlefields. Now they burned their furniture for heat and spent winters eating turnips because their armies had requisitioned all the potatoes. The lightning wars of annihilation brought by Napoleon to Europe had become bogged down, effectively becoming costly wars of attrition. The early phase of Britain's Industrial Revolution that had brought forth looms, "satanic mills," and railways was now surpassed by the products of the second Industrial Revolution in Germany in the last third of the nineteenth century.

Lightweight steel replaced iron. Bursting cordite shells replaced the solid iron balls of an earlier day. Accurate rifles with spiral grooves in the bored-out barrels rendered archaic the muskets of revolutionary France. Water-cooled machine guns enabled one man to stand guard over acres of bleak gray land. Telegraph lines were laid out so that generals could direct the course of battle from reinforced bunkers behind the fronts. Railways delivered fresh recruits with a speed unimaginable in Clausewitz's day. And submarines were employed to blockade whole countries from receiving shipments from across the North Sea and the Atlantic Ocean. War, once conducted by military geniuses on a battlefield of limited scope, had come to embrace whole continents and to involve citizens at the home front in the era of total warfare.

At one level the advent of total, technological warfare confirmed Clausewitz's observations about the inherent strength of the defensive position. Witness the stagnation resulting from trench warfare on the Western front. The ensuing stalemate seemed to drain any element of politics from the equation, leading the forlorn military strategists of the day to exhaust their troops in carnage in the hopes of outlasting the adversary. But of course military technology did not rest with the achievement of the machine gun. New forms of mobile firepower, particularly the tank, raised hopes that after years of stalemate, a breakthrough could be achieved.

For some strategic visionaries, that breakthrough would come not on the ground but through the air. The advent of heavier-than-air flying machines made it possible to believe that Clausewitzian friction could in effect be overcome and that the offense could acquire – or reacquire – a prominent place.

The most fervid advocate of aerial power was a former Italian artillery officer, Giulio Douhet (1869–1930), whose persistent agitations on behalf of air power landed him an appointment as general and head of his country's Central Aeronautical Board in February 1918. His scattered essays, first published together in book form in 1921 as *Il dominio dell'aria* (*The Command of the Air*), provided the first systematic analysis of the strategic uses of air power. The volume celebrates the ability of military power in the third dimension to deliver enormous quantities of offensive firepower at civilian or military targets. Indeed, the genius of Douhet's peculiar vision is that he located operational debates about air power within the larger context of fundamental transformations in the very nature of warfare. Even though his estimates of aerial bombardment proved wildly optimistic, his overall vision of the future of war proved frighteningly prescient.[37] Douhet's concern was to draw lessons from World War I, where a regard for defensive positioning led to years of unnecessary carnage. "There is no doubt now that half of the destruction wrought by the war would have been enough if it had been accomplished in three months instead of four years. A quarter of it would have been sufficient if it had been wrought in eight days."[38]

Unlike land warfare, air power knows no limits. "Since war had to be fought on the surface of the earth, it could be waged only in movements and clashes of forces along lines drawn on its surface. Hence, to win, to gain control of the coveted area, one side had to break through the fortified defensive lines of the other and occupy the area."[39] The expansion of the industrial means of warfare and war-preparation meant that the civilian economy became fully integrated into national strategy. Indeed, one of Douhet's crucial arguments is that classical distinctions between combatant and civilian, and between the front and everyday life, have effectively broken down under the material requirements of modern industrial warfare. Thus the advent of the term "home front" to describe the dependence of the military upon steady supplies from the national population and industrial base. The need to protect wider and wider spheres of life vital for sustained military exertion meant, argued Douhet, that "the fighting went on, to a point where, as in the last war, the lines extended over practically the whole battlefield, thus barring all troop passage either way."[40]

The new force to be unleashed enjoys the extraordinary freedom of open space. Much of the book reads as an Italian futurist manifesto. The key is the ability of air power to deliver "units of destruction" that effectively eliminate all targets within a 500-meter radius. There follows by Douhet some basic operations research, guided by a fantastic overestimation of accuracy from the air. Douhet effectively calculates pinpoint accuracy, with no regard for equipment failure, weather glitches, mission attrition, or for the psychological affect of losses – in other words, friction. It is a pure case of achieving command of the air and the subsequent ability to destroy civilian targets by virtue of aerial counterforce. Douhet distinguishes tactical combat aircraft missions from strategic bombardment missions. The first simply clears the air for the second to deliver the coup de grâce.

A key strategic point, picked up later by the pioneer theorists of nuclear strategy, is that in strategic bombing, offensive operations are economically and militarily more efficient than defensive operations. In a fundamental reversal of a crucial Clausewitzian principle, air power enables the virtually frictionless delivery of overwhelmingly destructive firepower. The small toll taken upon incoming aircraft through ground-based artillery and flack guns can scarcely diminish airborne arsenals. So long as tactical fighter planes can gain operational superiority of the air and clear a path for incoming bomber planes, a country is left defenseless. In effect, then, Douhet's optimistic assessment of the accuracy of air power ushered in an idea which would liberate war from the limits of two-dimensional, terrestrial battle. We have here, then, the absolute triumph of offense over defense. The goal of air power is to utilize sheer offensive power and to "[i]nflict the greatest damage in the shortest possible time.[41]

But where Clausewitz explains the emergence of Napoleonic warfare in terms of the social history of armies, Douhet reverts to simpler, technologically driven images that naturalize militarization. The political nature of warfare, which Clausewitz incorporates into his military history, is reduced by Douhet to a world driven by the sheer instrumentalities of war. From the earliest reconnaissance planes in the World War, he writes, "aerial combat developed spontaneously, in the natural course of events."[42]

The naturalization of military technology, without regard for its social basis, was then applied by Douhet to the very object of war. For he introduces into the strategic equation a new military objective, the will, the morale, of enemy civilians. Writing in 1926, Douhet observed that

> It seems paradoxical to some people that the final decision in future wars may be brought about by blows to the morale of the civilian population. But that is what the last war proved, and it will be verified in future wars with even more evidence. The outcome of the last war was only apparently brought about by military operations. In actual fact, it was decided by the breakdown of morale among the defeated peoples – a moral collapse caused by the long attrition of the people involved in the struggle. The air arm makes it possible to reach the civilian population behind the line of battle, and thus to attack their moral resistance directly. And there is nothing to prevent our thinking that some day this direct action may be on a scale to break the moral resistance of the people even while leaving intact their respective armies and navies.[43]

Douhet succumbed to the temptation of which Clausewitz warned. The three elements comprising the "remarkable trinity" of war – popular will, armed forces, and political leadership – are now all reduced and brought to bear against the one, civilian sentiments, as the sole target of strategy. The result is to reduce warfare to a technocratic enterprise in which human will and social life are transformed to mere instrumentalities, indeed, to objects of the war effort itself. The whole earth is thereby transformed into a strategic map, and the give and take of global politics are all funneled conceptually into their contribution to the war effort. The much-heralded advent of the home front as a desideratum of strategic operations in World War I now sees its literary apotheosis in Douhet's pure totalizing discourse of strategy. Cities are construed as targets of opportunity for reducing enemy morale. The ability of a country to sustain successful aerial operations is measured in its capacity for producing "a constant flow of replacement planes" – while nothing is said of pilots.[44] The world is thus analyzed in terms of "units of destruction" and "units of combat." This is the unacknowledged birth of operations research, or at least of thinking in terms of operational *materiél* and capacities without regard for human agency and purpose. To the extent that political goals are anticipated, they are construed in terms of a utilitarian morality designed to get a war over as quickly as possible with the greatest possible destruction packed into the least possible time. Most importantly, we witness here the strategicalization of public life, the rendering of habitations and workplaces into targetable opportunities.

Civil society is now strategic society. This, perhaps more than his celebration of air power, is Douhet's enduring legacy to strategic debate. Without it, it would literally be impossible to talk as if a nuclear revolution pertained to human life.

The nuclear revolution

Bernard Brodie, more than anyone else, established an understanding about nuclear weapons as different from all other weapons. His particular genius was to take this seeming banality and convert it into what became a dominant mode of analysis in the postwar era. Brodie's work legitimates the shift from classical military studies of defenses to the political study of security. Indeed, the very idea of Strategic Studies as an academic discipline was made possible by taking political–military affairs from the hands of the generals and handing it over to political statesmen and bureaucrats in a liberal world trying honestly to manage the blind forces of uncontrollable violence that, amidst the nuclear revolution, portended the destruction of mankind. From this explicitly military genesis, it was, as Stephen Walt has reminded us, a short yet decisive step to the emergence of Security Studies as an academic discipline, replete with the private foundation support and intellectual respectability lacked by its analytical forbearers.[45]

The book in which Brodie first outlined the concept – though not the phrase – of a "nuclear revolution" betrays through its title its rootedness in Clausewitzian traditions: *The Absolute Weapon*. Writing in the immediate aftermath of the destruction of Hiroshima and Nagasaki, Brodie argued that in the nuclear age defense was effectively neutralized by the overwhelming force of whatever few nuclear weapons successfully penetrated defensive air nets. The German aerial bombardments of London during the Second World War were not ultimately successful, thanks to something like a 10 percent attrition rate of attacking aircraft being shot down by the RAF and coastal defenses. Such a rate decimated Luftwaffe forces over time. The gradual exhaustion of personnel, aircraft, and morale that resulted was sufficient to hamper and ultimately erode German war efforts.[46]

There would be no such luck in the nuclear age, for here offensive power would achieve "absolute" superiority over the defensive. Clausewitz's claims for the inherent virtue of defensive land forces was to be thereby rendered obsolete in an era when nuclear weaponry was conveyed via air power. Thus the title of Brodie's visionary book. The "absolute weapon" had arrived.

The ensuing view of strategy would come to be known as one of

59

"minimal deterrence," sometimes, and for the most part misleadingly, associated with US Secretary of Defense Robert McNamara's force posture of "Mutual Assured Destruction."[47] The minimalist position most accurately captures the innovative impetus of a political–military force whose basic function was less to be used actively in the course of an ongoing battle than to be deployed in a manner designed to assure that no winner – indeed, no conflict – would ultimately emerge, least of all the aggressor who had introduced nuclear weaponry into the fray at the outset. The resulting strategic picture adumbrated by Brodie in 1946 and subsequently associated most prominently with the work of Robert Jervis (himself a student of Brodie) counselled the judicious deployment of nuclear forces so as to avoid their use as war-winning weapons and to rely upon them, instead, solely for purposes of retaliation. Nearly a half century after they first appeared, Brodie's words remain the clearest expression of this orientation. "Until now the purpose of armed forces has been to win wars. From now on, it must be to prevent them. They can have no other purpose."[48]

Several elements define this new strategy.[49] To begin with, there must be "no first-use" of nuclear forces. The presumption here is of a clear and unproblematic distinction between conventional and nuclear forces, and that crossing the boundary from one to the other represents so monumental and monstrous a shift of weaponry and strategy that there can be no justifiable reasons for doing so. The introduction of such "absolute" weaponry threatens to escalate levels of conflict to such unmanageable proportions that the side under attack would be justified in reverting on its own part to overwhelming levels of nuclear forces designed, not in Clausewitzian fashion, to escalate and to disarm the adversary, but, through a process of leap-frogging, to annihilate the attacking party altogether. To use nuclear weapons first is to cross a threshold that is both strategic and moral. A country facing a state that has reverted to nuclear weapons cannot be assured, once the weapon has been used, of its own survival. The justified use of nuclear weapons then, can only be retaliatory, not initiatory.

A second element is that in the nuclear age, there should be "no defense." A strange maxim in a Clausewitzian world, certainly, but in the nuclear era, argued Brodie, defense was simultaneously futile and dangerous. Futile, because the mechanisms of aerial transport could readily outwit any defensive systems that could be designed. And dangerous, because the possession of a defense that did work would make it impossible to reassure other countries of one's own peaceful purposes.

Writing in an era of long-distance bomber planes, when there was not yet the capacity even for intercontinental rocketry, Brodie understood that the effects of even a few nuclear warheads eluding defensive emplacements would be tantamount to unparalleled destruction. The point was not that defenses against airborne bombs wouldn't work. The argument, rather, was that unless the defenses were absolutely perfect, they might as well not exist at all. And if these principles upheld in an era of airplanes and artillery defenses, they were all the more relevant a decade later with the advent of rocket-borne warheads.

But Brodie went further than arguing the mere futility of defenses; he also argued that they were dangerous because they might pose the illusion of invulnerability, or worse yet, pose the real threat of invincibility to a country. If a country could indeed hide behind an effective defensive shield, what would assure its rivals that they would not ultimately be subject to attack? In the deracinated logic of the nuclear strategists, vulnerability was thus a virtue insofar as it assured all countries that no one of them might achieve impunity should it choose to seize the initiative and attack. A country that sought – or found – invulnerability would have abandoned its ability to be humbled through the threat of retaliation. With nothing to stop it, its leaders would have no reason to fear retaliation. Thus no country would feel safe from it. To forestall the possibility of a country ever achieving absolute defensive invulnerability, other countries might decide to resort to military force in an effort to ensure that the fully functioning defensive shield were not yet established in operational terms. In other words, the most dangerous and threatening moment for world affairs would come in the build-up phase as a country accumulated the defensive forces prior to full invulnerability. Countries seeking to preserve a modicum of operational breathing room might be tempted to attack pre-emptively in order to forestall final implementation of full defensive plans. In this manner, the pursuit of defensive forces would be both futile because unworkable and dangerous if successful. The road to stability and order, then, resides in the virtues of vulnerability. In other words, "no defense."

How, then, to "defend" oneself in the nuclear age? The answer, simply, was to engage in a *political* relationship of bargaining with a potential adversary so that the country would be dissuaded or deterred from launching an attack in the first place. For this, only a certain number of missiles were needed, a number sufficient to deliver such overwhelming destruction upon that potential aggressor that no rational actor would be tempted to believe it possible to strike with impunity in the first place. To the question, "how much is enough?", the only feasible answer was the quantitatively indeterminate yet politically crucial response: "'X' is enough".[50] "X" equals that number of strategic warheads that would suffice to create a relationship of stable deterrence. Whatever the particular number, its importance lay in the fact that from the standpoint of requirements for deterrence, an unlimited proliferation of warheads was not in principle necessary, so that deterrence could be achieved with finite levels of armaments.

The function of "X" number of missiles would be confined to the act of retaliation in response to any first strike. Or, to be more politically precise, the rationale for the existence of those warheads would be to represent the existence of a threat of retaliation sufficient that they would never need to be used in response. Whether they would actually be deployed in retaliation was less important for purposes of strategy than the psychology of perception on the part of an adversary that they might be used, and that a potential aggressor would have no choice but to assume that indeed they would be used. The credibility of their likely use existed by virtue of their existence as weapons of retaliation.

What, then, was the strategic purpose of this force posture? For theorists of minimal deterrence, the answer was to demark the limits of classical strategy. In the nuclear age, went the argument, the level of destruction that would likely afflict all parties to a conflict would leave none of them in a position of victory over the other. The whole issue of winning a war, in other words, had been rendered infeasible by the sheer levels of destructive power contained in the nuclear arsenals of the world's major powers. In other words, "victory is not possible." The idea of vanquishing an opponent, of literally "disarming" an adversary in Clausewitz's sense, no longer made sense. As soon as both sides in an adversarial relationship acquired nuclear capacities, classical strategic notions of winning and losing, of defeating an enemy, were rendered obsolete. The vulnerability of states to air power bombardment, and the uncontrollable character of both prompt and long-term consequences of nuclear detonation, ensured that civilian populations were hence vulnerable to but a few weapons, successfully delivered. Classical balance of power considerations, including relative deployments of offensive and defensive weapons systems, were less important given the simple existence of overwhelmingly offensive weapons – and the means available to deliver them.

So overwhelming was the imminence of such destructive power that one of the early postwar champions of realism, John Herz, argued in 1957 – precisely the year when the Soviet Union acquired a transcontinental missile capability – that in the age of aerial nuclear power, the classical sovereign, territorially bounded nation-state had been rendered obsolete. Herz invoked a fascinating trope in accounting for the manner by which the "hard protective shell" of the early modern state had become vulnerable to nuclear missiles leaping over traditionally defensible surface borders.[51]

The maximalist response

From the very outset of the nuclear age, voices were heard which sought to assimilate nuclear weapons within conventional categories of strategy as usable instruments of war. William Borden, for instance, writing in 1946, quickly perceived that contrary to claims about a revolution in strategic affairs wrought by nuclear technology, such weapons of mass destruction could readily be incorporated within a classical framework as instruments of war.[52] He thus foreshadowed subsequent alternatives to the minimalist position articulated by such renowned strategists of a "maximalist" position as Albert Wohlstetter, Herman Kahn, Colin Gray, and Paul Nitze. Even such moderate strategists as Henry Kissinger, William Kaufman, and Secretary of Defense Robert McNamara variously articulated positions sharply critical of the minimalist position such that a variety of flexible, nuclear war-fighting strategies would be made available to Western strategists. Most of these arguments arose during what Gray has termed the "golden age" of strategy, 1955–65, when in his view, there was an extraordinarily fecund outpouring of critical thinking about basic issues of deterrence, arms control and nuclear strategy, with the basic arguments governing respective positions on nuclear strategy effectively cast.[53]

Among the chief concerns for critics of the minimalist position is that it abandoned initiative to the aggressor. According to the charge, this was a peculiar attitude to take in the midst of heightened Cold War tensions, when a series of assumptions made about an implacable totalitarian foe destined to strive for world domination provide the starting point for arguments about the need for nuclear deterrence in the first place. To place in the hands of a potential aggressor the power to start a war is problematic enough under any construct of a global security dilemma. But when the adversary in question is so ideologically driven, or when the representation of the potential aggressor is so ideologically overdetermined, it seems politically problematic to then argue on behalf of a strategy which explicitly places faith in the hands of that foe that it will not attack. The prevailing discursive resources of Cold War international politics were thus incompatible with such an account. Something had to give. Either the Soviet Union was not especially troubling, or so precarious a foundation for security as mutual deterrence would have to be revised. From the standpoint of political debate, as well as basic military strategy, leaving the initiative in the hands of the aggressor was too much to ask of liberal strategists of minimalist deterrence.

Moreover, such an orientation was incompatible with basic military training. The point of minimal deterrence was to ask the professional military, particularly the Air Force, to stand back and wait for an attack and then to heap nuclear weapons upon defenseless citizens, urban and industrial targets, and non-military assets, all in order to make the point that aggression does not pay. Douhet's emphasis upon sustained aerial terror bombing comes to the fore here, but now the goal is more ambiguous than to exploit command of the air and force the enemy to surrender. One could always argue for aerial strategic bombardment designed to eliminate the willpower of a nation in arms. However difficult this would prove to be operationally, and however fleeting its results in the Second World War, such a goal held out the promise of forcing a persistent adversary out of the war. But what, by contrast, was the point of retaliatory bombing after the fact of a (presumably) devastating first strike? The internal logic of the minimalist position could offer little convincing reason for actually carrying out such an counter-attack once deterrence had been breached. Perhaps, one could argue, the goal would be to affirm the credibility of retaliatory threats in case of future aggression. But if that were the case, went the counter-argument, why not establish credibility through a variety of subtle maneuvers below the threshold of all-out retaliation, and do so in the midst of actual war-fighting rather than after the fact?

This line of argument exposed a fatal flaw in the minimalist logic: namely, that striking in retaliation had no discernible strategic purpose. What counted was the credibility of the threat to retaliate, but strategists on both sides of the debate were forced to deal with a basic conundrum of the nuclear age, namely that the affirmation of credibility beyond mere technical capability was an inherently unsolvable problem having far more to do with elusive interpretive dimensions of strategic perception and representation than with nuts and bolts issues of conventional military hardware.

Perhaps the most influential critique of the minimalist position was that it was strategically and politically inflexible. The uncompromising form of the minimalist position had been taken up, curiously enough, by John Foster Dulles. Driven by traditional Republican budget-cutting concerns, as well as by the need to establish a global military presence consistent with United State postwar multilateral trade commitments, Secretary of State Dulles articulated a primitive form of punitive retaliation, with the significant deviation from the Brodie-esque formulation that such overwhelmingly retaliatory nuclear power might well be used in the face of conventional as well as nuclear aggression. Dulles' refusal to discriminate was part of the genius of his position, for it harnessed nuclear firepower to strategic bombing in a manner that could scarcely be challenged by any adversary.[54] Greatly aiding this strategy was the fact that the USSR had no ability to respond in kind to any US attacks. The Soviet Union might well have had the A-bomb, but it was scarcely noticed at the time that it hardly had any means of delivering it, and certainly not to the United States until the late 1950s at the very earliest.

But despite the recurrent propaganda about America's homeland vulnerability (and the subsequent need for everything from civil defense shelters to lead-lined underwear), the critical issue in US strategic planning was always those areas abroad to which forms of security through deterrence needed to be extended. The issue was brought home most clearly during the mid-1950s debates about NATO's manpower and weapons systems requirements.

Hopes of building adequate conventional NATO troop strength faltered due to the extraordinary demands on the population and labor markets that would have been necessary. The requirements of economic rebuilding proved more important than those of meeting security by traditional means, and none of the Allied powers would agree to divert its working-age labor force. President Eisenhower's own restraint in budget policy made nuclear guarantees for Europe all the more attractive. But in devising such a policy, Dulles drew the crossfire of critics who complained that the West was now saddled with no real alternative to Soviet territorial expansion.[55] US paralysis in the face of the 1956 Hungarian uprising brought home to many the hollowness of claims about strategic retaliation against levels of aggression below the threshold of direct territorial attacks upon the West. In phrases that carry enormous interpretive weight regarding gender roles and phallocentrism in strategic discourse, the argument was raised about the inability of minimalists to act when confronted with "salami tactics" by totalitarian forces that were designed to "nibble" or "chop" away at regions of marginal interest to the West. The primary strategic concern here was not a direct nuclear assault upon the US homeland but rather, a series of smaller, lower threshold maneuvers of aggression aimed at Korea, Hungary, Vietnam and the like. Against such measures, the West would be paralyzed. The tacit assumption of such engendered discourse was that a country or statesman unwilling to "stand up" to aggression did not have what it takes in the tough world of strategic relations. They were "soft" on Communism, wimps, and unable to wield sufficient thrust and fire-power when it was needed.[56]

Massive retaliation was criticized as particularly inflexible and undiscriminating; the critique was directed not simply at Dulles' policies, but at the larger idea of confining nuclear deployments to the case of direct homeland attacks. What, after all, did the minimalist position countenance when confronted with levels of conventional violence short of direct nuclear assault, and that took place in peripheral but yet crucial areas of the world, whether in Central Europe or throughout the Third World? The maximalist response varied widely, and by no means did all parties agree on developing a full nuclear war-fighting capacity as an alternative to retaliation. Wohlstetter's arguments, for instance, about "the delicate balance of terror" were intended to strengthen retaliatory deterrence by arguing that considerable measures would have to be undertaken merely to ensure a survival second-strike capability. Strictly speaking, this was not an argument for nuclear war-fighting, but rather, for enhancing the minimalist position. But his modifications, introduced in the name of enhancing credibility, required a series of shifts that enabled the strategy to slide imperceptibly into one that was indistinguishable from possessing the operational capability to conduct counterforce nuclear wartime operations.[57] Indeed, Wohlstetter's intervention introduced a fundamental problem about the terms of debate between the minimalists and the maximalists. Efforts undertaken to ensure the ability to deter, in the name of dissuading a potential aggressor, moved the strategy closer and closer to what was in effect a war-fighting posture.

Implicit in these maximalist criticisms was the understanding that the minimalist position suffered from a fatal historical innocence. It was, after all, technological stasis to assume that nuclear retaliation was the only feasible operational deployment appropriate to the nuclear age. Second-strike attacks only made sense, for instance, in an era of inaccuracy, when little more than transcontinental lob shots were possible, with little chance of selecting and pin-pointing hardened (concrete reinforced) military outposts or key command and communications centers. The argument presupposed that such weapons could not be deployed with uncanny accuracy, for instance. Yet instead of, in effect, dumping weapons indiscriminately upon regions known to contain huge populations and critical industrial centers, why not rely upon increases in accuracy through inertial guidance, laser and honing devices, satellite guidance, computer mapping and so on in order to be able to develop pinpoint accuracies – a "circle error probability" of a few hundred feet, even when launched from submarines or land-based silos thousands of miles away? Moreover, the minimalist position ignored miniaturization of the weapons themselves – the ability to build smaller, lighter, more mobile and in effect more efficient, perhaps even less-destructive weapons suitable to smaller jobs than long distance strategic and terror operations. The minimalist position ignored, or even condemned, the use of battlefield tactical weaponry. It was so concerned with the absolute divide between conventional and nuclear weaponry that it ignored the incorporation of smaller weapons into battlefield operations. By so doing, it would willingly forgo the likely operational advantages of lighter, more flexible weaponry that could conceivably be used in theater operations.

With the gradual advent of a credible Soviet nuclear capability, the one-sided Western reliance upon massive nuclear guarantees lost its feasibility, since it is unlikely that Washington would have been willing to put Boston at risk for Frankfurt, or more precisely, London or Paris at risk for freedom fighters in Budapest. But with lower yield, more mobile field weaponry launched from the ground or from regionally based bomber planes, strategists might be able to gain crucial advantages in efficiency of firepower while reducing the economic and manpower commitments required to mount robust military action. Moreover, reliance upon such weapons in a variety of war-fighting scenarios would actually enhance the credibility of deterrence by making threats of nuclear escalation and use more plausible than would be the case if such weapons were to be threatened solely in cases of post-aggression retaliation. A potential adversary is less likely to believe the retaliatory threat of a massive strategic counter-strike in the face of successful conventional probes below the threshold of the absolute levels. When harnessed to operational battlefield plans and when used in conjunction with robust conventional ground and air operations, a flexibly integrated nuclear capability strengthens the political nature of deterrence by filling gaps in the various escalatory options available to military planners. The minimalist position forgoes this whereas the maximalist position readily seizes this as an important moment in the completion of deterrence strategies. In this manner, the need to confirm the credibility of deterrence slides imperceptibly but decisively into measures designed to guarantee war-fighting capabilities.

The effect of such measures advocated by maximalists is to reverse the strategy of minimal deterrence. In lieu of "no first-use," the maximalist counsels "first-use," though this is carefully distinguished from what came to be known as "first-strike." Critics of the maximalist position often blur the distinction between the willingness to be the first to use nuclear weapons in a conflict, and the ability to inflict such a crippling opening salvo that no meaningful strategic (retaliatory) response is possible. But NATO strategy is a good example of a "first-use" orientation in the face of superior conventional forces that no one could ever have mistaken as sufficient for a pre-emptive attack upon Warsaw Pact forces. Indeed, the longstanding dilemma of NATO strategy was precisely its inability to be the first to introduce nuclear weapons without being able to guarantee that the war wouldn't escalate out of control.

The point of a "first-use" orientation is that it enables one side to rely upon enormously efficient levels of military firepower without having to match arsenals of conventional deployments possessed by an adversary. The capacity to "go nuclear" first and early in the battle, it was assumed, would actually enhance the credibility of deterrence by making it more likely that a potential aggressor would face an overwhelming response, even if that response were a significant escalation to the nuclear realm. Of course, this did not eliminate the question of credibility, for now the deterrer would have to assume that the likelihood of escalating to a nuclear response first would have the same credibility as responding in kind with conventional weaponry. The mere threat to resort to nuclear weapons in the face of a conventional attack did not alone suffice to deter unless the aggressor were also convinced that such a threat was both militarily and politically credible. Advocates of this maximalist position quickly found out that the problems of enhancing deterrence were not solved by moving from the threat of conventional power to a response at the nuclear level. But whatever the credibility problems of a "nuclear first-use" posture, and these proved to be considerable throughout NATO's history, the importance of this was it showed how difficult it was to sustain the minimalist position of "no first-use" altogether.

The maximalist response to "no defense" was likewise to invert the posture and to argue on behalf of both passive and active defenses. Passive defenses refer to a range of measures for reducing the vulnerability of a society to nuclear attack. Back in 1946, Bernard Brodie concluded his account of the revolutionary nature of nuclear offenses with an argument that the US might consider dispersing its industrial and housing facilities to make urban patterns less attractive as targets.[58] In the mid-1950s, more specific measures for civil defense shelters were widely circulated. The Gaither Report, issued in 1957, developed extensive plans for both private and public shelters so that the United States could survive a direct Soviet attack.

At the same time, the Pentagon was working on a variety of active defensive systems designed to suppress incoming aerial attacks. The early measures were intended to fend off long-range Soviet bombers. Plans for coastal ground-to-air anti-aircraft artillery were eventually abandoned in favor of an extensive system of early warning radars installed across the northern Canadian frontier. This became the forward front of active US defenses based upon air-to-air interception. With the advent of a Soviet intercontinental ballistic missile capacity by the end of the 1950s, attention had to be turned away from fighter planes and toward antiballistic missiles as the basis of active defenses. Successive attempts at deploying Nike, Sentinel and then Safeguard were supposed to provide what was known as "point defenses" – covering a pre-given area to reduce the damage of incoming missiles and ensure that a survivable, retaliatory second-strike arsenal would remain operational after a first-strike attack. The reliance of ballistic missile defenses was intended not to provide an invulnerable shield against incoming weapons but rather, to reduce the destruction by suppressing a certain number of the missiles.[59]

Advocates of the various programs acknowledged the difficulties of providing for a comprehensive defense and argued instead for a far more limited program. At one point, when faced with the objection that such a limited "point defense" system could be readily overwhelmed by increasing the number of incoming missiles and by relying upon decoys, proponents reverted to the counter-argument that such a system would nonetheless be useful in the face of limited, accidental launchings or from a surprise attack emanating from the People's Republic of China. In any case, the idea of active defenses, usually in conjunction with an extensive program of civil defense sheltering, proved an attractive option for those who had been suspicious of the minimalist position.

The concern to provide strategic defenses was part of a larger sensibility regarding the apparent laxity with which minimalists confronted the peculiar dynamics of the nuclear era. Indeed, the basic problem was that advocates of a purely retaliatory posture did not see international strategic relations in terms of a dynamic process at all. Instead, the image was one of world politics having reached an entirely new technical realm, from which there was no escape and within which the only rational posture was to rely upon retaliation.

69

The condition became known as one of "existential deterrence," as if there was no way out of the nuclear dilemma other than to accept its existence and to live within its constraints. In other words, there was no escaping the nuclear age other than to adapt revolutionary strategies of retaliatory deterrence. After all, the "no escape" clause pertained not merely to the existence of nuclear weapons, but to the condition of vulnerability as well. While disarmament would be naïve and foolish, full-scale war-fighting militarization would be, from the opposite side, equally fraught with danger and faulty innocence. No level of armaments could circumvent one side's vulnerability in the face of a retaliatory second-strike capacity by another country. Nor could arms racing achieve sufficient levels of certainty in targeting to achieve an assured first-strike capability. Without such an arsenal, deterrence was now an existential fact of modern life, since no other means of achieving security was obtainable.

As Jervis emphasizes, the minimalists' claim that strategic relations had been fundamentally transformed renders irrelevant the issue of relative balance of forces. What counted was the achievement of a secure second-strike capacity. Thus the term "nuclear revolution" was somewhat misleading, since the critical variable was a survivable retaliatory arsenal, not necessarily the fact that the weapons were nuclear in character.[60] Nonetheless, the invocation of "existential" to characterize the new strategic relationship tended to naturalize the political and technical relationships, as if they had become indelibly imprinted upon the texture of modern life. Precisely such an understanding was encouraged in 1983 by the Harvard Nuclear Study Group, comprising leading moderate strategists fashioning their own response to the rising influence of anti-nuclear peace groups. The title of their work, *Living with Nuclear Weapons*, neatly captures its argument, that regardless of any state's efforts to squirm out of the unfortunate world of nuclear weapons, these weapons of mass destruction were – and ought to be – here to stay, and countries were better off with them than without them for the security against nuclear war which they ensured.[61]

Maximalist critics of such a position had already been arguing for nearly three decades that such an attitude regarding the "existential" character of deterrence needlessly counseled complacency when vigilance would have been the more appropriate mode. The issue became paramount when it came to targeting doctrine and the appropriate number of weapons required to ensure deterrence.

The minimalist position has long been that a certain number of missiles – "X" is enough – suffices to cover the "soft" industrial and demographic targets required to impose crippling damage upon a society. But the difficulties of assuring retaliation through survivable arsenals had been pointed out with great skill by Albert Wohlstetter in 1959.[62] He had criticized the minimalists' presumption that survivability would be relatively unproblematic and argued that the ability to maintain an arsenal sufficient for deterrence would require far greater measures than advocates of basic retaliation had ever acknowledged. The forward-basing of strategic bomber bases, for example, made them vulnerable to enemy attack. The improved accuracy of incoming ballistic missiles raised the likelihood that at least some of them would strike retaliatory arsenals. Even those second-strike weapons that were released would not all get through. Systems might simply fail. Enemy aircraft and artillery defenses, alerted to an impending second-strike, would be able to destroy a certain number of second-strike forces. And the dispersal of "soft targets," along with the protection of others through camouflage and reinforcement, would help reduce the effectiveness of a retaliatory strike. A potential aggressor aware of this delicate balance of forces would likely be emboldened to tempt a first-strike if convinced that the response could be minimized. Under such precarious conditions, countries need continually to upgrade and expand their arsenals – in the name of maintaining deterrence. The advice to limit one's forces to a certain number – "X" – would leave one vulnerable to attack. Instead, a country wishing to strengthen deterrence could never have enough.

Concerns about the limits of the minimalist approach included not only quantitative dimensions of weapons acquisitions but strategic considerations of targeting doctrine as well. The retaliatory, second-strike emphasis of this strategy was widely criticized because, in effect, it constitutes no strategy whatsoever and leaves the would-be deterrer with no flexibility. The same problems that faced the doctrine of massive retaliation in the mid-1950s can be seen to undercut the credibility of any purely minimalist strategy. The ability to deter rests entirely on a set of political relationships and the subtle psychology of assessments by which adversaries weigh both the technical ability of a country to respond and the likelihood – or credibility – that it would. But the one persistent question which defenders of minimal deterrence have never been able to answer satisfactorily is the question that cuts to the heart of its logic – namely, what, in the aftermath of a successful opening salvo, is the point of retaliating at all since it is obvious from the initial strike that the deterrent threat has (now) proven impotent to forestall an attack? To this question, the defender of pure retaliation has only been able to answer that the question itself

71

represents a kind of heresy, and that instead of asking what the point is of retaliating, the proper question is how can deterrence be firmed up to the point where its credibility would never be doubted in the first place.

The answer, of course, is to ensure a retaliatory arsenal sufficient to ride out an opening attack and to be able to deliver a significant level of damage to civilian industrial and population centers. In this manner, no matter how successful the first strike, the aggressor would face devastating punishment that in all likelihood would far outweigh the gain achieved through nuclear aggression.

But increases in intercontinental missile accuracy emboldened maximalists to raise the possibility that a first-strike could be so well coordinated and precise that it could effectively eliminate a crippling second-strike arsenal. Even the far-flung dispersal of nuclear forces onto land-based missiles, aircraft, and seaborne vessels might not, on this account, ensure the survivability of a robust second-strike capacity. A carefully coordinated attack upon key military assets that was able to preserve the discrimination between counter-force targets and such counter-value targets as cities and vital centers of industry would scarcely be an attack meriting a retaliatory response. The reversion to such a secondary response would merely target the aggressor's cities and economic centers, thus forcing that country to respond in kind with levels of destruction that would far exceed the losses entailed in the initial pre-emptive attack.

But perhaps more importantly – and more likely – than this scenario of a perfectly coordinated "bolt out of the blue" pre-emptive attack were the political problems raised by relying largely on retaliatory nuclear forces. What, for instance, is the appropriate strategic response to attacks that are less than all-out examples of direct homeland aggression? Would large-scale retaliatory attacks upon cities be the appropriate response to a limited nuclear deployment against key Western interests in, say, Central Europe or the Persian Gulf? And what of NATO's promised nuclear response to an attack by the (former) Warsaw Pact's quantitatively superior conventional armaments? It was one thing in the mid-1950s to rely upon such a threat, in an era when the Soviet Union had no ability to bring nuclear weapons to bear against the United States. But with the Soviets' developing ability to threaten the European continent and then the US homeland with direct nuclear bombardment, such a retaliatory threat was drained of all credibility. This was precisely the strategic dilemma faced by NATO strategists in the early 1960s. The threat of nuclear retaliation against the Soviet Union for attacks, whether conventional

72

or even tactical-nuclear in the European theater, would have raised the likelihood of a direct Soviet counter-retaliatory attack, this time aimed at domestic population and industry.

Instead, it made more strategic sense to slide over from a retaliatory targeting doctrine to one based more on the counterforce targeting of key military and political assets. This would actually enhance the credibility of deterrence by making it more likely that the threat of a nuclear response would be credible to a potential aggressor. That way, instead of needlessly putting civilian populations at risk and making more likely the mutual escalation of destruction to levels that far exceeded the value of the initial conflict, the strategic relationship could be confined to efforts of destroying enemy forces. Such a targeting doctrine would be more credible than retaliation, reduce the likelihood of one's own population suffering damage in the course of war, and at the same time reduce the enemy's ability to carry out aggressive warfare.

Such a counterforce targeting doctrine enjoyed the additional virtue that it actually was more consistent with moral standards of conducting war insofar as it reflected an attempt to distinguish civilian from military targets. It was, of course, ironic that weapons of mass destruction made it more difficult than ever, perhaps impossible, to uphold the strictures of *jus in bello*. In a curious turn around, however, advocates of counterforce were able to claim the high moral ground in their argument that their own strategy was more morally acceptable than the minimalist's attempt deliberately to target innocent civilians.[63]

And what was the point of such a maximalist strategy? Simply stated, to win. The argument was put most straightforwardly in a 1980 *Foreign Policy* article by Keith Payne and Colin Gray, entitled (in order to leave no doubt) "Victory is Possible." Ever since Brodie, the minimalists had been claiming that the certainty of mutual destruction had effectively rendered obsolete any classical military notions of winning and losing. Such zero-sum final accounting made no sense when even a country suffering a devastating first strike would possess the ability to unleash a devastating retaliatory blow. The resulting mutual deadlock, characterized during the McNamara years as a condition of assured destruction, meant that in the course of nuclear war, victory was not possible.

The maximalist claim, by contrast, was that classical principles of war-fighting, offense and defense, and victory and loss, nonetheless persisted in the nuclear era. In what amounted to a "conventionalization" of strategic considerations, war-fighters argued that nuclear weaponry and targeting practice could be assimilated within a conventional mode. Intercontinental missiles could be deployed much as long-range artillery had been deployed in battlefield conditions – with the strategic purpose of preparing enemy ground for a counter-offensive, or for directly targeting the adversary's artillery batteries in an attempt to reduce the damage the other side could inflict on one's troops and military installations.[64] Crucial in such a strategy was the ability to destroy the adversary's command, control and communications facilities – a strategy appropriately characterized as "decapitation." As Payne and Gray argued, a combined and coordinated attack in the early course of wartime operations could significantly reduce the adversary's nuclear arsenals and allow one to prevail militarily. Instead of passively riding out the first wave of attacks, they argued, the United States should be willing to seize the initiative and rely upon its relative technological advantages in terms of accuracy and intelligence reliability to suppress the Soviet's ability to respond while denying it the ability to launch a blinding, pre-emptive attack.

The operational feasibility of implementing such a war-winning strategy became subject to a raging debate throughout the early 1980s. Whether it was actually possible to "prevail" in the course of a nuclear war was widely discussed, particularly as the Reagan administration publicly advocated further development of initiatives that had been more quietly pursued by the defense strategists in the Johnson, Nixon, Ford and Carter administrations.[65] A series of strategies and weapons systems was developed in an attempt to implement such a war-winning strategy: anti-missile defenses, silo-busting intercontinental and submarine-launched ballistic missiles, a comprehensive civil defense shelter program, the upgrading of command and control facilities to ensure survivability, and the proliferation of targeting lists to ensure redundancy against hardened military installations. Whether such a capability was indeed operationally feasible was less important than the fact that the effort was undertaken at all. The developments represented a decisive shift away from the minimalist presumption that such an undertaking would simply be futile. Yet both critics and defenders of these moves rightly argued that this did not represent such a fundamental break from the precepts of a nuclear revolution since efforts had been underway since the very advent of the nuclear age to circumvent the minimalist position.

The uneasy synthesis

Which account more accurately reflects the state of nuclear strategy, the minimalist emphasis on the nuclear revolution, or the maximalist

74

claim of conventionalized war-fighting? For over forty years, debate has oscillated between – or within – these two perspectives, as each claimed to represent a more comprehensive account of existing, and prospective, nuclear strategy. Each weapons system developed or proposed, and each turn in the strategic relationship between the United States and the Soviet Union, could be convincingly interpreted within the analytic framework of the one view, while the other would be subjected to devastating criticism.

The first thing to be said about this recurring great debate is that certain ways of posing the question are more useful than others. For instance, an empiricist framing of the question, as if an externally given, objective realm of nuclear relations "as they really existed" had some autonomous existence, which it then was the task of one or the other account of strategy to capture and describe, can be understood as the most misleading presentation of the whole issue of postwar politics. For such an account of the question presupposes that the strategic universe has a clear and unambiguous structure which can be rationally apprehended by a given body of knowledge. There is, after all, a strong empiricist streak in Strategic Studies which continually tempts the analyst to pose the world in realist, materialist terms, as if questions of political intention could be hived off from those of measurable military capability. On such a behavioral account, the task of the social scientist is exhaustively to describe the world, and to separate such an explanation from messy issues of interpretation and the contestability of its meaning. Only then, with a full account of strategic relations in hand, can it be possible to propose alternative sets of policy questions so that prescription can rationally follow the prior task of understanding.

There are two sorts of difficulties to this approach, and each one of them deals a crippling blow to such an attempt. The one concerns data, the other perceptions. The first is that the field of nuclear deterrence is, thankfully, short on empirical data regarding actual cases of nuclear war. For a policy science that has located itself so confidently in practice, this is one of those ironies of life that should go a lot further than it does toward undercutting received wisdom. The raw material from which definitive conclusions can be reached about the nature and consequences of nuclear war simply does not exist, and all statements or conclusions made about it are necessarily based upon a combination of extrapolation, guesswork, hypothesizing, and analogizing. The medieval wizardry involved in so speculative an enterprise has been often pointed out, but has managed only to glance off the considerable political and discursive armour accumulated by strategic practitioners.

Even the literature on deterrence stability is based upon peculiar foundations, since it is, in one sense, never possible to know with accuracy why something has not happened. To some extent, this has given the field of contemporary Strategic Studies a kind of literary and intellectual freedom that other areas of International Relations have not been so lucky to enjoy. At the same time, the theoretical underpinnings of the whole strategic enterprise acquire distinct political resonance, since so much of the ensuing debate turns on the acceptance of several basic claims about the nature of conflict among states in an anarchic states system.

The only time that nuclear weapons were used was under conditions in which mutual deterrence did not obtain. Since then, of course, there have been a number of important attempts to specify the conditions under which deterrence has been achieved.[66] Some draw more heavily than others on pre-nuclear, conventional relations, and all have contributed significantly to creating a body of case studies. But what is remarkable about this extensive literature is the extent it must continually make a series of assumptions about the interpretations, perceptions and understandings of key actors and decision-makers in the various examples – and the extent to which such assumptions elude the self-imposed boundaries of the empiricist rendition of such a project. In effect, these interpretations by participants are themselves part of the raw data which analysts must digest and make sense of. A large part of deterrence, after all, is aimed at influencing, shaping, and altering the perceptions of decision-makers.

And this brings us to the other difficulty of dealing with deterrence – the realm of perception. This is, of course, the particular interest of those rooted in the school of perception–misperception in nuclear strategic relations. Yet while scrupulously sensitive to issues of interpretation and perception on the part of policy makers who seek a firm basis for action, analysts such as Ken Booth, Robert Jervis and Steven Kull have all been committed to rationalist readings of the strategic universe, so that there can be, at base, no question of the deeper structure of the nuclear revolution or of the anarchic political structure among states in which that "revolution" has taken place. Deviations from the pre-given rationality of the world of "the nuclear revolution" are construed by these analysts as distortions of reality. Booth, for example, explains systematic deviance of interpretations and expectations in terms of ethnocentrism, and his task is to create a more empathetic environment so that strategists can disabuse themselves of their own cultural biases and thereby more rationally confront the strategic universe. Jervis, the most lucid and comprehensive advocate of the nuclear revolution thesis, has characterized deviations from such a reading as "illogical." Kull, the most uncritical of those who adhere to such a reading of strategic relations, continually interprets attempts to conventionalize strategy in terms that would suggest outright irrationality or neurotic evasiveness on the part of the policy-maker in question.[67]

One way to answer the question of which is the real nuclear strategy, then, is to point out that deterrence, whether minimal or maximal, has always required a combination of material hardware and linguistic articulations and therefore cannot be reduced to purely empirical representations. One need only look back at an influential article published in 1956 by none other than Paul Nitze, the architect of the position earlier expressed in document NSC-68 calling for a tripling of the US defense budget and the nuclearization of US global commitments. For a variety of reasons, Nitze's ambitious plans in NSC-68 were not fully adopted, and by the time of Dulles' reversion to a more limited strategy of massive retaliation, Nitze, along with many other critics in the mid-1950s, began to point out the limits of such an approach. Nuclear strategy, Nitze indicated in the pages of *Foreign Affairs*, consists of both "action policy" and "declaratory policy." "Action policy" consists in the operational conduct of strategy in the course of actual wartime operations. "Declaratory policy," by contrast, deals with national rhetorical strategies designed to impress upon a potential aggressor the seriousness of potential threats. If action policy deals primarily with technical capabilities in the face of aggression or threats, declaratory policy emphasizes political relationships of credibility designed to impress foreign audiences while providing a domestic political rationale for budgetary priorities and weapons acquisition.[68]

As a number of detailed historical studies have shown, at no time can American nuclear strategy be described as meeting the criteria for either the minimalist or maximalist description.[69] The distinction between action and declaratory policy already suggests that the practical composition of nuclear policy was always more complicated than advocates on one side or the other of the debate were willing to acknowledge. Since the advent of the nuclear age, and with various permutations along the way, US nuclear strategy has been a hybrid of the two strategic orientations highlighted here, with several elements of one predominating, until overtaken or surpassed by the (re-) emergence of elements prevailing from the other orientation. For the simple truth of the matter is that the minimalist orientation, emphasized on the declaratory side, has never been politically adequate to the global

77

functions undertaken by extended nuclear strategy. Meanwhile, the maximalist variant, highlighted as action policy, has been operationally infeasible, however much it represents the teleological goal toward which weapons acquisitions and targeting doctrine tend. It is as if the maximalist position represents the achievement of Clausewitz's absolute war – a theoretical impossibility to be sure, but politically desirable given that it fits so neatly with the larger political purposes of nuclear strategy in the first place.

This, then, is the paradox of strategy since the very advent of the nuclear era. For it turns out that the debate about nuclear strategy has abstracted deterrence from a broader political context involving structures of both civil society and world order. This is evident when the dynamics of nuclear deterrence are examined in terms of their genesis within domestic political economy as well as their function or role within the whole postwar articulation of global politics and trade. But a comprehensive account of strategy as organized violence cannot afford to abstract weapons of mass destruction from questions of their origins and purpose. A debate which focuses exclusively on the deterrence of a direct homeland attack is the most likely to ignore these questions. In this respect, proponents of a maximalist, war-fighting strategy at least attempt to place nuclear weapons within the broader ambit of political and social relations. The whole issue of extended deterrence, for instance, is impossible to understand without seeing that US strategy is crucial to the development of postwar multilateral trading blocs and the need to incorporate these into spheres of security interest as guaranteed by various military alliances.

But that is not to claim some identity or one-to-one correspondence between nuclear strategy and American economic interests. Rather, the connection is mediated through a dense network of strategic discourses in which violence is legitimized as a global practice. And it is precisely here where the on-going policy debates between maximalists and minimalists prove so important, for as much as they dominated the terms of discussion within US policy circles throughout the Cold War era, they simultaneously affirmed a shared commitment of American power while excluding as tangential and irrelevant critical perspectives on their enterprise. It is illuminating, then, to explore in detail the terms of debate between these two viewpoints because in doing so we can appreciate the extent to which they are engaged in a common undertaking. To be sure, there are certain differences of style or attitude toward strategic violence. The minimalist position, while more rationalist, is also less culturally ambitious with respect to extending American power worldwide. It is also less optimistic that,

78

under certain conditions, the strategy will work. The maximalist position, more suspicious of potential adversaries, displays a greater faith (or need for faith) in technology over political bargaining. It seeks, in a sense, to overcome the slippage in strategy which it continually admits exists. In other words, the maximalist position tends toward greater exertion of effort, whether through technological initiative or invasiveness of planning, in order to cover the gaps and aporia which are unavoidable in nuclear strategy. Much of the innovation and need for modernization in nuclear strategy can be understood not as response to developments by a putative adversary but as self-generated attempts to mask or shore up weaknesses internal to the strategy itself.[70]

It would be easy to overstate the differences between these perspectives, as if the terms of their debate exhausted the realm of political discourse in matters of nuclear strategy. What is significant here, however, is not so much their differences, but the way in which the debate has been shaped by debates about the utility of classical principles. Clausewitzian assumptions about the uses of military force have thus been subjected to fundamental questioning in the nuclear era. Classical understandings about military policy and the nature of battle, friction, and the superiority of the defensive position have all been challenged by students of postwar strategy who have argued instead for the revolutionary character of the nuclear era. Such accounts have led to the development of a nuclear strategy of minimalist retaliation which has represented, in effect, the apotheosis of this perspective. Adherents of a classical perspective, by contrast, have continually criticized such an understanding as unduly naïve and rationalist: in short, as neglectful of the basic and abiding purposes of political–military strategy. The ensuing terms of debate have characterized not merely the intellectual field of Strategic Studies but the various policies of nuclear deterrence itself. Indeed, the history of nuclear strategy has been characterized by recurring attempts to transcend the relative simplicity of a narrowly retaliatory orientation and to develop one of war-fighting and nuclear conventionalization which would embody with weapons of mass destruction the classical principles articulated one and a half centuries ago by Clausewitz. That such a project has proven so elusive to realize has not prevented successive generations of strategists from trying.

Classical and modern postwar strategic relations share more in common than normally appreciated. Arguments focusing on the nuclear revolution tend to obscure the technological and strategic dynamics at work that inform, indeed, that generate strategic relations in the first place. For this, we need to re-examine the history of strategic relations and to explore not merely the external manifestation of strategy in terms of war-fighting/war-deterrence but the place of armaments in domestic and international society. Toward that end, the following chapter embeds strategic considerations within the making and remaking of postwar global structures.

4 MILLENNIAL LIBERALISM AND DUAL MILITARIZATION

"Nuclear Weapons: Power Through Modernization" (*New York Times*, May 23, 1983)

The development of nuclear strategy and its extension to the far corners of the globe in the postwar world were made possible only through the optimism and enthusiasm of American power and culture. While Soviet policy played no small role in the subsequent development of nuclear militarization, the leading edge role assumed by US strategy established a precedent that deserves attention in its own right, even though it cannot alone be held accountable for the ensuing scope of the world military order that developed in the postwar era. Nonetheless, as the self-appointed post-colonial power responsible for liquidating colonial holdings worldwide, and as the sole world power whose economic, industrial, military and political capabilities enabled it to assume global functions, the US bears particular scrutiny. Moreover, the accessibility of source material to researchers in the field has enabled students of strategy to achieve a far more detailed picture of American strategic policy than has been possible with respect to the Soviet Union, Britain or France. For all of these reasons, a sustained look at the American contribution to postwar militarization is appropriate, though it should not be mistaken for a "burden of guilt" argument placing exclusive responsibility for subsequent militarization on American shoulders.

It is not, of course, customary to equate liberalism with militarization. Indeed, a vibrant literature has lately placed much emphasis upon the relationship between democratization and international peace.[1] While advanced industrial democracies do tend to be peaceful toward other advanced industrial democracies, this does not tell us much either about relations toward the Third World, nor of the historic processes of militarization, often times at levels below those of overt aggression, that have been associated with the major powers – the advanced industrial democracies. Moreover, the postwar development of both nuclear strategic relations and a global arms trade emanating largely from these countries in question suggests that the issue of liberalization and militarization has not been decisively settled. Indeed, a major thesis of this study is that Western political and social practices were able to become the basis of postwar order only through a series of ambitious strategies of invasiveness and extensiveness. This enterprise evolved not only through world-revolutionary market forces, but also through the armature of scientifically micromanaged military power.

A certain kind of optimism and rationalism surely distinguished liberalism on a world scale from its colonial and imperial predecessors. But an examination of the rise of the American republic reveals that such a nascent entity, however "exceptional" its condition at the founding, could scarcely afford to do away entirely with the basics of state power and armaments. What distinguished the American strategic project from that undertaken by the Continental land powers was the code of civilian militarization that shaped it from the beginning and that stamped it through to the era of nuclear deterrence. While this chapter cannot exhaustively account for the history of the American military, it can insert that theme into an account of the liberal strategic vision which America championed. It was a celebration of its revolutionary power that distinguished it from all other world-historical attempts at globalism.

At the sake of spawning another clumsy neologism, it helps to characterize the phenomenon in question as that of "millennial liberalism."[2] In this chapter, I explore how such a liberalism came to usher in postwar militarization along two simultaneous, complementary tracks. The one concerns invasive militarization of allied states and developing regimes. The other entails the extensive militarization of postwar relations under the rubric – and protective wraps – of extended nuclear deterrence. The concern here is less an exhaustive account than an analytical treatment of the origins of the postwar world military order. Only by understanding its historical and theoretical constitution does it become possible to see how deterrence strategy therein functioned as a distinct social practice underpinning world order. The function of nuclear strategy cannot fully be captured in a Strategic Studies model of mutual deterrence and the fending off of major power aggression. At least as important in explaining the internal ironies and dynamics of deterrence is to see it as part of the ongoing making and remaking of a postwar order in which sovereign states have been integrated, at times forcibly, within a global market system.

American power projection

After some thirty years of uninterrupted disorder in global affairs, the United States overtook the monetary, political and military leadership of the Free World after World War II. The USA was, at that point, the single power capable of assuming such a responsibility. It understood itself as liquidator of the old colonial system and of that unenlightened condition of imperial competition among the European powers that had led to two world wars. The Second World War was to be the final manifestation of irrational, bellicose nationalism and militarism. From then on, the chaotic jungle of international relations, in which economic protectionism and national self-interest had led to recurrent crises, would be replaced by a cosmopolitan system of open, multilateral trade relations, with the United States as guarantor of a newly stable order.

The theoretical justification for such a strategic concept can be found first in the classical economic theory of Adam Smith. It is no mere historical coincidence that his most famous work, *The Wealth of Nations*, appeared in the same year as did the United States. Both represent important new stages in the transition from mercantile trade and policies to something approaching a more market-oriented civil society and polity. In this sense, they both stand for the creation of new, liberal structures. According to the liberal tradition to which Smith's work gave rise, capital embodies two basic properties. It is essentially international in scope, and it is peaceful.

Like later sociologists of the modern state, including Herbert Spencer and Joseph Schumpeter, Smith argued that free capital knows no national borders and is dependent upon a condition of peace among nations. The true capitalist, in this sense, is neither nationalist nor militarist. There is no transcendent sensibility at work here, no idealism of the sentiments. Instead, enlightened self-interest suggests that war, as well as preferential tariffs and interventions, disturbs the free flow of goods and spoil opportunities for business. The logical consequences, and the ultimate goal, of such a view might be a world in which narrow-minded national governments no longer existed – a world, in other words, in which all of humanity could partake undisturbed in the civilizing and peaceful consequences of trade. In such an international civil society, wars would be relegated to remnants of a pre-modern past – to a world, in other words, in which the natural law of free competition had not been fully recognized or had been repeatedly violated. It was as if those who did not share in the bountifulness of a liberal world order were not fully able to participate as human beings at all in the world. This, at the core, is what came to

83

constitute a certain millennial tradition of American liberalism – a liberalism of international free trade that was ideologically a center-piece of the postwar strategic project of the American Century.

Yet such an ideological understanding of market political economy in the modern world was not what the early makers of American strategy foresaw. For even starting with Adam Smith, and clearly in the seminal works collectively published as *The Federalist Papers*, there was a profound pessimism about the transformative power of trade and a keen sense of the need for the new republic to rely upon its naval power as it sought a place in the world community. Smith himself did not share the optimism of a Richard Cobden or John Bright regarding the pacifying character of liberal trade, and was an ardent supporter of a vigorous standing armed force – not merely to protect trade, but also to protect the homeland against the threat of direct aggression. "The first duty of the sovereign," wrote Smith in *The Wealth of Nations*, "that of protecting the society from the violence and invasion of other independent societies, can be performed only by means of military force."[3] While there could be no doubt that economic power provided a considerable measure of security in its own right, it also contributed to a country's ability to field a sufficient armed force. Moreover, as liberal contract theorists such as Hobbes and Locke had been arguing for over a century, a stable and secure civil society was the indispensable precondition for the flourishing of domestic trade. Without military security, commerce would prove short-lived. When it came to protecting the commonwealth, wrote Smith, "defense is of much more importance than opulence."[4]

The United States entered world affairs on terms that differed fundamentally from those that prevailed on the Continent. Its geographical isolation ensured it would remain outside the immediate sway of the balance of power system. Two vast maritime buffers insulated it from the threats of invasion which had so characterized European power politics. While its leadership was inexperienced in court diplomacy, they understood that with its rich abundance of land and raw materials it held forth the promise of inexhaustible commerce and trade that could distinguish it from all other countries. That "the first new nation" also encountered few internal barriers to expansion and development only further whetted the appetite of its political leadership in the years after independence was won from the British.[5]

In his "Farewell Address" of 1796, George Washington noted the peculiarity of these conditions when he suggested that the United States need not follow the classical Continental powers with their complicated alliance commitments necessitating standing armies and extensive navies. By contrast, the United States should rely upon its commercial prowess and trade with all nations. This, rather than diplomatic and political obligations, would constitute the primary involvement of the US. "The Great rule of conduct for us, in regard to foreign Nations is in extending our commercial relations to have with them as little *political* connection as possible."[6]

Several of the Federalist Papers by John Jay and Alexander Hamilton had already expressed concern about whether such an expressly liberal strategy would be at all feasible. The difficulty of providing for the common defense and of minimizing the risks of war to the homeland was, in fact, one of the primary reasons to endorse a unified nation rather than a looser confederation of sovereign states as had been encouraged through the Articles of Confederation. But the trade rivalries engendered by American commerce abroad would certainly bring the country into conflict with foreign rivalries no matter how politically unified was the United States. In this regard, the Federalists drew upon arguments about the need for national defense which Adam Smith had already foreseen in arguing for the necessity of a strong navy. Wrote Jay in Federalist #4, "[t]he extension of our own commerce in our own vessels cannot give pleasure to any nations who possess territories on or near this continent."[7]

The Federalists foresaw that increased global trade would not lead to an end of war but rather, would bring with it a new set of conflicting interests over which nations would compete. As Hamilton asked, "[h]as commerce hitherto done any thing more than change the objects of war?"[8] The American strategy of pursuing commerce rather than politics or diplomacy abroad would raise particular questions about possible US interference with European navigation. It would also raise more diffuse concerns, rooted in mercantile perceptions of the relationship between trade and power, regarding the growth of American commercial greatness. Moreover, the historic role of British maritime supremacy would unavoidably be challenged in the course of an American attempt to create overseas networks of trade. Hamilton argued that in the face of such rational suspicions, the United States would have to forego a truly *laissez-faire* policy of "passive commerce" and pursue instead what he called "active commerce" by means of a national navy that would protect US trade interests at sea and abroad. "The necessity of naval protection to external or maritime commerce, and the conduciveness of that species of commerce to the prosperity of a navy, are points too manifest to require a particular elucidation. They, by a kind of reaction, mutually beneficial, promote each other."[9]

Until the end of the nineteenth century, however, American naval strategy was not prepared to pursue such an active policy. As established under President Jefferson, the US Navy was limited to coastal defense, countering piracy close in to shore, and dispatching landing parties of Marines, such as to the Barbary Coast in 1806. Only with the doctrinal innovations propagated by Capt. Alfred Thayer Mahan around the turn of the century did the United States acquire a protracted naval war-fighting capacity along the lines suggested by Hamilton's call for "active commerce." As Mahan showed, American commercial policy required an active defense policy capable of defeating enemy forces at sea. Such a strategy, operationally offensive in its capacity to deliver concentrated firepower ("never divide the fleet") and to choke off the enemy's key internal lines of operation, was militarily offensive in capacity but politically defensive in its larger aims – to protect the homeland and its own commercial fleet. In an argument that would be reprised in the nuclear era regarding the politically defensive character of a militarily offensive, war-fighting capability, Mahan argued against confusing political goals with military operations. "A navy for defense only, in the *political* sense, means a navy that will only be used in case we are forced into war." This was not to be confused with a self-restricted naval policy capable only of defensive operations in and around one's own coastline – as had been the case for the US for decades. This kind of limited "navy for defense only, in the *military* sense, means a navy that can only await attack and defend its own, leaving the enemy at ease as regards his own interests, and at liberty to choose his own time and manner of fighting."[10] The appropriate naval strategy was not coastal patrol but extended global operations, for "the enemy must be kept away not only out of our ports, but far away from our coasts."[11]

Mahan's importance extends far beyond his contribution – vital though it was – to the expansion of the US battleship fleet. For it was as a visionary of sea power, not just of naval strategy, that he stamped his mark on the evolution of America's role as a world power. In arguing the case for naval forces in the service of open sea lanes, Mahan developed an important position on the social function of military power. Whatever the specific contribution he made to naval history, his legacy to both American strategy and to the study of military strategy resides in his singular emphasis upon how sea power shaped, indeed, in his view, decided, the fate of nations and empires.

Consider, for instance, Mahan's understanding of the very concept of "sea power." While much of his work concerns the details of naval history and warfare, one can fruitfully follow Mahan's own advice and ask the analytically decisive question for naval operations without detailing the history of great maritime battles, namely "How did the ships come to be just there?"[12] By this Mahan means to broaden the question of naval conflict and to move away from the idea of the grandeur and tragedy of single engagements to a more sociological account of sea power as a dimension of general history.[13] This is where narrative history begins to assume theoretical proportions. Thus, in his systematic treatment of sea power in the opening chapters of *The Influence of Sea Power Upon History, 1660–1783*, Mahan reveals the seamless interweaving of commercial strategy and military policy. His object, he says, is nothing less than to provide "an estimate of the effect of sea power upon the course of history and the prosperity of nations."[14] He achieves this less through an empirical elaboration of colonial trade policy than through a conceptual fusion of naval armaments with maritime commerce.

What Mahan refers to as "sea power" embraces two different phenomena simultaneously. On the one hand, there is the basic form of superior naval power exhibited in military confrontation: what he referred to as "that overbearing power on the sea which drives the enemy's flag from it, or allows it to appear only as a fugitive."[15] The other side of sea power concerns the sources of commercial greatness, namely "(1) Production; (2) Shipping; (3) Colonies and Markets – in a word, sea power."[16]

From the standpoint of a strict logician, such an account of sea power might seem hopelessly ambiguous. Yet Mahan's boldness of vision inheres in his refusal to understate or finesse what was really an argument about the political economy of grand strategy. This becomes clear in his theoretical account of "The Elements of Sea Power," where he draws together claims about geopolitics, national character, and forms of government to arrive at an overview of the way sea power shapes national wealth and greatness. The effect of the argument is to celebrate the state's power to mobilize all of civil society and to coordinate the flow of resources so that the character and capabilities of the social body instantiate themselves in the unmistakable form of a robust maritime presence. Mahan's work provides a crystaline example of what Robert Cox argues concerning the nature of classical realism, namely that it derives its validity from its historically situated representation of civil society's subordination to the mercantile state. Mahan's account, as with geopolitics in general, is an attempt to adapt to the increasingly transnational character of state trading policy through a vigorous overseas extension and incorporation of those earlier mechanisms of control. In this sense, it represents a liberalization of policy, though it maintains in place all of the political and

87

military mechanisms of territorial sovereignty and control. This "diffusion" of realism helps explain its ability to adapt to contemporary conditions of global market relations. The theoretical relationship between mercantile strategy and foreign empire was embraced, among others, by Mahan's contemporary, Max Weber, in his work on "national economy."[17]

Mahan elaborates six constituent elements of sea power: 1) "geographical position" with respect to various international bodies of water and to potential naval rivals; 2) "physical conformation" of the interior, in terms of riparian and overland access to the marine frontier; 3) "extent of territory," in terms of the length of the coastline and the character of harbors; 4) "number of population," including its propensity to seafaring; 5) "national character" of a people, especially as regards their willingness to engage in commerce and overseas settlement and trade; and 6) how the "character of government" enables it to marshal domestic resources and popular will in the name of a sustained maritime presence.[18]

Mahan's peculiar combination of military, geopolitical and commercial power in the form of sea power marks him not (simply) as an imperialist of capital expansion but as a new breed of global strategist, for whom "political, commercial, and military needs are so intertwined that their mutual interaction constitutes one problem."[19] The answer to the question, does commercial strength determine naval capability, or does naval military power determine the extent of commercial empire?, is "yes." On this view, the imperative for overseas expansion has a dual impetus, the one in pursuit of classical trading outposts, the other as a search for way stations and repair posts so that national naval power can come to the defense of a far-flung commercial fleet. The link between the two is made explicit in terms of the main mission of the fleet, which is to clear the sea lanes and maintain open lines of transit and communication. Jomini's earlier arguments for maintaining clear interior lines of communication and supply were thus hauled out to sea by Mahan. "If navies, as all agree, exist for the protection of commerce," he wrote in 1897, "it inevitably follows that in war they must aim at depriving their enemy of that great resource, nor is it easy to conceive what broad military use they can subserve that at all compares with the protection and destruction of trade."[20]

It was far from clear whether the United States was in a position to pursue a strategy of the magnitude which Mahan thought required to sustain the project of commercial greatness. The Civil War had revealed the limits of the Union's navy, with military operations undertaken close in to ports and the country vulnerable to a Confederate blockade. Admiral Perry's exploratory ventures, first into Japan and then forty years later into Manila Harbor, were symbolic displays rather than demonstrations of US naval superiority.

Mahan's plaint about the nation's ill-suitedness at sea combines the lyrical imagery of romantic flight with a drumbeat call for national greatness in the midst of the imperial age.

> Having therefore no foreign establishments, either colonial or military, the ships of war of the United States, in war, will be like land birds unable to fly far from their own shores. To provide resting-places for them, where they can coal and repair, would be one of the first duties of a government proposing to itself the development of the power of the nation at sea.[21]

A rapid succession of events conspired, in effect, to settle the issue on behalf of the blue water navy hoped for by Undersecretary of the Navy Theodore Roosevelt. The Spanish–American War, the opportunity to move onto Hawaii, Spain's weakening position in the Philippines, and plans for a canal across the Panamanian Isthmus all gave the US the chance to make something substantive out of Secretary of State John's Hay's Open Door Notes regarding China. The result was a fleet flung far westward out into the Pacific, and a growing fleet in the North Atlantic which less than a generation later would turn the tide against the Central powers. This strange concatenation, of liberal America and global power, was to intensify its presence among the nations of the world. The exceptional trading nation designed by the Founding Fathers became, just over a century later, a growing industrial power with worldwide strategic outposts. As Mahan's writings made clear, this development had to do not with balance of power politics but rather, with the linkage between military strategy and global trade. American strategy over the next century was to soften the relationship between the military and international commerce. Indeed, in the nuclear era, the interaction between the two would seem to have lost all interdependence. But a look at the nature of American versions of liberal development and modernization suggests, in ways that are not available through the lens of Strategic Studies, that deterrence itself was engaged in the making and remaking of a liberal world order.

The violence of liberal modernization

In the aftermath of the Great War, President Woodrow Wilson tapped a sentiment that lay at the heart of progressive or enlightened liberalism, namely that the irrational, nationalist autocracies were ultimately

89

responsible for war and imperialism. The United States, by contrast, was executor of a natural or universal rule of law by which orderly trade and democratic self-determination prevailed. Perhaps worst of all was the secret diplomacy behind closed doors, the kind that insisted on *Realpolitik* and that stood in the way of democratic, market-oriented ways of life. The US was really the only country in the world which was capable in its foreign actions of preserving, indeed, advancing, human striving and progress. This corresponded to the American national interests, even if it also required military intervention. To make the world safe for democracy was, by definition, exactly the opposite of imperialism or despotism.

This was the basis for Wilson's famous "Fourteen Points."[22] The statement expressed his commitment to assist all peoples and nations of the world in their struggles for justice and self-determination. He was convinced that people long subordinated to despotic rule would, if granted self-determination, necessarily strive to organize themselves in the image of the United States. Yet as became obvious in subsequent decades – and as was apparent to those who looked with concern upon America's policy in that era toward the Mexican Revolution – the promise of American liberalism was often accompanied by a darker, malevolent side. Liberal society, based on a conception of domestic order often required that state mechanisms of power be applied against the body politic in an attempt to secure public life.

This, after all, had informed the core of social contract theory from Hobbes to Locke and Rousseau. Democracy requires particular conditions, and the inherent dynamics of political life do not bode well for the persistence of civic virtue in the absence of state repression. The state, even the liberal state, does not come about *de novo* but has, instead, to be constructed and maintained. Crucial to the ability of that state to patrol public space and ensure its receptivity to peaceful trade and exchange is its willingness, at times, to deploy violence strategically, economically, in defense of liberal order.[23]

In an American context, this willingness to rely upon violence in defense of liberal order can be seen in what might be called the Janus-character of American foreign policy.[24] The one face that is presented is friendly, prosperous, future-oriented and democratic. It generously presides over its own affairs and throughout the world as well. When problems emerge, money is sent, and the young, idealistic sons and daughters of middle class prosperity are dispatched via the Peace Corps to these regions of the world that have not come so far in their development as the US. The basic issue of foreign policy is how to distribute the available surplus and how to ensure that others can create for themselves what the country is blessed to enjoy. The world's people are thereby shown how, through a combination of self-confidence and creativity, they can alleviate their misery and perhaps even enjoy some prosperity.

But should one of these countries entrusted with its own fate decide, whether through orderly parliamentary procedure or through a violent revolution, to address its own social problems through state-controlled mechanisms, then Janus-headed liberalism shows its other face. This one is unpleasant and impersonal, unsympathetic and aggressive. In a word, violent. This other face is capable of showing the most profound intolerance and aggression. This is the other side of the US, the other side of that liberal and tolerant civil society that was so exceptional in the New World. Its brutality expressed itself in the decades-long pursuit and destruction of Native Americans.[25] Simultaneously with these measures of internal colonization began a series of overseas interventions, particularly in Latin America under the protective cover of the Monroe Doctrine and the Roosevelt Corollary. Reports in the *US Congressional Record* from 1969 document, for instance, that since 1789, the United States had been involved in over 200 distinct overseas military engagements, the overwhelming majority of them in areas of the Third World, and a significant number of them directed against revolutionary governments, including Mexico (1914–17), the Soviet Union (1918–20 and 1920–22), Nicaragua (1926–33) and Vietnam.[26] Moreover, in numerous cases of domestic unrest, the US government covertly participated on the side of counter-revolutionary forces, as in Iran (1953) and Guatemala (1954). The bloodiest example came in Indonesia (1965–66), where no less than half a million communists were executed.[27] Furthermore, one needs to consider the support, often for decades, which the United States extended to brutal military regimes under the auspices of various "security partnerships:" Spain under Franco, Greece during rule by the military junta (1967–74), and for various periods of military domination, Chile, Iran, Iraq, Korea, Turkey and more recently, China. These examples help illustrate an argument that pertains not merely to US foreign policy but to the whole school of contemporary Strategic Studies, namely how a political practice that understands itself as liberal and enlightened has been prepared to defend – and pursue – its vital international interests with an extraordinary degree of violence. The disproportion between US casualties and the loses incurred by both civilians and soldiers in Vietnam and – most recently – Iraq, offers vivid testimony to the price which strategic leadership is willing to exact, so long as the price can be enumerated as a non-Western body count.

How, then, does liberal strategy maintain the two sides of its character? What, specifically, is the theoretical substance which binds the classical Wilsonian vision of millennial liberalism with the strategic violence by which the West, in large measure under American leadership, has constructed global order?[28]

A clue can be found in the practice of "modernization," that influential school of the 1950s and 1960s allied with developmental economics. In essence, modernization was little more than an elaborated refinement of classical Enlightenment universalism, merged with Wilsonian liberal ideology and structurally coordinated to the needs of an emergent postwar multilateral trading system in which the postcolonial lands were to assume their allocated space at the bottom of the international hierarchy and at the margins of the international division of labor.

The hope among Western planners was that an orderly postwar environment could arise out of the destruction that had characterized European politics and society for some thirty years. The wartime mechanisms of postwar economic steering would now be applied in peacetime as the Keynesian consensus, supplemented by a (liberal) measure of social welfare statism, became the norm across the north Atlantic.[29] The advent of the Bretton Woods agreements of 1944 dealt a deathblow to the attempted phases of mercantile protectionism that had characterized the 1930s. Such state-centered measures were officially abandoned, to be forever replaced by international organizational regimes of cooperation on monetary and trade policy.

The panoply of transnational institutions set up after World War II had as their goal not merely to coordinate the trade policies of the major industrial market economies, but to provide as well a mechanism for the orderly integration of the newly emergent developing world. Yet the fragile, peripheral economies of the world, on the verge of postcolonial status as nominally independent states, would need subtle but invasive ties of military assistance, economic development, and political institution-building in order to be able to partake – though not as equals – of the emergent multilateral world order. As David Harvey later wrote of this era, "[i]t was almost as if a new and revivified version of the Enlightenment project sprang, phoenix-like, out of the death and destruction of global conflict."[30]

The difficulties of institutionalizing the modernist project were recognized in a 1948 text by George F. Kennan concerning the European Recovery Plan, the ERP.

> This is the significance of the ERP, the idea of European Union, and the cultivation of a closer association with the U.K. and Canada. For a

truly stable world order can proceed, within our lifetime, only from the older, mellower and more advanced nations of the world – nations for which the concept of order, as opposed to power, has value and meaning. If these nations do not have the strength to seize and hold real leadership in world affairs today, through that combination of political greatness and wise restraint which goes only with a ripe and settled civilization, then as Plato once remarked: "... cities will never have rest from their evils, – no nor the human race, as I believe."[31]

Kennan's famous "Long Telegram" of 1946 concluded with the observation that "Much depends on health and vigor of our own society. World communism is like a malignant parasite which feeds only on diseased tissue."[32] Despite his view at the time of the Soviet Union as an implacable, ideologically closed-minded foe, Kennan's analysis of the specific threats facing Europe and the developing world focused largely on political instability rather than overt military aggression. One searches in vain throughout his work at the time for a claim that the Soviet challenge manifests itself in terms of military intent – or capability, for that matter. In this sense, the medicalized representation of Soviet policy as parasitic displaces attention from a critique of identifiable Soviet interests to an account of how vulnerable certain countries are to outside interference. By depoliticizing strategic concerns and invoking instead a medical discourse, Kennan's account creates a sanitized space for legitimate intervention by concerned public officials whose task is more akin to humanitarian rescue than political decision-making.

This medicalized discourse was to find a more sustained account in the work of W.W. Rostow, the architect of modernization theory and a key figure in the articulation of a comprehensive strategy by which modern Western identity, which reaches its apotheosis in the form of advanced industrial capitalism, can export itself to other countries as the only plausible model of development. The only hindrance to this free unfolding of human productive force is confronted when dissident social groups tap social unrest and channel it toward radical purposes. The chief culprit here, of course, are the communist revolutions in the Third World. Appropriately, Rostow gave his most influential work, *The Stages of Economic Growth*, the immodest subtitle, *A Non-Communist Manifesto*. In a phrase that combines both medical and teleological representations to valorize Western identity, Rostow writes that "Communism is a disease of the transition" from traditional to modern society.[33] It would require forms of Western military involvement at a threshold lower than overt military intervention, particularly anti-guerrilla insurgency, to stanch the infection before it spread and poisoned all of the body politic.

Reconstruction after the Second World War, while bringing the rest of the world along, would require therapies of "modernization." These would prove crucial in the development of a recognizably Western world order, for "to modernize" would come to mean to improve, to upgrade, to make something better by technical refinement and scientific know-how. The application of master-planning, a broad, urbane and future-oriented, growth maximizing perspective, would be needed to ensure that peoples are not allowed to rest in their traditional forms of life. Late-nineteenth-century German sociology had identified this transition as a move from "Gemeinschaft" to "Gesellschaft," literally, from "community" to "society." The shift refers to a whole range of deep-seated transformations in values, modes of household economy, and in the spheres of life in which people circulate. Weber, in particular, explored the ambiguities of the process as involving a certain mundaneness and rationalization of social practice. The advent and widespread deployment of instrumental forms of thought indicated, for Weber, that modernity was not a simple matter of progressive human unfolding. In fact, his writings are characterized by a deep-seated anxiety about the social costs of the subsequent "disenchantment of the world" and the loss of a certain familiarity with traditional forms of authority and work. Weber himself looked upon bureaucracy as both the *sine qua non* of modernization and as evidence of the loss of personal responsibility and initiative. For him, this indicated a level of moral uncertainty, indeed of Nietzschean anxiety, that was incompatible with his self-assigned role as social scientist. Weber himself never reconciled the tension between these two positions, but postwar modernization theory was to prove far more confident in its affirmation of these processes.

Economic modernization has come to refer to the process of enforced changes, implemented from above by a secular state, that strategically alters the social landscape and that prepares the way for a capitalist, market-oriented political economy. Its stylistic motif is that of streamlined, mobile flow, with an explicit value placed upon accelerated social change. The look and feel, architecturally speaking, is linear, of large scale, and establishes both vertical and horizontal dominance over natural land forms. It is conspicuous in its presence as an object of human design and engineering, featuring straight lines over complex curves, and favors a readily maintainable look rather than the complexities of minute variation. In industrial production, this is the triumph of Fordist mass production over the craftwork of

94

the guild worker or artisan. In public housing, modernism takes the form of huge urban renewal projects that sweep aside brownstones and the smaller units comprising distinct neighborhood styles. The broad urban avenues that Georges Haussmann designed for Bonapartist Paris exemplified how strategic modernization yields public architecture in the name of social control.[34] The need for security officers to patrol the streets and to prevent effective use of barricades in the aftermath of the Paris Commune induced officials literally to reconstruct the streets in the name of public order. The redesign also enabled the police to make use of the machine gun as an instrument of social control. This aesthetic finds its developmentalist analog in the urban fantasy of a hyper-modern Brasilia deep in the heart of the Amazon jungle. Under the megalomaniacal vision of a Ceaucescu in Bucharest, such a fantastic vision assumes brutalist proportions in the name of urban renovation.

It is, perhaps, something of a leap to move from the international politics of Western postwar strategy to modern urban design. Yet the cultural underpinnings of modernization and Third World development drew heavily upon the images and values of the European and American experiences. Indeed, the master plan for this reworking of international life was the self-consciously proclaimed path of achievement realized by the most advanced Western industrialized democracies. Their leadership consisted in their ability in the postwar, post-colonial world to bring to the newly liberated peoples of the Third World the latest in applied social engineering. Rostow's stages of growth present the clearest version of an attempt to draw the post-colonial world into the Western orbit, with the path of industrialization, urbanization, and the creation of a rigorous division of labor all based self-consciously on emulating the serial phases of industrial and social revolution experienced by Great Britain, Germany, the USA and other Western powers.

Rostow's paean to impending affluence is a useful example of how "modernization" draws its sustenance from particular representations of life. Implicit in this celebratory account of development is a series of conceptual commitments that need to be brought out into the political foreground if practitioners concerned with "developing" societies are fully to understand what analysts have in store for them. "Traditional" societies are seen as mired in a pre-Newtonian world, confined to natural horizons with a fixed "ceiling on the level of attainable output per head."[35] Such a delimiting cosmology has to be transformed if modernization is to proceed. This "pre-modern" worldview is to be replaced by a recognizably "modern" one of unlimited growth. Nature thereby becomes a resource for use by human beings who now stand at the center of all things.

A network of representations is called into play here: mutually dependent conceptions of nature, man, goods and society. A set of dichotomies is invoked, with the "pre-Newtonian" world on one side of the divide and "modern" affluent cultures on the other: traditional society/modern society; nature/science; subsistence/wealth. Only by tacitly invoking these dichotomous representations and invoking one side continually against the other is Rostow's discourse of development possible.

The ensuing social scientific delineation of isolable stages of economic growth results in Rostow's five steps on the stairway to modernist heaven. The telos of this civil society is market-oriented consumerism, with the ultimate vision that of a panoply of luxury goods available to those who work less and less and are able to devour more and more. But what Marx had aspired to as socialist freedom becomes in Rostow's hands transformed into a living Sears catalog without any pretense to democracy.

The first stage, for instance, that of traditional society, depicts those cultures languishing in "the present." Their millennial deliverance from the natural given-ness and boundaries of their repetitive life only results from their "contact" with Western industrial powers. It should be noted that these advanced industrialized powers are already well-traveled on the Rostovian locomotive of history and are fully developed by the time they encounter these traditional societies. Their own wealth and power cannot be explained as the product of a history of colonial conquests. Indeed, a peculiarity of Rostow's model is that each of the advanced industrial countries has developed in hermetic isolation from the rest of the world, whereas their contemporary younger brethren in the developing world are fully dependent on the expertise and assistance of the more mature of the world's powers. In a global version of conservative welfare state politics, the message is clear: since these countries made it on their own, why can others not follow in their footsteps?

And what will countries experience which adopt the sweeping changes in their social order proposed as necessary by Rostow? Here is how he explains the ennobling moral drama of economic growth as it takes hold in the second stage, marked off as "the preparation for take-off."

> The second stage of growth embraces societies in the process of transition; that is, the period when the preconditions for take-off are developed; for this is the time to transform a traditional society in the

ways necessary for it to exploit the fruits of modern science, to fend off diminishing returns, and thus to enjoy the blessings and choices opened up by the march of compound interest.[36]

The treatment is thoroughly devoid of drama, or existential struggle. The "march of compound interest" refers to a market economy set in motion, able to enlarge due to growing productivity and to the widespread social practices of capital accumulation and reinvestment as they are poured back into productive infrastructure. Now countries that had squandered whatever surplus – beyond mere subsistence – that they had been creating are pouring back that surplus into an expanding stock of productive capacity. Yet such a transition, revolutionary in its domestic social implications, is reduced in this treatment to a series of technical alterations, measured in terms of expanding per capita output and savings. There is no acknowledgement of the power relations, the struggles involved in the process of change – the (re-)creation of ownership, control over land and manufacturing, distribution of the social product, or access to capital and purchasing power. Moreover, the state's function in this process is essentially an administrative one, overseeing market infrastructures, educational systems, and proving reliable streams of revenues for the public projects needed to maintain orderly growth. All of this proceeds without partisan politics, devoid of ideology, and within a consensualist framework that looks suspiciously like the well-scrubbed consumerist world represented in such period-piece black and white television programs as "Leave it to Beaver" and "The Donna Reed Show."[37]

Insofar as Rostow recognizes that the changes associated with modernization are violent and disruptive, the assumption of moral rectitude and rationality is so squarely placed upon the shoulders of the modernizers that those benighted parochialists who would oppose it are dismissed as irrational atavists. In short, political power does not manifest itself. The march of progress is a friendly one, and it promises equal delivery to all.

Rostow's developmental discourse draws upon a key assumption: that modern, Western, developed societies are simply better and more desirable than traditional, pre-modern societies. The philosophical point is so deeply embedded that it never once is even acknowledged, much less questioned as (potentially) problematic. Nor is the question raised: desirable for whom? The ethnocentrism of the whole analysis arises from its refusal to take seriously the indigenous cultures and identities of particular peoples and countries. Instead, the reference point is the self-evident superiority of Western goods, the Western economy, the Western way of life. Ever the economist, Rostow calls this "the demonstration effect" of modern technology and lifestyles. But the mediation of these values and the transition processes of adopting them that is required of developing countries are by no means politically neutral. They are strikingly violent. The world's people really do want Western products, we are told. Of course there is a back-up just in case they do not. Not surprisingly, this is where Rostow's text gets murky. Malcontents can always look over the shoulder of traveling salesmen and see battleship guns in the harbor. Surely, this is an impressive sight, one that demonstrates the (potentially) superior effects of modern Western society. Spurred on by these "demonstration effects" of Western goods, the peoples of the formerly colonial world are induced to follow along and to develop themselves in the footsteps of their uninvited guests.

Yet the violence at work in the modernization process is not merely the strategic–instrumental one of armed forces waiting to move in should the auto-suggestive power of "demonstration effects" not work on their own accord. The violence also occurs at the level of everyday life, as longstanding, traditional forms of life are transformed into modern, commodity-based exchange economies of mobile labor markets and class-based relations of labor and capital. It is, perhaps, characteristic of the discourse of modernization that it does not acknowledge the essentially violent transgressions of the land and the human body required by economic development. Roads, port cities, a transport network, electrification, an educational system, trained labor, a police force, agribusiness, multi-storey buildings, tourist hotels and golf courses for the expatriates all have a dramatic effect on the shape of land and the tenor of everyday life. So, too, does the infusion of foreign businessmen, and of landholders eager to make deals with them. A whole class of compradors and hangers-on of the new elite is inherently part of the process. Interestingly enough, however, this does not qualify for Rostow as "violence," but rather, as the normal evolutionary flow of modernity.

Small wonder that local resistance may develop, and a political opposition begin to organize. Civil disorder and social unrest invariably accompany such changes. But Rostow treats these very selectively. Modernization is peaceful. Resistance is violent. Only that which reacts against such a naturalistic dynamic of social processes expresses itself as "violence" and thus may legitimately be put back violently in its place through reliance upon domestic militia and security. Recall here, from another context, the refreshingly honest words of Michael Howard, who at least acknowledges, as Rostow cannot, that "I myself am one of those fortunate people for whom the existing order is tolerable, and I want to maintain it." The proper role of strategic violence is to preserve the global distribution of power. "If the existing framework of international order is to be preserved, a deterrent capacity must be maintained against those, whatever their ideological persuasion, whose resentment at its injustices tempts them to use armed force to overthrow and remould it."[38]

Underdeveloped countries are particularly susceptible to social unrest in the first transition phase, from "traditional society" to the "preparation for take-off." Here the basic problem is the restructuring of long-standing work and life forms into market and exchange-oriented practices. The ensuing dislocation can often lead to militant nationalism and has to be held in place, lest it become the basis for militant, radical oppositional movements. Rostow understood that the process of domestic change could not be carried out on its own accord. Though he sanitizes the power relations embedded in the global division of labor, he concedes that the internationalization of postwar capital and the construction of a truly international trading order require a strong political hand to lead the developing countries through the first precarious stages toward "take-off." Charismatic political leadership alone cannot provide the investment capital required for creation of the necessary infrastructure: the most important goal during the first phase of the modernization process creating stable political institutions.

Rostow, writing in the heady days of development theory, was characteristically optimistic about the likelihood of this process succeeding. Aside from the unfortunate obstacles posed by Communist insurgents, there seemed little to worry about as the stages of growth unfolded in their evolutionary naturalness. That there may have been some connection between the West's ability to have developed economically and its historic dependence upon colonial labor power and raw materials never enters the analysis.[39]

Even the most ardent celebrants of the development model acknowledge that the emergence of the postwar, post-colonial lands has encountered considerable difficulty that has had to be negotiated by state elites. In an especially influential work on this issue, *Political Order in Changing Societies*, Samuel P. Huntington has argued that in most Third World lands, only one social constellation is available to provide the stability, values, national commitment, and loyalty necessary for building up the reliable political institutions necessary for participation in multilateral trade: the military.[40] Its social and class background has qualified it for the task of nationally oriented modernization. Their professional education stamped them as disciplined, dedicated nationalists with strong ties toward Western models of stability and economic values, and they were best prepared among all available collegial groups to forge the kind of internal political stability that would carry a society through the wrenching early phases of modernization and growth.

In order to transit the precarious stages of growth, and thus to ensure seamless social and economic development, it is necessary to stabilize governments through military assistance: police training, weapons transfers, technological instruction, and military-strategic coordination at the level of national armed forces. This link between liberal America and Third World military elites would be the price to be paid for the modernization of the developing world. The Pentagon undertook this through a sustained program of civil-military training throughout the Third World involving the Military Assistant Program (MAP), International Military Educational Training (IMET), and Foreign Military Sales programs (FMS).[41]

The strategic importance of the ensuing ties between the US and the Third World was stressed in 1968 by Secretary of Defense Clark Clifford in testimony before the Senate Foreign Relations Committee.

> If we are to maintain the type of relationship we want with some of these newer countries, we can do so many times through the use of military aid and in some instances through military sales. It brings us into a relationship with them that has proved valuable, particularly, as I have mentioned, when they send their younger men over here for training. We also have advisers and technicians overseas, so it results in a type of intercourse between the two countries which has proven to be valuable.[42]

As Rostow's and Huntington's work suggested, Third World modernization could well require military regimes as a necessary step on the way toward mass consumption and Western-style political democracy. This could only be legitimate, however, to overcome the difficulties of the transition stages and to achieve self-sustaining economic growth. But what should happen if the desired modernization process did not take full effect? What policies could be expected from the leading advanced liberal democracy when its promise of an "age of high mass consumption" proved illusory for those countries on the periphery of the global division of labor? That, as it turned out, would depend far less on whether the country was a military (or democratic) regime and far more on whether its government was interested in aligning itself with the basic military–strategic and economic network of the postwar liberal trading order. Whether effective, widespread social development and modernization resulted turned out to be far less important than whether a stable regime could be entrusted to side with the articulation of Western order. In short, human rights became less significant than the international loyalty of the regime in question when choosing sides in the Cold War conflict. The performative success of the developing regime in generating widespread social benefits became subordinated to the strategic role of the country in postwar alliance structures. Developing regimes, facing modes of social violence in the course of the modernization process, were thus subjected to a second form of violent coordination, engineered on a global scale.

With the United States having displaced the British in the Middle East as guarantor of regional peace, American strategic considerations established political dominance within the Alliance. The Truman Doctrine consolidated this role for the US and presaged the country's role as postwar political–military hegemon. While France proved recalcitrant in its abandonment of colonial holdings in Vietnam, Algeria, and throughout French West Africa, the clear dominance of the US within the Western orbit required it to assume leadership of strategic–military protection and thereby to provide an effective umbrella over the whole of the multilateral trading system. Recurring support for Third World military–developmental governments – as in Iran (from 1953) South Korea (1953), Pakistan (1958), and Brazil (1964) demonstrated that there need be no antithesis between such assistance and the long-term liberal universalism which motivated Western planners.

This really was the greatest achievement of the short-lived "American century." That the US could articulate and underpin a transnational strategic architecture gave enormous political legitimacy to its concomitant project of a multilateral trading bloc. The example in 1991 of Corazon Aquino fighting against her own Senate in its decision to close Subic Bay and Clark Air Field testifies as much to the political credibility extended to her fragile government by this foreign military presence as to the immediate economic cash-out to Philippine employees servicing the troops.

Strategic Studies has long focused on the military as an instrument of warfare. The Clausewitzian legacy, of analyzing armed force as an instrument of political purpose, has, however, limited the vision of strategic analysts in seeing war in terms of its "use value" rather than as a critical element in the general discursive economy of a country's overall development and state-building.[43] What distinguishes nuclear strategy from all other political–military strategies, beyond the destructive potential which it has drawn upon for both deterrence and war-fighting, is the ambitiousness of the social project which it under-takes. For in ways that have never been articulated within the thou-sands of monographs and journal articles on arms control and deter-rence, nuclear diplomacy in its political character is visible evidence of the arrival of modern industrial and scientific culture. Its presence, in the corporeal form of weapons systems and support bases, and in its mediated form through Western-trained armed forces and alliance guarantees, is part of its discursive form as a means of cultural incorpo-ration. The "umbrella" held out to Western allies thanks to the good graces of extended deterrence is part of a cultural absorption whereby legally sovereign states are recruited within a cultural ambit of modernism. The technical control afforded by nuclear strategy is paradigmatic for the larger project of instrumental rationalism and a collective Western project of a shared historical identity.

The issue in this regard has been partially addressed by radical critics of weapons systems development who have pointed to the supporting weapons culture – an infrastructure of armaments experts, technologists, and generally pro-Western bureaucrats in both the mili-tary and industrial sectors concerned to adopt the whole panoply of advanced industrial culture embodied in state-of-the-art weaponry.[44] This transnational class, the bearers of armaments culture, is part of the growing ties between metropole and periphery that link the advanced with the developing world. It was just such ties through military–political institutions that Rostow and Huntington foresaw as crucial if the critical early stages of development were to be safely negotiated in the Third World. And it was just such ties of infrastructural depend-ence that President Nixon drew upon in his strategy – modestly announced in July 1969 as "the Nixon Doctrine" – of holding back on the direct deployment of US troops overseas and relying instead upon regional allies – Iran, Nigeria, Pakistan, South Korea – to provide not only for their own security but for Western strategic security as well throughout vital points in the global economy of resources, labor, and markets. The policy was part of an explicit attempt to recognize that "[t]he postwar period in international relations has ended."[45] In an explicit repudiation of the Truman Doctrine, and in a rhetorical appeal that specifically reversed John Kennedy's 1961 inaugural promise to bear all burdens and assume all costs, Nixon proclaimed as "the central thesis" of his doctrine that

> the United States will participate in the defense and development of allies and friends, but that America cannot – and will not – conceive *all* the plans, design *all* the programs, execute *all* the decisions and undertake *all* the defense of the free nations of the world. We will

102

help where it makes a real difference and is considered in our interest.[46]

Addressing himself indirectly to the Rostow–Huntington thesis of military institution building as a central component of economic development, Nixon reiterated the liberal paradigm as the foundation of American postwar strategy. But unlike the immediate postwar days, the United States was not in a position to sustain the kind of broad-ranging global support of its multilateral commitments. The economic burdens were mounting. Military credibility suggested the need to rely upon local forces. And the politics of military intervention was becoming increasingly difficult to legitimize before domestic audiences. All of this contributed to a need for shifting some of the burden for political–military stability onto the host country itself. Among the lessons of Vietnam were that the country threatened with subversion would have to assume chief responsibility for its own internal security.

> we cannot expect US military forces to cope with the entire spectrum of threats facing our allies or potential allies throughout the world. This is particularly true of subversion and guerrilla warfare, or "wars of national liberation." Experience has shown that the best means of dealing with insurgencies is to preempt them through economic development and social reform and to control them with police, paramilitary and military action by the threatened government.[47]

One significant effect of the shift in strategy toward burden sharing among Third World states was to alter the terms of aid, from outright grants and military aid through the Military Assistance Program (MAP) to direct sales of equipment under the category of Foreign Military Sales (FMS). In the case of US aid to Pakistan, for instance, during fiscal years 1950–66, FMS totaled only $33 million compared with $650 million in MAP funding. The ratio reversed dramatically in the following years. Between fiscal years 1967 and 1980 the assistance was shifted entirely to the FMS, with some $291 million in sales directed toward Pakistan and none under MAP.[48] The statistics pertaining to Pakistan are reflected in overall US policy worldwide. Of the $54.6 billion in MAP reported for fiscal years 1950–85, $52.7 billion (96 percent) was incurred in the years 1950–75. By contrast, of $94.6 billion in FMS reported for 1950–85, only $19.6 billion (30 percent) was reported for 1950–75, with the rest ($75 billion) reported for the ten-year period 1976–85.[49]

While the Carter administration made a much-publicized effort to restrict military assistance to states in violation of human rights, it nonetheless endorsed the basic parameters of postwar military assistance to Third World regimes. A clear explanation for the Carter administration's overall approach was made at the time by Lucy Wilson Benson, Under Secretary for Security Assistance, Science and Technology, in testimony before the Senate Committee on Foreign Relations in February 1979 regarding the value of ties between the US government and Third World governments created through military sales and associated staff training.

> Since 1950, we have trained almost 500,000 foreign nationals under various military training programs. These programs contribute to the military proficiency of allied and friendly countries and strengthen our communications with the current and future military leadership of those countries.
>
> A recently completed review of the current positions held by IMET/FMS trainees for the five-year period fiscal years 1974–78 indicates that many trainees have achieved positions of prominence and influence in their respective countries. In 47 countries for which information is reasonably complete, more than 1,100 former IMET students have achieved general or flag rank. Approximately 1,000 former IMET students occupy high positions in the military or civilian sectors of their country. The latter positions include several heads of state in government, cabinet ministers, members of parliament, and ambassadors.[50]

Throughout the postwar era, the superordinate goal of American strategy was the maintenance and reconstruction of a multilateral economic order in which the post-colonial lands of the Third World could be integrated. In this manner, the political–military "security" concerns were seen as inseparable from the political–economic. Drawing on the one hand from a security discourse and on the other hand from a discourse of political economy, the postwar multilateral world was forged under the aegis of American protection. In particular, American power projection established itself both extensively, in terms of extended nuclear deterrence, and intensively, through strategies of military assistance and preparation for a panoply of low-intensity, anti-guerrilla insurgencies. Beyond the immediate concerns of homeland nuclear deterrence and war-fighting, generalized security guarantees of American nuclear deterrence were vital for the successful reconstruction of the core industrial powers – Great Britain, West Germany, France, Italy, and of course Japan. There is no other way to account for the meticulous emplacement of American nuclear weapons throughout Western Europe, especially since the documentary record makes only the most cursory reference to the likelihood of a Soviet operational capacity to advance on Western ground. Far more realistic, and far more politically compelling, was the accompanying political argument that the weakened social fabric of the Western industrial world made it susceptible to internal Communist influence and control. That these invocations took place at a time of spectacular electoral successes of the Communist Party in France and Italy lends credence to the overwhelmingly political rather than military–strategic character of the postwar Soviet threat.

The eagerness with which this argument was greeted by the *avant-garde* of postwar modernists was simply indispensable to the subsequent success of regional economic reconstruction. The domestic Keynesian–Fordist consensus on the fate of these industrial economies ultimately required that state managers and regulators accept American protection as a bulwark against the resurgence of interwar militancy from both the left and the right. Nominally directed against outside aggression, it was part and parcel of a broader, more ambitious strategy to recapture and reconstruct the basic trajectory of Western industrial and political culture and to fend off domestic challengers as well. In this sense, liberal strategy embodies two antagonistic attitudes, the one open-minded and generous, the other brutal and violent. Undertaken in the name of peace, it relies upon deeply embedded processes of domestic and international militarization. This Janus-faced quality can be found in the ability of Strategic Studies to fuse together the two seemingly disparate phenomena of liberal generosity and violent brutality. The self-proclaimed aspirations of modern political–military strategy embody the paradox or tension of these two modes. The ability of liberal society to threaten destruction in order to forge peace created a puzzle that lay at the heart of nuclear deterrence strategy since the first days of the postwar era.

5 DETERRENCE AS A SOCIAL PRACTICE

... nuclear weapons provide the glue that has held the Western alliance together. (James Schlesinger[1])

Baudelaire's much-cited essay of 1863, "The Painter of Modern Life," captures an ambivalence toward order that manifests itself in the tension between production and destruction: "By 'modernity' I mean the ephemeral, the fugitive, the contingent, the half of art whose other half is the eternal and the immutable."[2]

The promise of man's making and remaking the world brings with it a recurrent striving to distance life from tradition. All human achievement, all creativity and vision, finds itself unstable and subject to displacement. Yet for any one particular moment it is art as creativity that prevails in its promise to ensure a new order. The triumphs and durability of the modernist are short-lived, so that in the words of Marx, "all that is solid melts into air."[3] The momentary achievements of human imagination and culture are rapidly overtaken, displaced and rendered archaic museum pieces by the onward march of progress and modernization. The relentless pursuit of the streamlined – the more rationalistic and efficient – is both an expression of human creativity and a sign of destructive restlessness.

No greater example of creative tension, of imaginative destruction and the promise of rational control, has existed than nuclear weaponry. Indeed, one can argue that the existence and proliferation of these weapons of mass destruction in effect completed the modernist dilemma. In simultaneously offering both the hope of world peace and the promise of its apocalyptic demise, nuclear weapons have embodied the aesthetic and political antinomies to which Baudelaire referred over a century ago. Perhaps in this sense, the weaponry and various strategies of deterrence which have promised to tame that ambivalent character of creative destruction are more sophisticated and more interesting than articulated by either their most ardent defenders or their most relentless critics. Much of postwar nuclear opposition has been predicated on the basis of nuclear weapons as an unambiguously evil and destructive threat. The strategic community, by contrast, has embraced them as the long awaited solution to the centuries-long problem of recurrent warfare. Neither side has been able to incorporate within the central terms of its analysis the inherently ambivalent and multivalent character of these weapons – and of their manifold strategies of deployment. To have allowed some of that tone into a monochromatic room would have compromised the apparent clarity which both sides sought – from respectively different traditions of analysis. Perhaps with the emergence of global political structures in which nuclear weapons recede in immediacy, it is possible to locate nuclear weapons within a cultural and aesthetic domain that might earlier have seemed heretical or indulgent. Terms of debate about weapons and strategy focus on their instrumental character – whether they will create stability or not, ensure peace or promote militarization, and the logic of their production and distribution within a world military order that enhances or detracts from security. No doubt, these are important issues. But they do not exhaust possible avenues of inquiry. Nor, more importantly, do they fully account for the fluency with which these weapons and strategies circulate in political economies of representation. Nuclear weapons and deterrence strategies have helped constitute the cultural identities of major (and minor) powers throughout the postwar world. Only by examining how this construction of identity has taken place does it become possible fully to explore whether "the end of the Cold War" might bring about an altered manner by which the West can imagine and construct itself.

A particularly revealing example of this came during the debates about nuclear strategy that preoccupied NATO politics in the late 1970s and early 1980s. The emphasis on force "modernization" and the accompanying efforts promoting newer, more mobile and more accurate weaponry had the curious effect of publicizing whatever existing limitations may have existed concerning alliance strategy, all the while stoking public anxieties about the grisly likelihood of nuclear conflict. A basic rule of Alliance defense strategy, evident since the May 1955 debacle following the West German debate over the "Carte Blanche" exercises, had been that the public has difficulty dealing with the operational realities of nuclear strategy.[4] The destructive potential of the strategy momentarily outweighs its political intent as an instrument of reassurance. For reasons that deserve more attention than

107

they got at the time, popular confidence in the Alliance was shaken in the fall of 1981 when President Reagan, followed by Secretary of State Alexander Haig, ill-advisedly spoke up about one of several possible war-fighting scenarios confined to the European theater. It did not take much to rouse concern, for there is a thin line, or perhaps a chimerical one, between the promise of peace and the promise of annihilation.

Decision-makers have skated close to the edge of the nuclear precipice for years, and it is not clear, even to many of them, that the effort lives up to its promise. A whole literature of strategic confessionals by apostate strategists and would-be crisis managers confirms the growing doubt that strategy policy-makers had at the time they were involved in policy making about the actual utility of nuclear weapons as viable instruments of strategic bargaining. US Admiral H.G. Rickover, for years the architect of the American nuclear submarine arsenal, evidenced his disavowal of the prevailing strategy after leaving military service. In testimony before a Joint Committee of Congress, the retired officer undercut everything he had worked for during a forty-year tour of duty when he confessed that the world would be better off if all nuclear ships were sunk.[5]

NATO's experiences in the mid-1970s and early 1980s suggests a pervasive problem concerning the social function of nuclear deterrence. The immediate issue about preserving NATO's credibility in the face of recurring Soviet intermediate deployments was but a reprise of earlier debates within the Alliance concerning the reliability and credibility of American nuclear guarantees. Much of the intra-Alliance strategic debate concerned the need to assure the Allies themselves of US strategic reliability. The problem that was to bedevil NATO for four decades was also central to the domestic politics of nuclear strategy in many of its member countries since the advent of the nuclear era. The purpose, function and utility of these weapons of mass destruction have always been at question by those who have relied most heavily upon them. Kissinger's lament is worth recalling. "What in the name of God is strategic superiority?", he asked at a 1974 press conference. "What is the significance of it, politically, militarily, operationally ...? What do you do with it?"[6] might best be considered the central question of the whole nuclear era. Indeed, as suggested above in chapter 3, the major impetus behind the nuclear armaments process has been less a "realist" assessment of balance of power considerations than an internally generated anticipatory response to the absence of a compelling answer regarding the question of what one can do with one's arsenal. Regardless of its composition and operational capabilities, these questions will remain and have lain at the core of repeated efforts to find a meaningful purpose for nuclear arsenals. The utility of nuclear weapons as instruments of deterring aggression has proven notoriously difficult to establish. It is, after all, impossible to prove why outright aggression or a "bolt out of the blue" attack on a major power has not happened. Those who have presided over postwar foreign policy decision-making, meanwhile, have continually expressed wonderment at the effectiveness of nuclear weaponry as instruments of diplomacy. Even those who thought they were relying upon them – as in the midst of the Cuban Missile Crisis – turned out later, upon reflection and open discussion with their colleagues, to acknowledge that their ability to survive, much less master, the crisis had considerably more to do with conventional military forces, diplomatic bargaining, and the sheer play of personality and good luck than did reliance upon nuclear threats.[7]

The ability of nuclear threats to serve diplomacy constructively is likely to remain an open question that historians will long continue to debate. Yet attention should not be diverted from the way in which nuclear strategy has helped shape the domestic and international orders which it has purported to be defending. As I show in this chapter, the strategy has acquired the status of a social practice that cannot be exhausted by the regulative model of deterring aggression that is postulated in so much of the Strategic Studies literature. Indeed, far too little attention has been focused on the constitutive dimensions of nuclear strategy – its utility as an instrument of state-building and alliance-building and of forging the basic parameters of the world military order and modern global cultures.

The promise of technological salvation

Writing in the midst of the Second World War, a Russian *émigré* air force officer named Maj. Alexander P. de Seversky concluded his best-seller, *Victory Through Air Power*, a May 1942 selection of the Book-of-the-Month Club, with a call for the full unleashing of American ingenuity and power.

> Air power is the American weapon. It will not fail us, if only we unchain it and provide immediately the minimal conditions for its unhindered development. I know that I speak for all my colleagues in the aeronautical legions of the land – our gallant pilots, designers, engineers, and manufacturers, the aerial strategists and the humblest aeronautical mechanics – and especially for the millions of American young people born into the air-power age and attuned to its dynamic

rhythm, when I say, that we airmen feel frustrated by the artificial restraints. We are eager to serve and ready to act when our beloved America says the word.[8]

He had earlier in the text constructed a riveting image of America's newfound vulnerability in the aftermath of Pearl Harbor – written with all the patriotic ardor that only a naturalized citizen can muster, as if to play upon the imagery of the "Star Spangled Banner."

> From every point of the compass – across the two oceans and across the two poles – giant bombers, each protected by its convoy of deadly fighter planes, converge upon the United States of America. There are thousands of these dreadnoughts of the skies. Each of them carries at least fifty tons of streamlined explosives and a hailstorm of light incendiary bombs. Wave after wave they come – openly, in broad daylight, magnificently armored and armed, surrounded by protective aircraft and equipped to fight their way through to their appointed targets. Aerial armadas now battle boldly and fiercely just as great naval armadas used to do in the past, only with a destructive fury more terrifying.[9]

In the face of this challenge, strategists were forced to turn to air power for useful, peaceful purposes. They were to harness the strange new powers inherent in the aerial offensive and apply them for public good. It was far from clear, however, whether so liberal a polity as the United States would be able to muster the determination. Thus the stridency of his book. Seversky believed that the United States, as the leader of the civilized world, had no choice. Only by acquiescing in the imperative thrust of modern science and technology could there be found a release from the agonies of insecurity. Indeed, only by Americans turning themselves over to the irresistible force of modern technology would the world ever be able once again to live in peace. Thus the American people were to reverse the processes by which social forces constitute technology, and abandon themselves to the call of modern aeronautical and ballistic science. To overcome the unbearable anxiety of contemporary insecurity, Americans thereby needed only to hand their fate over to the naturalized impetus of a technologically driven strategy. This comes, it must be highlighted, on the eve of the nuclear era, before the actual advent of intercontinental missiles and furtively cruising submarines. But none of this would require a heroic act of imagination to usher in a world whose ocean beds were monitored, whose open skies were constantly under surveillance, whose outer space was filled with the armature of command and control satellites. It was but a prelude to a grand strategic project designed to domesticate and fill up every dimension with the imperatives of "power projection," and to do so in the name of security. And this, too, would become the logic of Star Wars, a logic whose dynamic has been passed down through the combined powers of American exceptionalism and American military strategy.

The presentation of armies as the singular face of state power does not begin to approach the scope of the ensuing strategic project. Nor, for that matter, can one readily identify some global blueprint, as if the magnitude and intensity of the ensuing postwar arrangement could have been systematically planned and detailed. What is clear is that despite all accounts of a "nuclear revolution" in contemporary strategic affairs, a dynamic of strategic expansion and intensification came to dominate the nuclear era. Its animating spirit was an optimism and enthusiasm about the export of American power and culture through means of scientifically managed military might. That this project was largely overseen by civilian rather than military strategists was one of the great ironies of the whole postwar era. If classical realism twinned statesman and general, modernist strategy fused the armchair rationalist with the liberal universalist. As one insider critic later noted, "In the wake of the First World War, war was seen as too important to leave to generals, and it was taken over by the politicians. They, having done little better in the Second World War, left the field to the academics."[10]

Theirs was to prove a distinctive battle, one in which the "use" of the absolute weapon took place at a far more subtle level than could ever be envisioned through scenarios of nuclear war-fighting and war-winning. Indeed, the whole concept of "use" of nuclear weapons needs to be refashioned, since so much of the recent literature pertaining to how the West won the Cold War revolves around the notion that it was done short of actually using nuclear weapons in battle. This should not overlook, though, the hypnotizing effect on world audiences of the US twice detonating nuclear weapons within the space of three days in August 1945. There is a certain, though immeasurable, quality of credibility derived from invoking threats that have already been carried out, however different those contexts were and however unilateral the advantage was to the US when it twice devastated Japanese cities without it having to worry about retaliation. Precisely because in subsequent decades the Soviet Union would acquire a sufficient arsenal to temper the most aggressive US plans for preemption or nuclear war-fighting, the West, under American guidance, required lower threshold, more invasive "uses" of nuclear strategy and strategic modernization to reassure itself and its adversary. William Borden, the first of the visionary nuclear war-fighters, had anticipated this structural, rather than instrumental, dimension of global nuclearized conflict when he argued in 1946 that "[t]he struggle for power will go on as before, but instead of focusing on chunks of territory vital to yesterday's strategy, the important competition will take place between laboratories."[11]

True, but this does not go far enough. Strategic competition during the Cold War involved decades of imaginary warfare, worst-case scenarios, and weapons development policies based largely on anticipatory reactions. Much of the substance of nuclear strategy involved a complex system of signalling, diplomatic maneuvering, perception management, and credibility reinforcement, designed, often enough, to persuade domestic audiences as well as foreign ones.[12] But it would be wrong to think of the ensuing symbolic "pas de deux" as an innocent semiotic exchange. The mutuality of the nuclear dialogue, its interactive dimension between the blocs as well as its constitutive action within the respective blocs, gave postwar strategy a character that had never been achieved – or achievable – through conventional, prewar military arrangements. Nuclear strategy was never simply part of a national security policy that anticipated imminent foreign aggression. Had that been the case, far simpler arrangements could have sufficed than were ultimately built in the name of deterrence. Nuclear strategy was also part of an ongoing social process of Alliance construction, definition, articulation and delimitation. It was part of a broad postwar strategy of securing the spheres of social reproduction required for maintaining the American – and Western – way of life. In ways that were never accessible to the Warsaw Pact, the Western alliance drew upon nuclear strategy to articulate a common political and cultural agenda. Thus the postwar era was marked by the political uses of nuclear weaponry as the leading edge of more pervasive strategies involving access to far-flung overseas military bases, the loyalties of the peoples in newly developing countries, the very processes of state-building and political modernization, and the values that were to guide Western liberal democracies. There is an underlying relationship between nuclear weapons and modernity, one that has been bypassed in much of the strategic literature that confines itself to instrumental issues of war-fighting, deterrence, arms control and crisis management.

A text on the world

In the immediate postwar era, deterrence was developed and institutionalized in the form of Strategic/Security Studies. The initial effort was profoundly Americo-centric.[13] Within a decade the logic of deterrence came to be accepted in Western Europe as a convenient means for linking the fate of the developed industrial powers under US sponsorship.

Strategic think tanks first developed in the United States immediately after World War II in order to coordinate the newfound power of nuclear bombs. The emergence of the think tank as a state-sponsored means of planning strategic doctrine and weapons acquisitions was the focal point in the larger development and proliferation of Strategic Studies as a recognized mode of inquiry into relations among states. It is not accidental that the development of Strategic Studies as a unique and legitimate subfield within the discipline of International Relations is coterminous with the nuclear age: with, that is, the development of global peacetime military alliances tied together by the sinews of extended nuclear deterrence. The prime sponsor of this effort was the United States Air Force, which maintained, until the mid-1950s, a monopoly of the means to deliver the weapon. A crucial discursive shift, from "defense" to "security," enabled a whole profession to emerge as a subdiscipline of International Relations and to rationalize the possession of weapons – not to win a war, as with past armed forces, but to prevent a war from ever (again) arising. The creation of Strategic Studies as a separate paradigmatic enterprise was consolidated by the development of specialized research institutes such as RAND, the MIT Lincoln Laboratory, the MITRE Corporation, the Airpower Research Institute, the Washington-based Institute for Defense Analyses, and Georgetown University's Center for Strategic and International Studies.

Nothing better exemplifies the quality of think-tank discourse than the shift from the "operations research" to "systems analysis."[14] Operations research, much used during World War II, had concentrated upon optimizing the utility of extant military equipment for an independently established operational strategy. Systems analysis, by contrast, was increasingly relied upon beginning in the 1950s. It transformed the instrumental question of fitting means to ends by asking what kinds of means could be devised in order to realize an indeterminant range of hypothetical missions – ends which analysts themselves were free to speculate upon as necessary to ensure national security into the future of global relations. The logic of this new inquiry seemed warranted in the postwar epoch of open-ended technological arms racing, for narrow advantages in weapons systems performance characteristics might be readily converted into exploitable advantages on the margin of vulnerability. When combined, as became inevitable in

113

the Cold War atmosphere of anti-Communism, with heightened anticipations of imminent technological breakthroughs, systems analysis became the intellectual framework for "discovering" a litany of vulnerabilities and recurrent crises. Analyses such as Albert Wohlstetter's important "vulnerability" studies of the 1950s simply dropped the question of political intent from the question of possible technical capabilities.[15] What was publicly debated in terms of impending "bomber gaps," "missile gaps" and "windows of vulnerability" was but the product of systems-analytical projections, extrapolations of highly contestable evidence, which became political capital for armed services seeking to expand their budgetary share and for up-and-coming politicians in search of new and usable issues. When American observers in Moscow during the Aviation Day festivities of July 13, 1955, noticed three squadrons of long-range Bison aircraft flying over, their reports fed into concerns back in Washington, DC of a serious "bomber gap" that threatened US security. The witnesses who observed first ten aircraft, then nine, then nine more flying overhead failed to note, as was later found out, that the same airplanes were merely returning over the field for purposes of impressing the audience.[16] This "Potemkin aircraft" scene worked all too well.

The resulting kind of thinking can be characterized as from the subjunctive to the indicative. Hypothetical scenarios, initially posited as little more than on the margin of possibility, are subtly transformed in their ontological status to an undeniable certainty, endowed with affirmative existence as actually existing conditions of strategic reality. This discursive shift, from "what if?" to "now that," constitutes a powerful rhetorical strategy that legitimated seemingly realistic readings of postwar Soviet behavior.

Consider one of the foundational texts of postwar containment strategy, "NSC 68: United States Objectives and Programs for National Security, April 14, 1950." The whole document is organized around the fundamental incompatibility of US and Soviet interests. The difference between the two powers is captured in the two brief opening sections, "II. FUNDAMENTAL PURPOSE OF THE UNITED STATES" and "III. FUNDAMENTAL DESIGN OF THE KREMLIN."[17] Not surprisingly, it counterpoises the difference as one of high moral purpose on the one hand and of cynical, absolute control throughout the Soviet-dominated world on the other. The difference in basic intent is further captured by the juxtaposition of the two sources of strategy, namely a country, the United States, versus a fortress-like center of Byzantine intrigue and malevolence on the other, called the Kremlin. The attribution of difference here is not simply one of contrary strategic goals, but is

114

embedded into the very character of the political body which lies at their source. The one is a politically self-conscious country, one animated by "the marvelous diversity, the deep tolerance, the lawfulness of the free society." Meanwhile, the other, at the metaphoric center of the entire Communist world, is but a devious cabal characterized by an unrelenting search for world domination under a single "slave state."[18] The anarchic quality of the international system posed a difficult enough problem for postwar strategists. But the realist's traditional concern for the international state of nature was now compounded because one world power threatened to resolve that anarchy on terms compatible with its own sinister designs. Relying upon the dichotomy between the free and the enslaved, the document is able to point to a foundational disparity in domestic political resource mobilization that seriously handicaps the attempts of the United States to protect freedom worldwide. "The free society is limited in its choice of means to achieve its ends." Meanwhile "[t]he Kremlin is able to select whatever means are expedient in seeking to carry out its fundamental design."[19]

Crucial for NSC-68's argument about Soviet postwar policy is that the account of military production and deployment capabilities is preceded by a lengthy analytical prologue whose literary strategy is, in effect, to depict Soviet intentions in the most sinister light imaginable. This accounts for the constant bifurcation whereby US purposes are pitted against Soviet designs. The comparison, in drawing out the strengths of an open political system, also highlights a fundamental weakness of democracies that puts "us" – as if were analytically clear who "we" all are – at a fundamental disadvantage to the USSR's command economy, namely that it is more difficult for the US to mobilize its resources. The message, then, of NSC-68, is that a "democracy can compensate for its natural vulnerabilities only if it maintains clearly superior overall power in its most inclusive sense."[20]

Crucial here is the extent to which claims about Soviet intentions take precedence in the analysis. Analysts such as George Kennan who took fault with NSC-68 because the document apparently focused on capabilities rather than intentions are nearly 180 degrees off the mark.[21] NSC-68 recurrently privileged intention over actually operational capabilities. Whatever fleeting claims it makes about current and projected arsenals are all framed within a discourse of the Soviet totalitarian state and its implacable worldwide ambitions.

No consideration was given, for instance, to the fact that with a land mass more than double that of the United States, the Soviet Union might have needs for homeland defense that differed from America's.

Instead, in an argument presuming that the Soviet Union should necessarily share America's view of Western strategic purpose, the claim is made that "[t]he Soviet Union is developing the military capacity to support its design for world domination. The Soviet Union actually possesses armed forces far in excess of those necessary to defend its national territory."[22] When it comes to development of its nuclear arsenal, NSC-68 cites CIA estimates anticipating a Soviet stockpile of ten to twenty bombs by mid-1950 and some 200 warheads by mid-1954. The USSR is also claimed to have "aircraft able to deliver the atomic bomb," though to where, and how far from Soviet bases, is a matter left entirely open to the reader's imagination.[23]

Then follows the crucial turn in the argument, from the subjunctive to the indicative. For here, NSC-68, having ranged over various estimates, and having repeatedly qualified them with acknowledgements that "[w]e do not know accurately ...",[24] makes a crucial shift – an argument that, in various forms will be repeated throughout the Cold War era. Having just run through a string of qualifiers, about what the estimates are, and about the range of probable outcomes regarding capacity, and having indicated as well the very questionable accuracy of Soviet bombers, let alone the question of range, which is left open altogether, NSC-68 then argues about what would happen if, as anticipated, the USSR did indeed acquire 200 weapons by mid-1954.

> At the time the Soviet Union has a substantial atomic stockpile and if it is assumed that it will strike a strong surprise blow and if it is assumed further that its atomic attacks will be met with no more effective defense opposition than the United States and its allies have programmed, results of those attacks could include:
> a. Laying waste to the British Isles and thus depriving the Western Powers of their use as a base;
> b. Destruction of the vital centers and of the communications of Western Europe, thus precluding effective defense by the Western Powers; and
> c. Delivering devastating attacks on certain vital centers of the United States and Canada.[25]

"If," "if" and "if" are thus suddenly transformed to become the basis of an annihilatory scenario. There is, however, no self-evident empirical basis for such extrapolations becoming the basis for a worldwide armaments policy. All strategic intelligence assessments, even those concerning military capabilities, require interpretations that are not beyond critical challenge by those who may read the evidence differently. Nothing speaks for itself, not even a missile silo. Yet the entire postwar era was characterized by estimates that continually – and

116

necessarily – invoked empirical data in an attempt to downplay the interpretive resources brought to bear in analyzing the meaning of putative threats. The brilliance of NSC-68 is not that it persuasively invokes such data, however, but that it provides the codes of attribution and intentionality which were to guide postwar strategy. For what enabled such readings of world politics to carry the day was a series of discourses about the nature of the Soviet totalitarian state and about its implacable global designs.[26] Not surprisingly, then, is NSC-68 lacking any analysis of actual Soviet capabilities. Yet in doing so, it must openly invoke – or perhaps, better said, establish – the interpretive grounds upon which postwar strategy will rely. But to do this would be to acknowledge an explicitly political dimension of strategy that cannot be accommodated within the conventional narrative of Strategic Studies. The code for such an interpretation, however, comprises the opening sections of the document. Why else devote the introductory section of a top secret national security memorandum to elaborating the differences in identity, values and worldview distinguishing the two major world powers? This sort of strategic Cold War realism, in other words, is animated by particular representations of self and other, without which the narrative could not be sustained.

Once the difference is established, it is a small but decisive move to establish the other country as the source of all that lurks ominously in the world. The inherent dilemma of anarchy in International Relations is thus displaced onto one of the constituent countries whose behavior – and military capabilities – can thereby be construed in terms of imminent danger. This is not to say that the Soviet Union was wholly innocent, or that its discursive representation is a false reading of its true character. Rather, this construction of an interpretive scheme enables certain accounts of Soviet behavior to take precedence over others, and thereby disables competing accounts which might be more critical of US policy, or more willing to see the space for diplomacy, negotiations, and political mediation of exiting differences.

Once the idea of a threat is established, it is only necessary to invoke the mere existence of military capability so that the conclusion then becomes incontrovertible. Subsequent invocations of "the bomber gap," "the missile gap," "the INF-gap," and the "window of vulnerability" all derive their value as significations of danger by drawing upon these claims, sometimes openly explicated, but more often allowed merely to reside in a tacit subtext concerning the alien-ness and other-ness of Soviet political culture.[27]

But the resources brought to bear in postwar strategic analysis nonetheless had to be disseminated and accepted among (potential)

117

allies if the nature of American postwar power projection was to be legitimately constructed. And, indeed, the academic subdiscipline of Strategic Studies become a decisive force in trans-Atlantic politics around the mid- to late-1950s. Crucial to the emergence of a unifying approach to strategy was the export of the field from the United States to Western Europe. Here it is impossible to overstate the importance of the London-based Institute for Strategic Studies, founded in 1958 and renamed in 1963 as the International Institute for Strategic Studies. The importance of the disciplining of the practice of strategic analysis as an instrument of postwar strategy is signified by the prepositional injunction that the institute was founded not only as a site in which the serious and scholarly analysis of strategic relations could take place, but also "for" the purpose of advancing this particular method of intellectual analysis. The IISS became a site for the articulation of a Western strategic consensus – not necessarily in terms of full and complete agreement, but in terms of the language and policy problems that came widely to be shared among responsible managers of Alliance affairs.[28]

The nuclear alliance

Throughout the first half of the 1950s there had been anything but agreement on trans-Atlantic defense strategy. The 1952 Lisbon Accords calling for NATO troop strength of 90 divisions immediately proved unworkable because of the economic and demographic toll that would have been entailed. Economic reconstruction and the need to draw upon a working-age labor force dictated that none of the West European powers would accede to such demands on its populace. When President Eisenhower's fiscal conservatism suggested nuclear guarantees of Massive Retaliation for Europe, John Foster Dulles immediately came under criticism for having articulated an inflexible non-strategy that lacked credibility in the face of conventional Soviet probes westward.[29] Such criticisms were heightened a short time later when the Soviets developed a thermonuclear capacity that could be delivered upon Western Europe (though not yet upon the US).

The difficulty of constructing allies was perhaps no more evident than with France's ambiguously independent place in world affairs.[30] Throughout the complex negotiations over the status of Berlin and Germany, France had made clear its reluctance to accept anything but division for its longstanding historic rival. "We like them so much we want to see two of them," De Gaulle is alleged to have said about his easternmost neighbors. Cold War accounts focusing exclusively upon

118

the Soviet Union's bargaining position *vis-à-vis* the United States overlook the importance of France's strategy to contain not only Soviet power but potential German power as well.[31] Nothing would have been more disastrous for a revived postwar French national economy than a repetition of the rivalry that had previously wracked its relations with Germany, especially over the Saarland and Rhineland. A peculiarly French quasi-imperial role was also evident in Paris' reluctance to liquidate its worldwide colonial holdings. Protracted postcolonial wars, first in Indochina, then in Algeria, were the immediate result of France's stubbornly traditional aspirations throughout the nuclear era. From 1960 on, France retained remarkable independence as a renegade power, free from various test ban treaties and arms control policies. It has enjoyed complete freedom when it came to patrolling Francophone Northwest Africa and New Caledonia, and freely utilized its holdings in French Polynesia for purposes of nuclear testing despite significant regional opposition.

Possession of an independent nuclear force enabled France to persist in its imperial pretense. Gaullism benefited greatly from the symbolic independence afforded by the strategy of "deterrence in all directions:" targeted westward, in other words, at the unreliable Americans, as well as eastward, at the Soviet Union. The peculiarity of French nuclear independence has been that the most likely target for the *force de frappe* was neither of the superpowers, but West Germany, whose easternmost border was as late as the mid-1980s the farthest that French land-based weapons could reach from their base on the Albion Plain. Beginning in the mid-1960s, France selectively extended its "sanctuary" to include southern Germany as well. But France's basic policy of enjoying an independent global strategy was accompanied by a nuclear force that, even with submarine-based missiles, had never been more than a threat of minimal retaliatory deterrence. Such a minimal strategy has been France's way of signalling its distrust of complex formulae for extended deterrence, flexible response, and ladders of escalation.

France's suspicions of Alliance strategy were well-founded. Leon Sigal concisely captured the infeasible operational nature of NATO's nuclear options when he wrote that "[t]he dilemmas of nuclear location, relocation, and dual capability suggest that if, as the saying goes, armies are designed by geniuses to be run by idiots, the reverse is true for short-range nuclear forces in Europe."[32]

Sigal's claim holds true for the history of NATO strategy. Small wonder the Alliance found itself recurrently enmeshed in crises of policy coordination.[33] No NATO strategy calling for use of any level of

119

nuclear forces ever showed any operational promise. The much-heralded formula of flexible response as enshrined in NATO planning document MC14/3 and the Harmel Report of 1967 was nothing more than a successful papering over of the divergent geostrategic interests of each of the NATO members. Flexible response was an agreement to disagree.[34] It was a political compromise, largely initiated by Europeans trying to bind reluctant Americans to come to their nuclear defense. The paradox of such a strategy is that it held out the promise of Continental, indeed global, destruction to fend off the possibility of a local attack. The essentially ambiguous quality of NATO doctrine was affirmed in a widely circulated manifesto, *Discriminate Deterrence*, published in 1988 by leading celebrants of America's containment strategy in Europe.

> However, a fateful ambiguity enshrouds this declaration. Sometimes, it has seemed as though NATO plans to use battlefield or even theater-wide nuclear weapons for their direct effect in repelling the Soviet invasion. At other times, NATO officials posit a different strategy – that what NATO really intends in threatening to use nuclear weapons is to point up the perils of escalation and, in effect, concentrate the minds of Soviet leaders on the apocalypse at the end of that road.[35]

This then raises thorny issues. For decades, the US rightly feared being brought into the fray too early and argued for a more robust conventional deterrent. The European allies were unwilling to expend funds for full conventionalization, but were also anxious that American nuclear guarantees might be confined to a Continental war while preserving the major powers as sanctuaries. These differing interpretations and interests characterized Alliance politics as a set of intractable dilemmas throughout the Cold War period. It would be mistaken to see these political disputes as merely military–technical in nature, as if the debate were solely about getting the right operational strategy. Nor, for that matter could such debates be counted as evidence that NATO was ever weak and on the verge of breaking up. Since its advent in 1949, the North Atlantic Alliance has derived its strength less from the plausibility of its externally directed deterrence posture than from the shared – and constructed – cultural nexus of distinctly modern forms of political identity which it has championed.[36] Indeed, public opinion polls have documented an historical suspicion toward any weapons-technical strategy and a manifest rejection of every particular force structure as unworkable and unacceptable. But such a suspicion toward rearmament should not be mistaken for a repudiation of what those strategies were primarily about. In this,

120

the guardians of Western strategy were always ahead of their critics from the peace movements. As polls throughout the 1970s and 1980s repeatedly showed, public opinion, while rejecting particular deployments, overwhelmingly endorsed the political purposes of the Alliance and supported NATO as a necessary means for the preservation of certain Western values.[37] This suggests an interesting problem. It seems that NATO has been more widely appreciated as a political practice than as a military one.

As it faces a very uncertain future, and as it examines its own past as well, NATO persistence can be explained not merely in terms of military security, but also through the consolidation of domestic consensus over dissident parties, labor movements, peace groups, and all those marginal or liminal groups whose aspirations could not find expression in the postwar order. The genius of NATO as a security alliance was the way in which its particularly modern accounts of development and security were enframed within a widely legitimate strategic discourse of deterrence. By effectively wedding itself to the defense of a distinctly modern, Western, Atlantocentric cultural project, strategic discourse enabled strategists to deflect criticism of the Alliance's extraordinary internal contradictions as a mechanism for deterrence and Western miliary defense. The only plausible account of deterrence was that it worked to fend off a major international war. Until proven wrong by the outbreak of such a war, NATO's strategy was thus the only feasible means of securing that precarious historical construct called "the Western way of life." The irony is that in order to strengthen the hand of deterrence, strategists had to acknowledge the apparent irrationality and absurdity of a security system which cultivated peace through structural intimidation and the threat of mutual annihilation.

NATO's problem is thus no different than the dilemma of American strategy. Millennial liberalism established a dynamic of strategic invasiveness and extensiveness whose ultimate logic was the ability to threaten destruction upon all that it had created. In an era in which the ostensible object of that strategy has now simply disappeared, the creative destruction inherent in deterrence strategy can be finally exposed for its fury. The end of the Cold War thus creates an important moment, both politically and analytically. In terms of security policy, it should now be possible to develop new, alternative arrangements and understandings concerning the role of the military in everyday life. To the extent this can be managed, it sustains the traditional realist reading of externally existing security threats. But if it turns out that despite the dissolution of the blocs, strategic practices remain largely intact, then this suggests another character to the nature of international life. It may turn out that the interpretive and discursive resources that animated the Cold War are more persistent and less amenable to restructuring than celebrants of a new world order might claim.

6 THE WEST OF ALL POSSIBLE WORLDS?

it is inappropriate to describe what is happening in terms of traditional Western categories. (Barbara Einhorn[1])

The internal disintegration of the Communist world and the ensuing fragmentation of the Soviet Union into constituent republics come as confirmation to some that they, or "we," have triumphed. These developments, which a decade ago one could only have fantasized about, and which no one would have thought could happen so precipitously, have lent new-found credence to the view proclaiming "the West of all possible worlds." This is the argument of those seeking to sustain, or revive, the Enlightenment project of a universalistic triumph of growth, progress, and modernization. Fukuyama's paean about the end of history is perhaps the clearest expression of a sentiment that has taken pride in its having defeated the Communist world and reduced it to ideological and geopolitical rubble. It is reflected, as well, in the internationalist aspirations of those who would destroy all foreign vestiges of protectionism and establish transnational regimes of free trade in their stead. Elements of it are at play, though perhaps with a touch of duplicity, when invoking the seeming inexorable march of democracy throughout the world. Indeed, so deeply embedded is the assumption as a commonplace of contemporary discourse about world politics that it can now be easily slipped in and evoked without being explicitly argued for or defended, as when Robin Wright and Doyle McManus write how in the post-Cold War era, the

> empowerment of the individual, as originally promised by the Enlightenment, was finally making its way down to the common man – and women – in the poorest and least developed parts of the world. The world's last serfs, at least in principle were being liberated; the last empires on the verge of formal collapse.
> ... the progress of the Scientific Era has given mankind

123

unprecedented knowledge and control of everything from space exploration and genetic engineering to the artificial intelligence of computers. Mankind no longer needed to depend on myths for sustenance or answers.[2]

The authors immediately qualify this claim and argue that in fact the promise of 1989 proved shortlived. "For a few glorious months we, like everyone else, hoped that the world was on fast track to peace and harmony, that a single universal form of democracy and free enterprise was being embraced on every continent".[3] While the substance of the ensuing text is of a promise betrayed by ethnic conflict, economic stagnation, environmental overload and refugee flows, the text draws all of its critical inspiration from a residual invocation of Reason and Enlightenment.

For the most sanguine analysts, the end of the Cold War is an occasion for congratulatory politics. The view, however, is not newly arrived, but essentially is driven by the same force that impelled much of the Western strategic tradition. Contemporary Strategic Studies, after all, is based upon the celebration of a distinct historical and cultural achievement: the West.[4] By "the West" I refer not (simply) to a spatially bounded North Atlantic realm, but to a cultural formation which primarily defines itself in terms of the values and practices of a secularized, growth-oriented, industrial order. Its intellectual heritage is presumed to derive from the classical world. Having dusted itself off from the Dark Ages, it emerged in the Renaissance as the foundation of recognizably "modern" state structures. Later it was absorbed within the scientific vision of the Enlightenment, enjoyed growing intellectual respect during the era of British hegemony, and held unchallenged worldwide prominence in the postwar days of American dominance.

The "celebratory" enterprise

Strategic Studies is part of the West's legacy. Since the advent of the Peace of Westphalia, strategic considerations, codified in the eighteenth-century balance of power, have been crucial in the maintenance and legitimacy of the modern states system. Though much of the classical balance of power politics thinking was altered in the course of the nuclear era, policy makers from Kennan and Nitze on acknowledged the centrality of strategic vision in steering America's place in the postwar order. While there was significant debate, for instance, concerning whether the US should have undertaken its new-found position along limited, particularistic lines or on an unlimited, universalistic basis, each of the claimants to a policy position could draw upon the strategic legacy in articulating a worldview.[5] As an essential component in the proposed world order, Strategic Studies functioned as a "celebratory" enterprise. Western values, institutions and political economies were valorized through the demand for an amenable postwar order, and it was the task of rational, technically trained arms controllers, strategists, and civilian experts fluent in the realm of the coercive arts of deterrence to serve as the guarantors of that world order.[6]

Small wonder that a similarly heady vision appears in the many essays published in various journals and learned pages explaining what to do now that "our" greatest foe has been vanquished.[7] It would, however, be a serious mistake to assume from the apparent triumph of "containment" policies that prevailing strategic practices can be much of a useful guide as we enter the post-Cold War world of the twenty-first century. For Strategic Studies represents a reification of the politics of Western culture, enshrined in a geopolitical, statist representation of the sovereign spaces within which that culture may legitimately pursue its projects. Its central presumption, that the sovereign state provides the legitimate political framework for nego-tiating the risks and uncertainties of international anarchy, makes less sense than it ever did.

It is helpful to recall that Continentally minded (and in some cases, Continentally trained) realists such as George Kennan, Hans Morgen-thau, Stanley Hoffman, Hedley Bull and Michael Howard were never quite comfortable with the atmosphere of strategic discourse as it unfolded in the US in the postwar era. Their traditional orientation, touted in balance of power politics, statesmanship, diplomacy and the give and take of politics among leaders of state, increasingly appeared marginal to the new-found nature of Cold War politics as a great contest among competing social structures. Kennan himself represents an endlessly fascinating case of someone who fell into circumstances that were far beyond his own comprehension on precisely this point. At one level a romantic and at another a classicist, he found himself thrust into the vortex of a country's foreign policy planning as it undertook to sponsor a quasi-imperial global strategy.[8] Try as he did to resist the transformation of *Realpolitik* into a discourse of competing bipolar social systems, Kennan's own work became readily susceptible to a re-reading that justified exactly the millennial "universalism" he argued so eloquently against. His own early analyses, in the "Long Telegram" and the subsequent "X" article, were always subject to precisely this reinterpretation – despite it betraying Kennan's express

125

intent – because Kennan's own studies had constituted the USSR as an unacceptable outsider, incapable of participating within the civil discourse of international society. It is difficult, after all, to construct a key actor as incapable of living by the normal rules of diplomacy and then to rue the day when policy advocates conclude that uncommon strategic means – beyond the bounds of conventional diplomacy and verging on full peacetime militarization – are thus appropriate in the face of such a presence.

"Containment" became a representative trope for the purpose of Western strategy. It is couched within a metaphysic that resembles plate-tectonics, by which the world is construed in terms of objects bumping into each other in the night, each of them "impacting" (to use a clumsy and therefore perfectly appropriate neologism) one another. In such a world, devoid of constitutive interpretations, communication and learning, adaptive behavior is non-existent, and the relevant variables are reducible to those collisions at the frontier of each self-contained, geopolitical entity. "It's a tough world out there," we are assured, and the spatial signification itself is a way of deferring uncertainty and the unknown into a realm beyond one's sovereign domain. Containment therefore means to impose external boundaries, to confine artificially, and by force where needed, so that the logic of conflict built in to the system is put on permanent hold – and must continually be held in place lest it break in, overtly or by stealth, and undermine security.

Throughout the Cold War, the basic difference between classical realism and hard-core Cold Warriorism was that the realist saw conflict inherent in international anarchy, whereas the Cold Warrior saw the dynamic emanating from within the Soviet Union. The difference proved important for policy debates, yet both views shared enough of a vision of physicalist violence in which sovereign states literally collided.

Kennan's analysis inadvertently sanctioned a more aggressive, less compromising reading of the Soviet threat than he himself had anticipated. But Kennan found few soulmates in the Washington, DC of his era when it came to the classical realist's predilection for preserving the inherent ambiguity of world politics. By relying so heavily – one is tempted to say "exclusively" – on psychological dimensions of security and popular perceptions of Soviet strategy, Kennan made himself vulnerable to hawkish critiques that he was not doing enough to console Western anxieties. The charge especially resonated when the Soviet Union developed an atomic capacity, and when US defense spending dropped all pretense of constraints in the second half of

Truman's last term. It thus was not quite as great a step to resolve all of the open and contestable dimensions of Kennan's version of world politics with the hard-headed, unambiguous tectonic version of "containment" sketched out in NSC-68 by Paul Nitze. The result was a loss of detail and particularity and a transformation to the universalism of a zero-sum world. Forty years later, it is the hawks who appear vindicated. And if the Soviet Union's loss is our gain, then the collapse can only mean our having been declared the winner in the greatest global contest of all.

Obviously, there are other views of the Cold War. Some analysts, for instance, have viewed the Cold War not in realist terms of states and military alliances but primarily as a great contest among social systems.[9] Such a conception, rooted in a critical political economy of world politics, goes substantially beyond the geopolitical domain of classical realism, and provides a powerful account of structural militarization. It also sidesteps overly voluntaristic accounts of world politics, particularly those forms of revisionist diplomatic history which explained the Cold War in terms of key statesmen, influential domestic interest groups, and lost opportunities of diplomatic initiative. It is precisely such a more structurally oriented perspective that in recent years has provided much of the impetus for critiques of armaments and national strategy. From this vantage point, nuclear deterrence is shorn of its guise as a protector of order in world affairs and becomes, instead, an active agent in the production and reproduction of that order.

What is distinctive about "strategicalization" is the extent to which state behavior becomes encoded within world views and then becomes the basis of whole bureaucratic apparatuses – of security analysis, intelligence estimates, and international surveillance.[10] This strategy – a strategy of strategy, if you will – becomes more apparent as one considers the question of what counts as part of the modern West – in other words, who – or what – "we" in "the West" are. For numerous forms of political life are simply ruled out of the picture as inconsistent with cultural claims of a singular, modern, progressive industrial order – as not befitting the stature of the developed, industrial pro-Western world, or as constituting a challenge to its identity and values. Fractures of class, gender and race – of partisan politics and religious identity, or of deviant social practice and political identification, all demark potential sites of domestic contestation within the Western Alliance. Yet these are acknowledged only insofar as they represent threats and challenges to the unity and "identity" of the West.

127

NATO as an embodiment of modern geopolitical space has presupposed an unproblematic singular human identity which all members of the West either embody or aspire toward. This is, after all, what is worth dying for, or in the modern age of deterrence, worth voting monies for in order to "secure." The classical strategic tradition has long enshrined this singular Western space as beyond political contestation. Those who would disturb it tamper with "order" and Western "stability." In the face of implacable threats, either emanating from the Soviet Union or appearing in the form of nuclear arsenals, there appeared good reason to focus on the unity of national and Alliance identity and to submerge or repress internal tension. This, in effect, is the discursive strategy which underlay the whole practice of national security in the postwar era.

For decades now, Strategic Studies, especially as articulated and practised in the United States, has constituted a celebration of the global modernist project. Its instrumental–technical defense of the postwar order of states and global multilateral trade has presented a particular cultural construction as if it were a completed historical act. In this sense it served, to paraphrase Clausewitz, as a continuation of classical balance of power politics, with the addition of other, considerably more destructive means. An exponential expansion in the radius of destruction was accompanied by an equally ambitious expansion in the power projection capabilities of the dominant states. Indeed, the nuclear era, replete not merely with atomic and thermonuclear warheads but also, with vast arsenals of intercontinental ballistic missiles, extended and deepened the ability of the major states to oversee global politics. In this sense, it was less the combined economic, political and military power of the US and the USSR that enabled them to assume the mantle of superpower status than it was the peculiar articulation of that power in the form of their respective nuclear arsenals. The idea, so appealing to the West, that the USSR could somehow be equated with the United States in terms of its postwar power, makes no sense when calculated on a classical mercantile scale of wealth. Nor could there be any presumed equivalence of the two when the overall strength of allies and alliances was thrown into the mix. Indeed, the significant disparities in wealth and power between the two countries were simply amplified when the respective Western and Eastern alliances, NATO on the one hand and the Warsaw Pact on the other, were included in the overall balance of East–West power.

Nuclear weapons were the central desideratum when it came to gaining "superpower" status. The very language of international politics reflects this, for possession of these weapons instantaneously endows the country that harbors them with enormous powers of bargaining and influence out of all scale to its demographic, economic or political profile. It is one thing to equate Saddam Hussein with Hitler. However expedient for propaganda purposes such a claim is, the same analog cannot possibly hold up if the message is somehow that Iraq is equivalent to the Third Reich. Yet the presence, or imminent appearance, or merely the signification, of nuclear capability instantaneously elevates the country in question to a member of that most prestigious and threatening of organizations – the nuclear club. It also legitimizes punitive action, especially when it is taken pre-emptively to forestall development of nuclear capability.[11]

The distinctive role assumed by nuclear weapons in the postwar relationship assumed, of course, pre-eminence in the hands of the two major "superpowers." Yet it must be acknowledged that the term "superpower" was largely a label of convenience for those within the West seeking to designate some external Other as an opponent worthy of national mobilization. In this sense, the debate about nuclear strategy that so occupied the strategic community, particularly during the 1950s and 1980s, functioned as a reifying shorthand notation for a larger and far more complex cultural contestation about the character and identity of life within the respective blocs. The importance of nuclear weapons consisted in their ability to short-circuit complex networks of cultural achievement by rendering them, in the briefest moment, into little more than hot ashes and dust. The threat they supposedly represented was thus abstracted from social processes and from issues of interests, national strategy and purpose. In the face of their compelling presence, it seems superfluous, or what is more dangerous, liberal, to enquire into such political issues as "intent." The mere fact of their existence, and the possibility that they could be deployed at a moment's notice with overwhelming and irreversible consequences, constituted enough of an issue in its own right that it tended to exhaust the scope of debate and to absorb the space that would otherwise have been occupied by discussion of alternative political and social arrangements.

The mutual character of this phenomenon was noted only by a small number of critics, most of whom were writing under the influence of post-Marxist sociological theory. C. Wright Mills argued in the late-1950s, for instance, that the causes of World War III would lie in the measures undertaken to prepare for it.[12] A decade later, in an argument that virtually spawned West German critical peace research, Dieter Senghaas drew upon cybernetics and systems theory to claim that nuclear deterrence produced a form of national strategic "autism," whose only product was the "organization of peacelessness" on a global scale.[13] E.P. Thompson later developed an influential account of the nuclear arms race as a new form of social reproduction, which he termed "exterminism."[14] Both the US and the USSR, he claimed, had engaged in a mutually reinforcing structural logic along lines that burst the traditional analytical categories of the whole Marxist tradition. Rudolf Bahro pinpointed the implications of such a form of militarization for Soviet strategy in Eastern Europe when he argued, against NATO's 1979 double-decision, that continued Western armaments would simply feed into the aggressively defensive orientation of the Soviet military. The Russians are not coming, he concluded, though their missiles might.[15]

Gorbachev as a critical strategic theorist

All of that began to change after Gorbachev's accession to power in 1985. Whether consciously or not, Gorbachev functioned as a critical strategic theorist insofar as his actions destabilized – and decentered – long-heralded givens of international life.[16] Under his guidance, the Soviet Union was able thoroughly to politicize a strategic relationship with the United States that had ossified into a mutually reinforcing structure of armaments and counter-armaments. Intermittent bouts of arms control measures had previously been significant for giving formal recognition to the mutually, indeed ritually, interactive and dependent character of US–Soviet nuclear strategic relations. In a number of significant ways, however, Soviet strategy, in large measure initiated by Gorbachev, was able to pose several fundamental new challenges to longstanding assumptions. In so doing, as it turned out, Gorbachev also made it possible for the Soviet Union to begin to address its internal dilemmas in ways that had been obscured by the demands of the nuclear arms competition. The resulting end to the standoff with the United States made it possible, indeed necessary, for the Soviet Union to address publicly for the first time in its history the question of its own political character.[17]

First of all, of course, Soviet policy under Gorbachev called into question the very idea of a Soviet threat, or at least, of an implacable one which could only be countered by the reciprocal threat of overwhelming counterforce.[18] Second, moves toward "transarmament" and structurally defensive military orientations promised a weapons-technical response to the problem of Continental security. These initiatives, inspired in part by European debates about non-offensive defense, were, curiously enough, an instrumental formulation that met long-heralded security needs on the very terms presented and championed within strategic analysis.[19]

Simultaneous developments in the democratic reorganization of East European countries had a palpable effect on defense-related debates insofar as they undercut the mutual effects of bloc strategic politics. Because much of the strategic debate concerned relations between the major alliances, *inter alia* NATO–Warsaw Pact, it had became awkward to acknowledge the internal socio-political role of military alliances on the societies which they nominally secured. While the express strategic intention had been to deter war, one discernible effect was to deter democratic politics as well. Indeed, particularly within the Warsaw Pact, the overriding emphasis upon regional security considerations made it difficult for dissident and democratic forces to mobilize themselves as a legitimate opposition. In the face of overwhelming military firepower, and with the threat of Continental war visited upon the Warsaw Pact literally on a daily basis, claims for autonomy and for security from the USSR, much of it arising from independent social and political dissident groups from within Eastern Europe, could be met only with repression from the Kremlin.

Gorbachev broke that internal bond and in so doing, he reversed the relationship that had obtained for forty years between regional security and regional quiescence. Gradual liberalization within certain Warsaw Pact countries was indispensable to a broader loosening up of Soviet policy toward its Eastern security glacis. With the Brezhnev Doctrine dashed for good, civic activism proliferated.[20]

For its own part, a remodernization of NATO defense efforts hardly seemed compatible with either public opinion or the imperatives of increasingly budget-conscious defense officials. Within a relatively brief period of time, NATO debates about a variety of new, innovative high-tech strategies – the Rogers Plan, AirLand Battle, Follow-On Forces Attack, or even something as straightforward as modernization of Lance short-range systems – were cast aside as politically unmarketable. The INF Treaty of December 1987 not only made substantial arms control progress; it also legitimized a more widespread politicization of security practices long-thought vital and sacrosanct to the integrity of the Western Alliance. One need not succumb to blandishments like "the greening of defense budgets" to see that the whole logic of military blocs became, and is still becoming, increasingly susceptible to questioning from the standpoint of a variety of critical attitudes. The dual effect of domestic liberalization within Europe and the downscaling of military arsenals across the (formerly East–West) German–

German border presented strategists throughout the Continent new opportunities that were simply unimaginable a decade ago.

Thirdly, and most importantly, the unraveling of Cold War representations has raised for the first time the fundamental issue of Western identity. It is no longer clear who is to be legitimately incorporated within the space of modern Western culture. The imminent reconstitution of Central Europe as a functioning entity is but one version of a larger overturning of categories of political space and culture that had enjoyed privileged status throughout the Cold War era. The divide between East and West was a divide between "us" and "them. For Europeans this was a more violent and arbitrary interpretation of world politics than for North Americans. Today, thanks in part to processes undertaken through the Conference on Security and Cooperation in Europe and affirmed in the Charter of Paris for a New Europe, the bifurcation works less well than it ever did. Whether these efforts can be extended onto the global plan is an issue which remains very much up in the air. Surely, the United Nations, with all its limitations and susceptibility to misuse by major powers, offers some prospects for multilateral cooperation that transcend the Alliance politics of the Cold War era – and of the immediate post-Cold War era as well.

The contours of Western identity and values are no longer clearly drawn. In both East and West, there are modernist orientations toward humankind and nature which are striving toward economic modernization through an expanded European community. Yet these cultures also claim a considerable share of orthodox, even fundamentalist, religiosity, including forms of nationalist essentialism that had been mistakenly thought more appropriate to the last century than to the next.[21] Nowhere is this more visible than in what used to be Yugoslavia – a country whose reprised Balkanization raises terrifying prospects for a new world order, and sustains for some a nostalgic return to earlier, simpler Cold War days.

It would therefore be wrong to assume that a new politics of European security can be exaustively defined in terms of universal strivings toward democratic national self-determination. The political movements that now shape Alliance politics and European security relations are not readily assimilable within the conventional analytical categories of postwar Strategic Studies. Perhaps the most enduring legacy of the peace movement was its ability to develop critiques of technology and technological discourse.[22] This effectively opened up a space within the logic of modernization that enabled social movements at odds with Atlanticist culture and political economy to secure a legitimate, if still decidedly subordinate, place among the ranks of oppositional politics, especially alongside feminist and environmental groups concerned to develop a politics of security that goes beyond strategic–military conventions.

These rearticulations occur simultaneously with what can be referred to as the respatialization of the Third World: the restructuring of despair and powerlessness, and an accompanying consciousness about it, so that poverty, hopelessness, starvation, unequal development and environmental exhaustion are not conditions confined to underdeveloped countries; they are endemic to modern, advanced industrial cities as well. The divide between First and Third World, itself a spatial representation of geopolitical space as homogeneous, is effectively breaking down. Sweeping global generalizations, whether about "us" and "them" or about "core," "semi-periphery," and "periphery," are increasingly drained of their plausibility. Who "we" are – what "we" are – is not as clear cut as claimed by analysts wedded to traditions of realism and empiricism, or for that matter, to traditions of materialism, have needed to believe.[23]

Questions raised about the identities of those whose "security" was supposedly ensured by weapons-technical strategies of deterrence are more relevant today than ever to a whole range of political developments that extend far beyond traditional frameworks of security. Simply put, the world created under NATO's guidance is no longer subject to containment. Its boundaries have now been eroded at the eastern-most margin. The result has been an unprecedented opening up of social and cultural politics. But this process is not confined to the member states of the (former) Warsaw Pact. It has been going on all along in the West – despite NATO's efforts to formalize a unitary identity as part of its strategic project. As for those who live beyond the pale of the Atlantic community and its newly incorporated neighbors, the end of the Cold War does not substantively change their security, though it does enable attention to shift to relations which were simply absorbed and neglected within the dominant strategic framework.

What it might really mean to end the Cold War

There has to be a cautionary note affixed to the basic historicist observation that because the world has changed our thinking must change along with it in order to adhere more closely to the "new realities" of the post-Cold War era. Of course, to a certain extent, there is some truth here, namely that the collapse of certain structures whose existence had long been thought immutable makes it possible for us to see things that were not possible to see earlier. But this can come uncomfortably close to the claim of "interdependence" theorists a generation ago (already!), that with the collapse of the Bretton Woods system and the growing power of the OPEC cartel, the traditional realist view of the world – while historically accurate in its own day – had suddenly to give way to modernist theories of International Relations that recognized the "growing" importance of transnational relations and the relative displacement of the state for regimes as basic units of world politics.

To make the claim for a particular theoretical framework on the basis of these new facts that have appeared for observation/measurement would be to rely upon an outmoded and indefensible methodological empiricism as the desideratum for testing theory. It would mean that on some observable scale, theoretical frameworks have the function of conforming themselves to an independent, empirically ascertainable external reality, whose flow and contour exist outside of the frameworks we bring to bear.

There is, of course, a strong empiricist urge to acquiesce in such thinking regarding the ways in which we analyze world politics today. But part of the theoretical perspective underpinning this study is that such a temptation, however seductive and historically opportune, must nonetheless be resisted. If new thinking is needed, it is not in some simple one-to-one correspondence, because the world has changed and therefore some have been proven right and others have been proven wrong. Rather, the relationship between thought and reality is far more complex – and this holds for strategic relations as well as for International Relations theory. Changes in the world do not so much prove one side suddenly right or wrong, but rather afford us opportunities to see more – or less – of what seemed to make sense, and to render plausible perspectives which might otherwise have remained marginal to the dominant interpretive frameworks.

Realism, for instance, had its moment with the great powers; neo-realism its greatest plausibility as a discourse of liberal hegemony. Likewise, postmodernity speaks to a fragmentation of political power and to the deterritorialization of social space, away from sovereign state-centered geopolitics and toward multiple dimensions of identity in time and space. Thus the clash of perspectives *about* world politics is given palpable reality through a confrontation of competing claims by participants *within* world politics.

In considering these questions, one cannot help but to keep in mind the particularly dramatic, indeed, world-historical, dimensions of these concerns recently. We face today an exhilarating variety of sea changes, having to do with the epochal collapse of communism, the apparent "triumph" of modern Western life forms, and at the same time a diminution in the organizing power of major states to patrol and discipline world affairs. Thus the disintegration and unrest within the many republics formerly comprising the Soviet bloc give rise both to democratic experimentation in Eastern Europe and to a fissiparous politics of ethnic, nationalist and religious differentiation in regions where democratic institutions are very much struggling to achieve institutional expression.

In 1989 the talk was optimistically about "the end of history." Yet it was not long before strategic analysts began longing for the simplicities and sharp edges demarcating political and ideological identities that had characterized Cold War politics. No sooner did we consider allocating the benefits of a "peace dividend" than war erupted, yet again, along the Persian Gulf, reminding us – as if some forgot – about a whole spate of questions concerning nuclear proliferation, regional arms races, the agony of military regimes, and the specter of renewed ideological conflict.

Nor can celebrations about having defeated the USSR or outlaw aggressors in the Middle East mask deep seated problems at home. Those raising the banner of a renewed and mature *Pax Americana* must simply turn their backs on the country's heightened state of internal disarray as it finds itself unable to house, educate and employ vast sectors of its own populace and deeply embedded in fiscal crises that extend to every state and local government.[24]

Meanwhile, the great promise of economic development, heralded thirty years ago as the dawn of a new age for vast stretches of the world's peoples, remains largely chimerical for most countries, and for most peoples within those newly industrializing countries where the Rostovian engine of relentless modernization had only begun to pick up steam. It turns out that there were only seats for the first-class passengers, and most of the ticket-holders (economy fare) were left stranded at the station.

The United States celebrated its successful prosecution of a coalition war as evidence of a new-found resurgence.[25] Yet it is sobering to recall that such a military victory, rather than affirming the return to operational greatness of American power, instead displays the monumental difficulties of doing so – requiring for instance, that some $60 billion be begged from allies. As the *Economist* observed in the immediate aftermath of the Gulf War, "[t]o defeat a country with the national product of Portugal took 75% of America's tactical aircraft and 40% of its tanks. Some unipolar gunboat."[26]

135

Attempts to forge for a post-Cold War United States the dominant position as arbiter of world order encounter certain structural limits. To be sure, there is a strong temptation in the wake of the USSR's break-up to seize what Krauthammer calls "the unipolar moment." But the political and economic costs are simply overwhelming, especially because the Cold War ideological consensus now having fragmented, it is increasingly difficult to manufacture domestic unity behind overseas commitments. Moreover, the basic logistical requirements of material supply, transoceanic deployments, and sustained involvement in regional conflicts make undue burdens on defense budgets – especially in an era of fiscal downscaling. An initial draft of the US Defense Planning Guidance for the Fiscal Years 1994–9, for instance, sketched out seven possible scenarios for American troop deployments. The US would need to be prepared to wage two of these major regional wars simultaneously as part of a broader strategic goal "to prevent the re-emergence of a new rival, either on the territory of the former Soviet Union or elsewhere," and to "show the leadership necessary to establish and protect a new order that holds the promise of convincing potential competitors that they need not aspire to a greater role or pursue a more aggressive posture to protect their legitimate interests."[27] The plan proved too controversial and too ambitious, as well. Ultimately, it was pared back somewhat; the language arguing for one superpower and for preventing the rise of any competitors in Western Europe and East Asia was softened, and some concessions were made (rhetorically, at least) to working with multilateral organizations, such as the United Nations.[28] A year later, the Clinton administration acknowledged further limits in meeting post-Cold War strategic goals. From now on, the US would no longer even be able to fight two major wars at once but instead would seek to fight them in turn – what it called a "win-hold-win" strategy. As one senior military official said, "The dilemma is that there are more requirements than there are capabilities to accomplish them. We have not found a way to bring these into line yet."[29]

This, of course, can be frustrating. After all, the end of the most recent great world war was supposed to usher in an era of peace, but that peace proved frighteningly transitory. Classical models of nation–state warfare hardly seem to exhaust the spectrum of overt conflict wracking world politics today. Moreover, security can no longer be measured in terms of the (momentary) absence of war, but has come to include a more ambitious social agenda, including questions of ecology, economic sufficiency, human rights, and gender relations. Finally, there is the increasingly complicated question of the relevant actors in world politics. In an age when classical realist principles were considered intellectual manna, the domain of significance extended only to the very closed circles of the sovereign state's power. But today, such a view is simply antiquarian, and even the most dedicated realist is forced to address the emergence of a whole panoply of non-state actors, including social movements organized around such constellations of identity and power as gender, race, culture, religion and class. It may well be that the most revitalizing intellectual force at work upon International Relations is coming from the many schools of thought that generally fall under the heading of "Feminist Studies." Particularly influential here are debates about the phallocentric quality of strategic discourse, the engendered nature of the development paradigm, and the patriarchal basis of the modern state.[30]

In such a world, the teaching of world politics becomes enormously complicated, particularly as leading scholars in the field explore different perspectives by which to understand recent developments and find out that among those points up for contestation are their very own claims to lead the discipline. There cannot, then, be a more opportune moment to open up methodological and pedagogical questions about International Relations. The last few years have taken us through a breathless series of events. The dismantling of the Berlin Wall has itself passed into history. It remains to be seen what precisely will be the nature of those successor states that had been cowering behind the Iron Curtain. The makeshift Commonwealth of Independent States will likely prove no more perdurable than a Yugoslavia or Czechoslovakia. The great bipolar conflict between two hegemonic superpowers finally – or so it seems for now – has played itself out. Once again, but this time for real, the Cold War is over. It is not clear, however, and it remains very much an open question, what will replace the old familiarities – whether something called a New World Order, or a new economic order centered around Japan and the European Community, or perhaps a revived *Pax Americana* venting its fury upon the same "ungrateful" competitors it had helped revive half a century earlier.[31] But in any case, it can fairly be said that even if the new has yet to be born, the old has simply passed away.

Yet for vast stretches of the globe, the breakup of the older world order offers no visible hope for the future. The talk of building a New International Economic Order has subsided as the Western world, politely referred to as the "multilateral trading system," has refused to acquiesce in a series of structural reforms. The result is that many national economies are stagnating, mired in growing debt. Some of these countries now find it more attractive to turn themselves into tourist outposts or to export drugs to the industrialized world.

The resilience of the classical Atlantic-centered order sustains those who see in classical realism timeless principles for the discipline. There is, it must be acknowledged, something powerful about the appeal of a doctrine which speaks so consistently about the nature of power and the role of competing states in the international system. Yet however ill-defined a new world order may be, this does not warrant confident reliance upon the versions of realism that have been deeded to us today. For the basic animating concepts of this perspective – power, the state, the state system – can all be seen to be far more internally complex than presumed by standardbearers of the idiom. One need only confront the primary works of those who have created the pantheon of realism to see that their thinking is, in fact, far richer and more ethically ennobled than as seen within contemporary textbook versions. Machiavelli wrestling with modernity, or Hobbes invoking religion in order to secure civil society – these are but two examples of thinkers whose intellectual richness threatens to break out of the Gothic straight-jacket into which they have been fitted by current champions of the tradition.[32]

All of this has meant something of a crisis for International Relations. The fundamental issue is that, like the Cold War and all the other old formulas for organizing world politics, the prevailing paradigms no longer seem flexible enough to accommodate the extraordinary changes that are taking place throughout the world. At the same time, we need to allow ourselves the possibility that the inadequacy of prevailing modes of thought pertains not simply to contemporary reality, but to the received wisdom about historic reality as well.

For some strategic policy analysts, there is no need to engage in a fundamental rethinking. The existing categories provide enough grist with which to confront even a radically altered security environment. As one observer has recently noted, for example, there is still a need for "nuclear policy without an adversary," even when that adversary, none other than the former USSR, has ceased to exist in its Cold War incarnation and no longer poses more than the most nominal or existential of threats.[33] The issue, then, is not the particular choice of a more stabilizing, minimal deterrent posture, but the analytical framework of security and strategy within which the policy option is couched. In effect, nothing really has changed in terms of the thinking brought to the table. Much of what passes for claims about the end of the Cold War, it turns out, falls into this variety of argument by default, according to which the Cold War furtively still rages, or in some cases, is actually extended and intensified into more domains of public life.

Consider certain claims for an expanded conception of security. It has not passed unnoticed among enlightened policy makers that

138

continued reliance upon a paradigm of "nuclear deterrence-strategy-security" is scarcely up to the complexities of modern global life. Especially in a world marked increasingly by international trade, resource dependence, ecological sensitivity, distorted patterns of development, food distribution problems and population growth, it seems quaint, or perhaps simply archaic, to adhere to national strategies in which military policy dwarfs other domains on the social agenda. For this reason, it is now commonplace for established circles to adopt expanded frameworks of security and national strategy, all in the name of meeting the changed nature of global policy in a post-Cold War environment. Most prominent, of course, have been calls for a renewed trade policy to confront the threats to national security posed by declining US international competitiveness and the prospects of rival power bases in Japan and Germany. But a similar motif is also recognizable among calls for attention to the threats posed by acid rain, global warming, and the ozone hole, as well guaranteed access to vital resources, especially oil.[34] Here it is common to see the threats articulated in terms of a national security model by which the state becomes vested with the power to manage the threat and assure macro-economic conditions so that national wealth can be promoted and established patterns of resource distribution preserved.

The point here is not that security should be narrowly construed. On the contrary, such efforts at expanding conceptions of security beyond the boundaries of nuclear deterrence and military policy are to be lauded as long overdue. But such a revisionist agenda, when couched in the particularly modernist and instrumental frame of "security," poses a range of political problems that need to be thematized. In this sense, what has passed for national security strategy is simply the clumsiest and most readily identifiable manifestation of a broader orientation toward man, nature and global politics which needs to be questioned. A critique of nuclear strategy and military policy that overlooks this dimension of Western practice betrays its claim to address the end of the Cold War.

The idea behind this analysis has been to question prevailing structures of strategic practice. The only way to do that is to interpret political-military strategy as part of a larger social and political project – indeed, as a network of linguistically saturated social practices about the violent making and remaking of the modern world. It is a discourse that presents itself as realistic, as dealing with the harsh and unmitigating surface turbulence of a world devoid of a centering principle. Because its *leitmotif* is anarchy, strategic discourse poses its own act of will as the solution to the immanent conflict which marks contemporary global affairs. Yet this approach to political will – in the name of establishing a modernist reign of "security" – has ended up sanctioning diverse forms of militarization in a heroic effort to contain it.

Increasingly today, there is a disjuncture between the scope of state power and the domain over which responsibility needs to be exercised. This does not necessarily mean that because security concerns are global in scope, only a world state can guarantee legitimate order. On the contrary, the multiple, overlapping and interlocking networks of work, production, distribution, ecology, culture, and personal identity require political structures and analytical schemes that are simultaneously less extensive and more far-reaching than the modern statist discourse of strategy can possible allow.[35]

Despite all the talk about the end of the Cold War, much of the discursive and representational structures of world politics remain in place from the Cold War era. Yes, the great adversary has collapsed, and the Eastern bloc countries are not ideological foes but aspiring democratic comrades. Yet at a deeper and more theoretically embedded level, the most essential categories of thinking about world politics remain firmly in place.

To talk about the end of the Cold War is to talk about more than US–Soviet strategic relations and the logic of this or that nuclear deterrent option. It is, rather, to confront the broader representational repertoire which make strategy and deterrence possible in the first place. The beauty of these polices is their scope and ambition, their breathless and admirably heady attempts to coordinate social life and political identity on a truly worldwide scale. The politics of deterrence, after all, is not exhausted by weapons-technical critiques of whether war-fighting or minimalism will suffice to deter a would-be aggressor. If this were the case, as many strategists had hoped and practised their craft for years in a political vacuum, there would be no need for theoretical reflection and no space for criticism beyond the narrowest imaginable terms. Indeed, the insularity and legitimacy of precisely such an argumentative posture is only possible because strategic discourse has stood in an intimate relationship with so many modernist conceits – the wall between public and private, the boundaries of inside and outside, the bifurcation of politics into the domestic and the foreign, and the mercantilist separation of state and economy. To reconstitute these bifurcations and to pose critical questions of how these boundaries are established and patrolled is to engage in a profound restructuring of Strategic Studies – and of world order.

NOTES

1 Introduction

1 Throughout this text, I have capitalized the academic disciplines of International Relations and Strategic Studies. This is to distinguish them respectively from such terms as world politics or strategic policy. By this manner, the general phenomena need not be exhausted by specific analytical approaches. For an extended argument about this, see R.B.J. Walker, *Inside/Outside: International Relations as Political Theory* (Cambridge: Cambridge University Press, 1993).

2 For a prime example, see James N. Rosenau, ed., *International Politics and Foreign Policy*, rev. edn (New York: Free Press, 1969).

3 Robert Gilpin, "The Richness of the Tradition of Political Realism," *International Organization*, 38:2, Spring 1984, 287–304.

4 Robert W. Cox, "Social Forces, States and World Orders: Beyond International Relations Theory," *Millennium*, 10:2, Summer 1981, 126–55.

5 Robert O. Keohane and Joseph S. Nye, *Power and Interdependence* (Boston: Little, Brown and Co., 1977); Stephen D. Krasner, ed., *International Regimes* (Ithaca: Cornell University Press, 1983); Robert O. Keohane, *After Hegemony* (Princeton: Princeton University Press, 1984); Robert O. Keohane, ed., *Neorealism and Its Critics* (New York: Columbia University Press, 1986).

6 A characteristic example of how strategy becomes subordinated to state-managed accounts of economic bargaining is Robert Gilpin, *War and Change in World Politics* (Cambridge: Cambridge University Press, 1981).

7 Cox, "Social Forces, States and World Orders"; Richard K. Ashley, "The Poverty of Neo-Realism," *International Organization*, 38:2, Spring 1984, 225–86; Mark Hoffman, "Critical Theory and the Inter-Paradigm Debate," *Millennium*, 16:2, Summer 1987, 231–49; Yosef Lapid, "The Third Debate: On the Prospects of International Theory in a Post-Positivist Era," *International Studies Quarterly*, 33:3, Spring 1989, 235–54; Jim George, "International Relations and the Search for Thinking Space: Another View of the Third Debate," *International Studies Quarterly*, 33:3, September 1989, 269–79; and Jim George and David Campbell, "Patterns of Dissent and the Celebration of Difference: Critical Social Theory and International Relations," *International Studies Quarterly*, 34:3, September 1990, 269–93.

8 Richard K. Ashley and R.B.J. Walker, "Reading Dissidence/Writing the Discipline: Crisis and the Question of Sovereignty in International Studies," *International Studies Quarterly* 34:3, September 1990, 384.

9 See the following works by Michael Foucault: *Madness and Civilization*, trans. Richard Howard (New York: Vintage Books, 1973); *The Birth of the Clinic*, trans. A.M. Sheridan Smith (New York: Vintage Books, 1975); *Language, Counter-Memory, Practice: Selected Essays and Interviews*, ed. Donald F. Bouchard, trans. Donald F. Bouchard and Sherry Simon (Ithaca: Cornell University Press, 1977); *Discipline and Punish*, trans. Alan Sheridan (New York: Vintage Books, 1979); *Power/Knowledge: Selected Interviews and Other Writings, 1972–1977*, ed. Colin Gordon (New York: Pantheon, 1980); *The Foucault Reader*, ed. Paul Rabinow (New York: Pantheon, 1984). For theoretically sophisticated applications of such an approach toward policy analysis, see Michael J. Shapiro, *Language and Political Understanding* (New Haven: Yale University Press, 1981); *The Politics of Representation* (Madison: University of Wisconsin Press, 1988); and *Reading the Postmodern Polity* (Minneapolis: University of Minnesota Press, 1992).

10 I follow here, with some elaboration, James Der Derian, "Introducing Philosophical Traditions," *Millennium*, 17:2, Summer 1988, 189–93.

11 E.H. Carr, *The Twenty Years' Crisis, 1919–1939*, 2nd edn (London: Macmillan, 1946), 22–88.

12 The same strategy of dismissal, whereby postmodernist forays are dispatched via second-hand treatment rather than directly analyzed and criticized, can be seen at play in Robert O. Keohane, "International Relations Theory: Contributions of a Feminist Standpoint," in Rebecca Grant and Kathleen Newland, eds., *Gender and International Relations* (Bloomington: Indiana University Press, 1991), 41–50; Stephen M. Walt, "The Renaissance of Security Studies," *International Studies Quarterly*, 35:2, June 1991, 223; and John Gerard Ruggie, "Territoriality and Beyond: Problematizing Modernity in International Relations," *International Organization*, 47:1, Winter 1993, 139–74. For examples of the understanding that Strategic Studies is in no need of theoretical reflection, see Hedley Bull, "Strategic Studies and its Critics," *World Politics*, 20:4, July 1968, 593–605; and Joseph S. Nye, Jr. and Sean M. Lynn-Jones, "International Security Studies: A Report of a Conference on the State of the Field," *International Security*, 12:4. Spring 1988, 5–27. An important early corrective to this view is Philip Green, *Deadly Logic: The Theory of Nuclear Deterrence* (Columbus: Ohio State University Press, 1966).

13 Edward Said refers to this as the "the worldliness" of texts. See his *The World, the Text, and the Critic* (Cambridge: Harvard University Press, 1983), 31–53. Jacques Derrida has explicitly addressed – and exemplified – the critical politics of deconstruction in *Of Grammatology*, trans. Gayatri Chakravorty Spivak (Baltimore: Johns Hopkins University Press, 1976); and "Racism's Last Word," *Critical Inquiry*, 12:1, Autumn 1985, 290–99. Traditional perspectives, anticipating a definitive alternative articulation, dismiss such a critical tack as mired in relativism. That criticism can explore the subterranean workings of power without necessarily replacing it, see David Campbell, *Writing Security: United States Foreign Policy and the Politics of Identity* (Minneapolis: University of Minnesota Press, 1992), 1–16, 245–62.

14 The term comes from Paul Fussell, *The Great War and Modern Memory* (New York: Oxford University Press, 1975), a book that explores literary represen-

tations of British experience in World War I. Fussell claims (p. 5) that he nearly subtitled his book "An Inquiry into the Curious Literariness of Real Life." His re-reading of military experience through such media as newspapers, diaries, memoirs and letters yields critical insights at odds with conventional understandings. Also, see Paul Fussell, *Wartime: Understanding and Behaviour in the Second World War* (New York: Oxford University Press, 1989).

15 Enrico Augelli and Craig Murphy, *America's Quest for Supremacy and the Third World: A Gramscian Analysis* (London: Francis Pinter, 1988); Stephen Gill, *American Hegemony and the Trilateral Commission* (Cambridge: Cambridge University Press, 1990); Stephen Gill, ed., *Gramsci, Historical Materialism and International Relations* (Cambridge: Cambridge University Press, 1993); and Ernesto Laclau and Chantal Mouffe, *Hegemony and Socialist Strategy* (London: Verso, 1985).

16 Jerome R. Ravetz, *Scientific Knowledge and its Social Problems* (New York: Oxford University Press, 1971).

2 The politics of Strategic Studies

1 Hedley Bull, "The Grotian Conception of International Society," in Herbert Butterfield and Martin Wight, eds., *Diplomatic Investigations: Essays in the Theory of International Politics* (Cambridge, Mass.: Harvard University Press, 1966), 68.

2 The clearest statement of the liberal position that arms sales enable Western powers to influence Third World politics in favorable ways is Andrew J. Pierre, *The Global Politics of Arms Sales* (Princeton: Princeton University Press, 1982). For critical expositions of the link among arms sales, underdevelopment and Third World militarization, see Nicole Ball, *Security and Economy in the Third World* (Princeton: Princeton University Press, 1988); Mac Graham, Richard Jolly and Chris Smith, eds., *Disarmament and Underdevelopment*, 2nd edn (Oxford: Pergamon Press, 1986); Mary Kaldor, *The Baroque Arsenal* (New York: Hill and Wang, 1981); and Herbert Wulf, ed., *Aufrüstung und Unterentwicklung* (Reinbek bei Hamburg: Rowohlt, 1983).

3 Stephen R. David, "Why the Third World Matters," *International Security*, 14:1, Summer 1989, 50–85; and "Why the Third World Still Matters," *International Security*, 17:3, Winter 1992/3, 127–59. Donald M. Snow, *Distant Thunder: Third World Conflict and the New International Order* (New York: St. Martin's Press, 1993), relies upon traditional state-centered security concerns, though delineates forms of domestic insurgency threatening international order in a post-Cold War context.

4 For a critique of this, see Caroline Thomas, *In Search of Security: The Third World in International Relations* (Boulder, Co.: Lynne Rienner, 1987).

5 George Orwell, "Politics and the English Language," in *A Collection of Essays* (San Diego: Harcourt Brace Jovanovich, 1953), 156–71, shows that form and content are not separable in terms of political analysis. For an account of how the lifeless prose of behavioral International Relations theory is intimately related to its worldview, see Bradley S. Klein, "Discourse Analysis: Teaching World Politics Through International Relations,"

in Lev S. Gonick and Edward Weisband, eds., *Teaching World Politics: Contending Pedagogies for a New World Order* (Boulder, Co.: Westview Press, 1992), 152–69.

6 Ekkehart Krippendorff, "The Victims – a Research Failure," *Journal of Peace Research*, 18:1, 1981, 97. This is largely why John Mueller, "Quiet Cataclysm: Some Thoughts on World War III," in Michael J. Hogan, ed., *The End of the Cold War* (Cambridge: Cambridge University Press, 1992), 39–52, refers to the recently concluded postwar era as World War III.

7 Eric Wolf, *Europe and the People Without History* (Berkeley: University of California Press, 1982).

8 Krippendorff, "The Victims – A Research Failure," 98.

9 John H. Bodley, *Victims of Progress*, 3rd edn (Mountain View: Mayfield Publishing, 1990), 39.

10 Jean B. Elshtain, *Women and War* (New York: Basic Books, 1987); Cynthia Enloe, *Bananas, Beaches and Bases* (Berkeley: University of California Press, 1989); Carol Gilligan, *In a Different Voice* (Cambridge: Harvard University Press, 1982); Rebecca Grant and Kathleen Newland, eds., *Gender and International Relations* (Bloomington: Indiana University Press, 1991); V. Spike Peterson, ed., *Gendered States* (Boulder, Co.: Lynne Rienner, 1992); Christine Sylvester, "The Emperor's Theories and Transformations: Looking at the Field Through Feminist Lenses," in Dennis Pirages and Christine Sylvester, eds., *Transformations in the Global Political Economy* (New York: St. Martin's Press, 1990), 230–53; J. Ann Tickner, *Gender in International Relations: Feminist Perspectives on Achieving Global Security* (New York: Columbia University Press, 1992); Marysia Zalewski, "Feminist Theory and International Relations," in Mike Bowker and Robin Brown, eds., *From Cold War to Collapse: Theory and World Politics in the 1980s* (Cambridge: Cambridge University Press, 1993), 115–44.

11 C.B. Macpherson, *The Political Theory of Possessive Individualism: Hobbes to Locke* (New York: Clarendon Press, 1962).

12 Perry Anderson, *Passages from Antiquity to Feudalism* (London: New Left Books, 1974); Perry Anderson, *Lineages of the Absolutist State* (London: New Left Books, 1974); Anthony Giddens, *The Nation–State and Violence* (Cambridge: Polity Press, 1985); Robert H. Jackson, *Quasi-States: Sovereignty, International Relations and the Third World* (Cambridge: Cambridge University Press, 1990); Friedrich Kratochwil, "Of Systems, Boundaries, and Territoriality: An Inquiry into the Formation of the State System," *World Politics*, 39:1, October 1986, 27–52; V.G. Kiernan, *State and Society in Europe, 1550–1600* (New York: St. Martin's Press, 1980); Michael Mann, *The Sources of Social Power* (Cambridge: Cambridge University Press, 1986); Michael Mann, *States, War, and Capitalism in Political Sociology* (Oxford: Basil Blackwell, 1988); Barrington Moore, Jr., *Social Origins of Dictatorship and Democracy* (Boston: Beacon Press, 1966); Gianfranco Poggi, *The Development of the Modern State: A Sociological Introduction* (Stanford: Stanford University Press, 1978); and Theda Skocpol, *States and Social Revolutions* (Cambridge: Cambridge University Press, 1979).

13 Among the clearer starting points for an appreciation of Machiavelli's contribution to what is here called "the indefinite state" are: Sheldon

Wolin, *Politics and Vision* (Boston: Little, Brown, 1960), 195–238; Martin Fleisher, "A Passion for Politics: The Vital Core of the World of Machiavelli," in Martin Fleisher, ed., *Machiavelli and the Nature of Political Thought* (New York: Atheneum, 1972), 114–47; J.G.A. Pocock, *The Machiavellian Moment* (Princeton: Princeton University Press, 1975); Hannah Fenichel Pitkin, *Fortuna is a Woman: Gender and Politics in the Thought of Machiavelli* (Berkeley: University of California Press, 1984); and R.B.J. Walker, "*The Prince* and 'The Pauper': Tradition, Modernity, and Practice in the Theory of International Relations," in James Der Derian and Michael Shapiro, eds., *International/Intertextual Relations: Postmodern Readings of World Politics* (Lexington: Lexington Books, 1989), 25–48.

14 Max Weber, "Politics as a Vocation," in *From Max Weber: Essays in Sociology*, ed. and trans. Hans Gerth and C. Wright Mills (New York: The Free Press, 1946), 78.

15 See note 12 above.

16 John Mearsheimer, "Correspondence: Back to the Future, Part III: Realism and the Realities of European Security," *International Security*, 15:3, Winter 1990/1, 220. The same view informs the article which spawned the exchange of letters. See John Mearsheimer, "Back to the Future: Instability in Europe After the Cold War," *International Security*, 15:1, Summer 1990, 5–56.

17 On the Peace of Lodi as a marking stone for the development of a recognizably modern states system, with particular attention paid to diplomatic practice, see Garrett Mattingly, *Renaissance Diplomacy* (Boston: Houghton Mifflin, 1971), 91–100. The case for the Ancient Greek world is often made by reference to The Melian Dialogue in Thucydides' *The History of the Peloponnesian War*. A clear case for the way in which contemporary problems shape historical interpretations can be found in a rigidly bipolar account of the conflict between Athens and Sparta by Peter Fliess, *Thucydides and the Politics of Bipolarity* (Baton Rouge: Louisiana State University Press, 1966).

18 Michael Howard, "The Causes of Wars," in *The Causes of Wars and Other Essays*, 2nd edn (Cambridge: Harvard University Press, 1984), 7–22.

19 Martin Wight, "Why is There No International Theory?," in Butterfield and Wight, eds., *Diplomatic Investigations: Essays in the Theory of International Politics*, 26.

20 Howard, "The Causes of Wars," 21.

21 Ibid., 9–10.

22 The difference between classical, historicist realism and modernist, technocratic structural realism is evidenced in the distance between two definitive statements of the security dilemma. John H. Herz, "Idealist Internationalism and the Security Dilemma," *World Politics*, 2:2, January 1950, 157–180, explores the dilemmas posed by revisionist social movements trying to escape the need to preserve security in an anarchic world. With Robert Jervis, "Cooperation Under the Security Dilemma," *World Politics*, 30:2, January 1978, 167–214, the relevant agents are state actors divorced from any ideological or social concerns except to maximize national security through limited forms of non-zero sum game cooperation. The difference between the two positions nicely illustrates the theoretical argument about

historicist and modernist realism found in R.B.J. Walker, "Realism, Change, and International Political Theory," *International Studies Quarterly*, 31:1, March 1987, 65–86.

23 Barry Buzan, *People, States and Fear: An Agenda for International Security Studies in the Post-Cold War Era*, 2nd edn (Boulder, Co.: Lynne Rienner, 1991).

24 Kenneth Waltz, *Man, the State, and War: A Theoretical Analysis* (New York, Columbia University Press, 1959).

25 Barry Buzan, *An Introduction to Strategic Studies: Military Technology and International Relations* (London: Macmillan and the International Institute for Strategic Studies, 1987).

26 On essential contestability, see William E. Connolly, *The Terms of Political Discourse*, 2nd edn (Princeton: Princeton University Press, 1984).

27 Buzan, *An Introduction to Strategic Studies*, 232.

28 Of particular importance when exploring the disciplinary character of modern academic disciplines are several works by Michel Foucault. See his *The Archaeology of Knowledge and the Discourse on Language*, trans. A.M. Sheridan Smith (New York: Harper Colophon, 1976); and *Discipline and Punish: The Birth of the Prison*, trans. Alan Sheridan (New York: Vintage Books, 1979). Foucault has developed the concept of "the specific intellectual" in "Truth and Power" in *The Foucault Reader*, ed. Paul Rabinow (New York: Pantheon, 1984), 51–75, to illustrate the two-fold character of modern disciplined man. The specific intellectual in not a "bearer of universal values" (p.73) but someone whose knowledge and power derive from an intensive mastery of a rational-technical policy practice (such as nuclear physics, criminology, or encryption). While such intellectuals may occupy crucial roles in policy making, they are not themselves vested with institutional protection and thus can quickly fall victim to an altered climate in values and lifestyles. For exemplary cases, see the parallel denouements of American atomic bomb developer J. Robert Oppenheimer and British mathematician/decipherer Alan Turing. Heinar Kipphardt, *In the Matter of J. Robert Oppenheimer*, trans. Ruth Speirs (New York: Hill and Wang, 1967); and Andrew Hodges, *Alan Turing: The Enigma* (New York: Simon and Schuster, 1983).

29 Michael Howard, "The Strategic Approach to International Relations," in *The Causes of Wars and Other Essays*, 36–48.

30 Kenneth Waltz, *Theory of International Politics* (Reading: Addison-Wesley, 1979), 66.

31 R.B.J. Walker, *One World/Many Worlds: Struggles for a Just World Peace* (Boulder, Co.: Lynne Rienner, 1988), offers a critical recasting of these categories, so that "the one" and "the many" do not exist in mutual exclusion of one another but in fact co-exist spatially and politically.

32 Waltz, *Theory of International Politics*, 88.

33 Realists and neorealists have deduced the identity and interests of states from their ontological status within a structure of "self-help." For a critique of this, and a counter-argument that states within a system of anarchic "self-help" are unavoidably engaged in processes of constructing their identities and interests, see Alexander Wendt, "Anarchy is What States

Make of It: The Social Construction of Power Politics," *International Organization*, 46:2, Spring 1992, 391–425.

34 For useful histories of the global strategic consequences of superior Western firepower, see Carlo Cipolla, *Guns, Sails and Empires: Technological Innovation and the Early Phases of European Expansion, 1400–1700* (New York: Minerva Press, 1965); Ekkehart Krippendorff, *Internationales System als Geschichte* (Frankfurt: Campus Verlag, 1975); William H. McNeill, *The Pursuit of Power: Technology, Armed Force, and Society since A.D. 1000* (Chicago: The University of Chicago Press, 1982); and John U. Nef, *War and Human Progress: An Essay on the Rise of Industrial Civilization* (New York: W.W. Norton, 1963).

35 W. W. Rostow, *The Stages of Economic Growth* (Cambridge: Cambridge University Press, 1960), 26–28.

36 Lawrence Freedman, *U.S. Intelligence and the Soviet Strategic Threat*, 2nd edn (Princeton: Princeton University Press, 1986).

37 Matthew Evangelista, "Stalin's Postwar Army Reappraised," *International Security*, 7:3, Winter 1982/3, 110–38; and John Mueller, "The Essential Irrelevance of Nuclear Weapons," *International Security*, 13:2, Fall 1988, 55–79.

38 Neil C. Livingstone, *The Cult of Counterterrorism* (Lexington: Lexington Books, 1990), 394.

39 E.V. Gulick, *Europe's Classical Balance of Power* (New York: W.W. Norton, 1967); Henry A. Kissinger, *A World Restored: Metternich, Castlereagh and the Problems of Peace, 1812–1822* (Boston: Houghton Mifflin, 1957); and Hans Morgenthau, *Politics Among Nations*, 5th edn (New York: Alfred A. Knopf, 1973), 167–221.

40 Waltz, *Theory of International Politics*, 73.

41 Michael Desch, "Turning the Caribbean Flank: Sea Lane Vulnerability During a European War," *Survival*, 29:6, November/December 1987, 528–51, manages to do so without the slightest irony or theoretical reflection. For critiques of such mental mapping that account for how such a strategic discourse is constructed, see Tzvetan Todorov, *The Conquest of America*, trans. Richard Howard (New York: Harper and Row, 1984); and Michael J. Shapiro, "The Constitution of the Central American Other: The Case of 'Guatemala'," in *The Politics of Representation* (Madison: University of Wisconsin Press, 1988), 89–123.

42 R.B.J. Walker, *Inside/Outside: International Relations as Political Theory* (Cambridge: Cambridge University Press, 1993).

43 For an example of what happens when a dissident voice infiltrates sites of strategic discourse and begins raising questions about the nature of the whole enterprise, see Carol Cohn, "Sex and Death in the Rational World of Defense Intellectuals," *Signs*, 12:4, Summer 1987, 687–718.

44 Richard K. Ashley and R.B.J. Walker, "Reading Dissidence/Writing the Discipline: Crisis and the Question of Sovereignty in International Studies," *International Studies Quarterly*, 34:3, September 1990, 367–416.

45 Philip K. Lawrence, "Strategy, the State and the Weberian Legacy," *Review of International Studies*, 13:4, October 1987, 295–310; and his *Preparing for Armageddon* (Brighton: Wheatsheaf, 1988).

46 John L. Gaddis, "The Long Peace: Elements of Stability in the Postwar International System," *International Security*, 10:4, Spring 1986, 99–142.

47 Karl Polanyi, *The Great Transformation* (Boston: Beacon Press, 1957), 3–19, argues that the absence of continent-wide war (along with the presence of numerous colonial wars) that characterized the Hundred Years' Peace can be explained in terms of emergent international market and monetary systems. "In other words, only on the background of the new economy could the balance-of-power system make general conflagrations avoidable" (p. 17).

48 Francis Fukuyama, "The End of History," *The National Interest*, 16, Summer 1989, 15.

49 Michel Foucault, "Practising Criticism," in *Politics, Philosophy, Culture: Interviews and other Writings 1977–1984*, ed. Lawrence Kritzman, trans. Alan Sheridan and others (New York: Routledge, 1988), 154–55: "Criticism is a matter of flushing out that thought and trying to change it: to show that things are not as self-evident as one believed, to see what is accepted as self-evident will no longer be accepted as such. Practising criticism is a matter of making facile gestures difficult."

50 Richard Eichenberg, *Public Opinion and National Security in Western Europe* (Ithaca: Cornell University Press, 1989); Mary Kaldor, ed., *Europe from Below: An East–West Dialogue* (London: Verso, 1991); Dorothy Nelkin and Michael Pollack, *The Atom Beseiged: Antinuclear Movements in France and West Germany* (Cambridge: MIT Press, 1981); and Thomas R. Rochon, *Mobilizing for Peace: The Antinuclear Movements in Western Europe* (Princeton: Princeton University Press, 1988).

51 Timothy Garton Ash, *The Magic Lantern: The Revolution of '89 Witnessed in Warsaw, Budapest, Berlin and Prague* (New York: Random House, 1990). On the complexities of German unification, see Günter Grass, *Two States–One Nation?*, trans. Krishna Winston and A.S. Wensinger (San Diego: Harcourt Brace Jovanovich, 1990); Thomas Kielinger and Max Otte, "Germany: The Pressured Power," *Foreign Policy*, 91, Summer 1993, 44–62; Peter Neckermann, "What Went Wrong: Germany After the Unification?," *East European Quarterly*, 26:4, January 1993, 447–69 and Amity Shlaes, *Germany: The Empire Within* (New York: Farrar, Straus and Giroux, 1991).

52 Fukuyama, "The End of History.".

53 John Mearsheimer, "Why We Will Soon Miss the Cold War," *The Atlantic Monthly*, August 1990, 35–50.

54 For a set of essays that moves more cautiously over this terrain than its editors initially claim, see Michael Klare and Dan Thomas, eds. *World Security: Trends and Challenges at Century's End* (New York: St. Martins Press, 1991).

55 Part of the debate about International Relations involves debate about the nature of paradigms. The ease with which the term paradigm circulates in academic discourse is surely attributable to the work of Thomas Kuhn – or at least to the Kuhn of 1962. In subsequent editions of *The Structure of Scientific Revolution*, and in the hands of other philosophers of science, such as Imre Lakatos and Stephen Toulmin, as well as philosophers of language and social science, including Richard Bernstein, "paradigm" assumes a less

definitive form. Instead of serving as a theoretical approach within a carefully circumscribed research program, paradigm functions in a more relaxed manner, something on the order of a set of questions whose assumptions are themselves subject to criticism and revision in the course of research. See Thomas S. Kuhn, "Postscript-1969," in *The Structure of Scientific Revolutions*, 2nd edn (Chicago: University of Chicago Press, 1970), 174–210; Richard Bernstein *Beyond Objectivism and Relativism* (Philadelphia: University of Pennsylvania Press, 1983); Richard Bernstein, *The Restructuring of Social and Political Theory* (New York: Harcourt Brace Jovanovich, 1976); Imre Lakatos and Alan Musgrave, eds., *Criticism and the Growth of Knowledge* (Cambridge: Cambridge University Press, 1970); and Stephen Toulmin, *Foresight and Understanding* (Bloomington: Indiana University Press, 1961).

The concept of "discourse" incorporates the contestable and interpretive dimensions of paradigm, but locates that contestation within the broader ambit of political power and social practice. It is language which conveys to us discourse; without language there could be no meaning. But discourses are not limited to language, though they cannot be meaningful outside of a linguistic medium. See Michel Foucault, "The Discourse on Language," in *The Archaeology of Knowledge and The Discourse on Language* (New York: Harper and Row, 1976), 215–237; Michael J. Shapiro, *Language and Political Understanding: The Politics of Discursive Practices* (New Haven: Yale University Press, 1981); and Michael J. Shapiro, ed., *Language and Politics* (New York: New York University Press, 1984).

56 Also variously called complex interdependence, transnationalism, neorealism, or (appropriately) modernism. See K.J. Holsti, *The Dividing Discipline: Hegemony and Diversity in International Theory* (Boston: Allen and Unwin, 1987); Robert O. Keohane and Joseph S. Nye, Jr., eds., *Transnational Relations and World Politics* (Cambridge: Harvard University Press, 1972); and Paul R. Viotti and Mark V. Kauppi, *International Relations Theory: Realism, Pluralism, Globalism* (New York: Macmillan, 1987).

57 Immanuel Wallerstein, *The Capitalist World-Economy: Essays* (Cambridge: Cambridge University Press, 1979); *The Modern World-System* (New York: Academic Press, 1974); and *The Politics of the World-Economy* (Cambridge: Cambridge University Press, 1984).

58 Robert O. Keohane, "International Institutions: Two Approaches," *International Studies Quarterly*, 32:4, December 1988, 379–96, sharply distinguishes a newly emergent "reflectivist" position from the dominant "rationalist" school of thought. While offering a cautious welcome to disciplinary interlopers, Keohane is careful to establish standards of judgment that are entirely rationalist. For detailed critiques of Keohane's argument, including his position that a basic epistemological identity can be detected among those embodying "reflectivism" against the dominant "rationalist" position, see R.B.J. Walker, "History and Structure in the Theory of International Relations," *Millennium*, 18:2, Summer 1989, 163–83; George, "International Relations and the Search for Thinking Space: Another View of the Third Debate"; Richard K. Ashley and R.B.J. Walker, "Speaking the Language of Exile: Dissident Thought in International

Studies," *International Studies Quarterly*, 34:3, September 1990, 259–68; George and Campbell, "Patterns of Dissent and the Celebration of Difference: Critical Social Theory and International Relations"; Ashley and Walker, "Reading Dissidence/Writing the Discipline: Crisis and the Question of Sovereignty in International Studies."

59 A basic statement of these themes is Richard Rorty, *Philosophy and the Mirror of Nature* (Princeton: Princeton University Press, 1980).

3 What nuclear revolution?

1 Giulio Douhet, *The Command of the Air*, trans. Dino Ferrari (New York: Coward-McCann, 1942), 153.

2 See the alternative reading of Thucydides by Daniel Garst, "Thucydides and Neorealism," *International Studies Quarterly*, 33:1, March 1989, 3–27, which argues that the neorealist (mis)appropriation of Thucydides' narrative misses entirely its performative, normative and sociological dimensions by which power is constructed and sent in circulation.

3 Otto Hintze, "Military Organization and the Organization of the State," in *The Historical Essays of Otto Hintze*, ed. Felix Gilbert (Oxford: Oxford University Press, 1975), 181.

4 For a detailed historical sociology of this, see Brian M. Downing, *The Military Revolution and Political Change: Origins of Democracy and Autocracy in Early Modern Europe* (Princeton: Princeton University Press, 1992).

5 Hintze, "Military Organization and the Organization of the State," 215.

6 Ibid., 201.

7 Herbert Spencer, *Principles of Sociology*, ed. Stanislav Andreski (London: Macmillan, 1969), 499–571, distinguishes between "militant" societies and "industrial" societies.

8 Thucydides, *The Peloponnesian War*, trans. R. Warner (Harmondsworth: Penguin Books, 1972), 47.

9 André Corvisier, *Armies and Societies in Europe, 1494–1789*, trans. Abigail T. Siddall (Bloomington: Indiana University Press, 1979); Downing, *The Military Revolution and Political Change*; Michael Howard, *War in European History* (Oxford: Oxford University Press, 1976); William H. McNeill, *The Pursuit of Power: Technology, Armed Force, and Society since A.D. 1000* (Chicago: University of Chicago Press, 1982); Geoffrey Parker, *The Military Revolution* (Cambridge: Cambridge University Press, 1988); and Hew Strachan, *European Armies and the Conduct of War* (London: George Allen and Unwin, 1983).

10 For Clausewitz's legacy to Western military strategy, see Raymond Aron, *Clausewitz: Philosopher of War* (New York: Simon and Schuster, 1986); Bernard Brodie, "The Continuing Relevance of *On War*," in Carl von Clausewitz, *On War*, ed. and trans. Michael Howard and Peter Paret (Princeton: Princeton University Press, 1976), 45–58; Günter Dill, ed., *Clausewitz in Perspektive* (Frankfurt: Ullstein Materialien, 1980); Michael Handel, ed., *Clausewitz and Modern Strategy* (London: Frank Cass, 1986); Michael Howard, "The Influence of Clausewitz," in Carl von Clausewitz, *On War*, ed. and trans. Michael Howard and Peter Paret (Princeton: Princeton

University Press, 1976), 27–44; Peter Paret, "Clausewitz," in Peter Paret, ed., *Makers of Modern Strategy: From Machiavelli to the Nuclear Age* (Princeton: Princeton University Press, 1986), 186–213; Anatol Rapoport, "Introduction," in Carl von Clausewitz, *On War*, ed. A. Rapoport, trans. Col. J.J. Graham (Harmondsworth: Penguin, 1968), 11–80; Hans Rothfels, "Clausewitz," in Edward Mead Earle, ed., *Makers of Modern Strategy: Military Thought From Machiavelli to Hitler* (Princeton: Princeton University Press, 1944), 93–113; Dieter Senghaas, *Abschreckung und Frieden*, 3rd edn (Frankfurt: Europische Verlagsanstalt, 1981), 43–70. For more general treatments of Clausewitz's work, see Werner Hahlweg, "Einleitung," in Carl von Clausewitz, *Verstreute kleine Schriften*, ed. Werner Hahlweg (Osnabruck: Biblio Verlag, 1979), ix–xxv; Michael Howard, *Clausewitz* (Oxford: Oxford University Press, 1983); and Peter Paret, *Clausewitz and the State* (Oxford: Oxford University Press, 1976).

11 For an extended critique of Clausewitz's appropriation of Kantian categories and how it shaped – and partially distorted – his distinctions between absolute and real war, and between total and limited warfare, see W.B. Gallie, *Philosophers of Peace and War* (Cambridge: Cambridge University Press, 1978), 37–65.

12 Chief among Bernard Brodie's works are: "War in the Atomic Age' and "Implications for Military Policy," in Bernard Brodie, ed., *The Absolute Weapon: Atomic Power and World Order* (New York: Harcourt, Brace and Company, for the Yale Institute of International Studies, 1946), 21–107; and *Strategy in the Missile Age* (Princeton: Princeton University Press, 1959). For Robert Jervis, see his: "Deterrence Theory Revisited," *World Politics* 31:2, January 1979, 288–324; *The Illogic of American Nuclear Strategy* (Ithaca: Cornell University Press, 1984); *The Meaning of the Nuclear Revolution: Statecraft and the Prospect of Armageddon* (Ithaca: Cornell University Press, 1989); and "Why Nuclear Superiority Doesn't Matter," *Political Science Quarterly* 94:2, Summer 1979–80, 617–33.

13 Herman Kahn, *On Thermonuclear War* (Princeton: Princeton University Press, 1960); Herman Kahn, *Thinking About the Unthinkable* (New York: Horizon Press, 1962); Paul Nitze, "Atoms, Strategy and Policy," *Foreign Affairs* 34:2, January 1956, 187–98; Paul Nitze, "Deterring Our Deterrent," *Foreign Policy*, 25, Winter 1976–77, 195–210; Colin Gray, *The Geopolitics of the Nuclear Era* (New York: Crane, Russak, 1977); Colin Gray, *Nuclear Strategy and Strategic Planning* (Philadelphia: Foreign Policy Research Institute, 1984); and Colin Gray and Keith Payne, "Victory is Possible," *Foreign Policy*, 39, Summer 1980, 14–27.

14 Carl von Clausewitz, *On War*, ed. and trans. M. Howard and P. Paret (Princeton: Princeton University Press, 1976), Bk. 1, ch. 1, 89. All subsequent quotations of *On War* are taken from this edition.

15 Hans Delbrück, *History of the Art of War Within the Framework of Political History, Vol 4: The Modern Era*, trans. Walter J. Renfroe, Jr. (Westport: Greenwood Press, 1985), 439–44, elaborates the distinction between a strategy of annihilation ("Niederwerfungsstrategie") and a strategy of attrition ("Ermattungsstrategie").

16 *On War*, Bk. 1, ch. 1, 79.

17 Ibid.

18 Ibid.

19 Ibid.

20 Clausewitz summarizes the inherent strengths of the defensive position in ibid., Bk. 6, ch. 12, 404–8. The long sixth book of *On War* deals in detail, at times excessively so, with each imaginable aspect of the defensive position: "Defensive Mountain Warfare," "Defense of Rivers and Streams," "Defense of Swamps."

21 Ibid., Bk. 1, ch. 1, 80.

22 Those who were wary of the vulnerability of America's strategic triad, or of the Minuteman land-based ICBMs, apparently ignored this concept of friction in assuming a perfectly coordinated first-strike by Soviet SS-18 missiles. See Committee on the Present Danger, *Can America Catch Up?* (Washington, DC: Committee on the Present Danger, 1984). Indispensable to this argument is the set of "dueling pamphlets" released by the respective defense ministries of the major powers. See US Department of Defense, *Soviet Military Power* (Washington, DC: US Government Printing Office, 1981); and USSR Ministry of Defense, *Whence the Threat to Peace* (Moscow: Military Publishing House, 1982).

The problems of friction involved in a coordinated first-strike across 6,000 miles and through a polar region of uncertain force fields are extraordinary. For a summary of the role of "friction" in modern conventional war planning, see James Fallows, *National Defense* (New York: Random House, 1981), 16–18. The botched attempt to rescue American hostages held in Teheran in April 1980 is a good example of friction. Subsequent debates about an impenetrable strategic defense shield relied upon a thorough neglect of friction. The illusory success of Patriot anti-missile missiles against incoming Iraqi SCUDs in the 1991 Persian Gulf War boosted, however momentarily, hopes that such a system might actually work. For an insider's very critical look that debunks the notion that the Patriot proved ballistic missile defenses to be feasible, see Theodore A. Postol, "Lessons of the Gulf War Experiment with Patriot," *International Security*, 16:3, Winter 1991/2, 119–71.

23 Clausewitz, *On War*, Bk. 1, ch. 1, 80.

24 Ibid.

25 Ibid., 86

26 Carl von Clausewitz, "Napoleon bei Belle-Alliance," *Politische Schriften und Briefe*, ed. H. Rothfels (Munich: Drei Masken Verlag, 1922), 217–19.

27 *On War*, Bk. 8, ch. 3B, 585–94.

28 Ibid., Bk. 4, ch. 2, 226.

29 Ibid., Bk. 8, ch. 3A, 584.

30 Ibid., Bk. 8, ch. 2, 580.

31 Ibid., Bk. 8, ch. 3B, 592–3.

32 Ibid., Bk. 7, ch. 22, 559–60.

33 Gallie, *Philosophers of Peace and War*, 37–65.

34 Clausewitz, quoted in Paret, *Clausewitz and the State*, 362.

35 John U. Nef, *War and Human Progress: An Essay on the Rise of Industrial Civilization* (New York: W.W. Norton, 1968), sees most of the breakthrough

military technology of industrializing Europe as having been derived from civilian economic production. Quite the opposite argument is found in McNeill, *The Pursuit of Power*, who sees military technology as having driven social change. For detailed studies of the military–technological background of World War I, see John Ellis, *The Social History of the Machine Gun* (New York: Pantheon, 1973); Marc Ferro, *The Great War, 1914–1918*, trans. N. Simon (Boston: Routledge and Kegan Paul, 1973); Howard, *War in European History*, 116–43; and Keith Robbins, *The First World War* (Oxford: Oxford University Press, 1984). On transformations in the nature of battle, see Manuel De Landa, *War in the Age of Intelligent Machines* (New York: Zone, 1991); John Keegan, *The Face of Battle* (New York: Viking Press, 1975), 204–336; and Paul Virilio, *War and Cinema: The Logistics of Perception*, trans. Patrick Camiller (London: Verso, 1989).

36 Quoted in Alistair Horne, *The Price of Glory: Verdun 1916* (Harmondsworth: Penguin, 1964), 22.

37 Brodie, *Strategy in the Missile Age*, 71–106; David McIsaac, "Voices from the Central Blue: The Air Power Theorists," in Paret, ed., *Makers of Modern Strategy*, 624–47; Michael S. Sherry, *The Rise of American Air Power* (New Haven: Yale University Press, 1987), 23–8; Barry Watts, *The Foundations of US Air Doctrine* (Washington, DC: US Government Printing Office, 1984), 5–15; and Edward Warner, "Douhet, Mitchell, Seversky: Theories of Air Warfare," in Earle, ed., *Makers of Modern Strategy*, 485–503;

38 Douhet, *Command of the Air*, 14.

39 Ibid., 8–9.

40 Ibid., 9.

41 Ibid., 51.

42 Ibid., 41.

43 Ibid., 126.

44 Ibid., 37.

45 Stephen M. Walt, "The Renaissance of Security Studies," *International Studies Quarterly*, 35:2, June 1991, 211–39. Edward A. Kolodziej, "Renaissance in Security Studies? Caveat Lector!," *International Studies Quarterly*, 36:4, December 1992, 421–38, takes Walt to task for his narrowly statist assumptions and for not exploring the state itself as a source of international insecurity. For a critical account of how military–defense studies were absorbed into postwar studies of strategy and security, see Bradley S. Klein, "After Strategy: The Search for a Post-Modern Politics of Peace," *Alternatives*, 13:3, July 1988, 293–318.

46 Brodie, *Strategy in the Missile Age*, 107–44.

47 "Minimal Deterrence" entails retaliation. Mutual Assured Destruction included a retaliatory component as part of a broader and more selective schedule of responses arrayed on an escalatory ladder that included limited first-use all the way to full-scale annihilatory war-fighting.

48 Brodie, "Implications for Military Policy," in Brodie, ed., *The Absolute Weapon*, 76.

49 The following account owes much to extended conversations with Allan Krass. See his "The Evolution of Military Technology and Deterrence Strategy," in *World Armaments and Disarmament: SIPRI Yearbook 1981* (Solna:

Stockholm International Peace Research Institute, 1981), 19–67; and "The Death of Deterrence" (unpublished manuscript, 1982).

50 Krass, "The Death of Deterrence."

51 John H. Herz, "Rise and Demise of the Territorial State," *World Politics*, 9:4, July 1957, 473–93. Unfortunately, Herz, "The Territorial State Revisited – Reflections on the Future of the Nation–State," *Polity*, 1:1, Fall 1968, 11–34, tried to refute his own argument a decade later when he argued that conventional military power was still a significant factor. Defense, he showed, was still a plausible strategy. He points to Israel's victory in the Six Days War of 1967 as proof, but this merely shifts the terms of his argument from nuclear missiles to conventional arms and does not really undermine – as he thinks it does – his earlier, seminal insight.

52 William L. Borden, *There Will Be No Time* (New York: Macmillan, 1946).

53 Colin Gray, *Strategic Studies and Public Policy* (Lexington: The University of Kentucky Press, 1982), 45–58. Lawrence Freedman, *The Evolution of Nuclear Strategy*, 2nd edn (New York: St. Martin's Press, 1989), xviii, writes: "Much of what is offered today as a profound and new insight was said yesterday; and usually in a more concise and literate manner."

54 John Foster Dulles, "Policy for Security and Peace," *Foreign Affairs*, 32:3, April 1954, 353–64; and "A Policy of Boldness," *Life*, May 19, 1952, 146–60.

55 William Kaufmann, ed., *Military Policy and National Security* (Princeton: Princeton University Press, 1956); Paul Nitze, "Atoms, Strategy and Policy'; Henry A. Kissinger, *Nuclear Weapons and Foreign Policy* (New York: Harper and Brothers, 1957); Maxwell Taylor, *The Uncertain Trumpet* (New York: Harper and Row, 1960); and Helmut Schmidt, *Verteidigung oder Vergeltung: ein deutscher Beitrag zur strategischen Problem der NATO* (Stuttgart: Seewald Verlag, 1961).

56 Cohn, "Sex and Death in the Rational World of Defense Intellectuals," *Signs*, 12:4, Summer 1987, 687–718; and Bradley S. Klein, "The Textual Strategies of the Military: Or, Have You Read Any Good Defense Manuals Lately?," in James Der Derian and Michael J. Shapiro, eds., *International/ Intertextual Readings* (Lexington: Lexington Books, 1989), 97–112.

57 Albert Wohlstetter, "The Delicate Balance of Terror," *Foreign Affairs*, 37:2, January 1959, 211–34.

58 Brodie, "Implications for Military Policy," 101–7.

59 Ashton B. Carter and David N. Schwartz, eds., *Ballistic Missile Defense* (Washington, DC: Brookings Institution, 1984); Franklin Long, Donald Hafner, and Jeffrey Boutwell, eds., *Weapons in Space* (New York: W.W. Norton, 1986); Craig Snyder, ed., *The Strategic Defense Debate: Can "Star Wars" Makes Us Safe?* (Philadelphia: University of Pennsylvania Press, 1986); and Samuel F. Wells, Jr. and Robert S. Litwak, ed., *Strategic Defenses and Soviet–American Relations* (Cambridge: Ballinger, 1987).

60 Jervis, *The Meaning of the Nuclear Revolution*, 9.

61 The Harvard Nuclear Study Group, *Living with Nuclear Weapons* (New York: Bantam Books, 1983). At an MIT/Harvard Summer Workshop on Nuclear Weapons and Arms Control held in June 1984, one of the co-authors, Paul Doty, publicly acknowledged his regret at the choice of the title.

62 Wohlstetter, "The Delicate Balance of Terror." The article was a declassified

distillation of the report by Albert J. Wohlstetter, F.S. Hoffman, R.J. Lutz, and H.S. Rowen, *Selection and Use of Strategic Air Bases*, RAND-R-266, April 1954. The best history of the relationship between the two studies is Fred Kaplan, *The Wizards of Armageddon* (New York: Simon and Schuster, 1983), 85–110.

63 Capt. Kenneth Kemp, "The Moral Case for the Strategic Defense Initiative," in D. P. Lackey, ed., *Ethics and Strategic Defense* (Belmont: Wadsworth Publishing, 1989), 39–45.

64 Hans Morgenthau, "The Fallacy of Thinking Conventionally About Nuclear Weapons," in D. Carlton and C. Schaerf, eds., *Arms Control and Technological Innovation* (New York: Wiley, 1976), 256–64.

65 This point constituted the core of Secretary of Defense James R. Schlesinger's 1974 request for additional options in US strategic targeting doctrine. See his testimony in *US and USSR Strategic Policies: Hearing Before the Subcommittee on Arms Control, International Law and Organization of the Commitee on Foreign Relations, United States Senate*, 93rd Congress, 2nd Session, March 4, 1974, 1–57. Also see Desmond Ball, "Development of the SIOP, 1960–1983," in Desmond Ball and Jeffrey Richelson, eds., *Strategic Nuclear Targeting* (Ithaca: Cornell University Press, 1986); "Carter Said to Back a Plan for Limiting Any Nuclear War," *New York Times*, August 6, 1980, A1; "Quick Outcome Is Not Expected On Fate of MX," *New York Times*, December 6, 1982, A1; Jonathan B. Tucker, "Strategic Command and Control: America's Achilles Heel?," *Technology Review* 86:6, August/September 1983, 38–49, 74–5; US Secretary of Defense Caspar W. Weinberger, *Annual Report to the Congress: Fiscal Year 1986* (Washington, DC: US Government Printing Office, 1986), 45–57.

66 Barry M. Blechman and Stephen S. Kaplan, *Force Without War: US Armed Forces as a Political Instrument* (Washington, DC: Brookings Institution, 1978); Alexander L. George and Richard Smoke, *Deterrence in American Foreign Policy: Theory and Practice* (New York: Columbia University Press, 1974); Robert Jervis, Richard Ned Lebow, and Janice Gross Stein, *Psychology and Deterrence* (Baltimore: Johns Hopkins University Press, 1985); John Mearsheimer, *Conventional Deterrence* (Ithaca: Cornell University Press, 1983).

67 Ken Booth, *Strategy and Ethnocentrism* (New York: Holmes and Meier, 1979); Robert Jervis, *Perception and Misperception in International Politics* (Princeton: Princeton University Press, 1975); Robert Jervis, *The Illogic of American Nuclear Strategy* (Ithaca: Cornell University Press, 1984); Steven Kull, *Minds at War: Nuclear Reality and the Inner Conflicts of Defense Policymakers* (New York: Basic Books, 1988); and Stephen Kull, "Nuclear Nonsense," *Foreign Policy*, 58, Spring 1985, 28–52. Booth, it must be said, has since been influenced by post-realist and post-empiricist conceptions of strategy and security. See his "Security and Emancipation," *Review of International Studies*, 17:4, October 1991, 313–26; "Security in Anarchy: Utopian Realism in Theory and Practice," *International Affairs*, 67:3, July 1991, 527–45; and "Strategy," in A.J.R. Groom and M. Light, eds., *International Relations: A Handbook of Current Theory*, 2nd edn (London: Pinter, forthcoming).

68 Nitze, "Atoms, Strategy and Policy." Desmond Ball, "US Strategic Forces: How Would They be Used?," *International Security*, 7:3, Winter 1982/83, 31–59, elaborates on the multi-dimensionality of nuclear strategy and finds five distinct elements – declaratory policy, force development policy, arms control negotiations, operational maintenance and preparation policy, and action or force employment policy. Each has its own history and dynamics, and some are at odds with other elements in the national strategic policy package.

69 Raymond Aron, *The Great Debate: Theories of Nuclear Strategy*, trans. E. Pawel (New York: Doubleday, 1965); McGeorge Bundy, *Danger and Survival* (New York: Random House, 1988); Freedman, *The Evolution of Nuclear Strategy*; Kaplan, *Wizards of Armageddon*; Gregg Herken, *Counsels of War*, exp. edn (New York: Oxford University Press, 1987); and Michael Mandelbaum, *The Nuclear Question: The United States and Nuclear Weapons, 1946–1976* (Cambridge: Cambridge University Press, 1979).

70 Michael C. Williams, "Rethinking the 'Logic' of Deterrence," *Alternatives*, 17:1, Winter 1992, 88, summarizes the philosophical dilemma of nuclear strategy as an unresolvable dialectical tension between two moments of apparently opposed strategic positions "Thinking about strategy and security has been reduced to a series of incomprehensible paradoxes or apparently unresolvable antinomies from which it seems unable to escape. That which has so often been claimed to be realistic is in fact a closed abstract system of idealism. In theoretical terms, it is incapable of meeting its own epistemological criteria. Moreover, it is incapable of even recognizing the sources of its own inability to do so; it is incapable of self-reflection upon its own confusion. Also see Michael C. Williams, "Neo-Realism and the Future of Strategy," *Review of International Studies*, 12:4. Spring 1988, 5–27, where the author demonstrates that despite their respective empirical aspirations, the minimalist position relies upon a tacit interpretive and subjectivist explanatory commitment, while the maximalist position masks its own appeal to culture. For a critique of the values inherent in deterrence thinking which impel it internally toward expansion, see Robert W. Malcolmson, *Beyond Nuclear Thinking* (Montreal and Kingston: McGill-Queen's University Press, 1990).

4 Millennial liberalism and dual militarization

1 Michael Doyle, "Kant, Liberal Legacies, and Foreign Affairs," Parts 1 and 2, *Philosophy and Public Affairs*, 12:3, Summer 1983, 205–35, and 12:4, Fall 1983, 323–53; Michael Doyle, "Liberalism and World Politics," *American Political Science Review*, 80:4, December 1986, 1151–69; and Francis Fukuyama, "Democratization and International Security," in *New Dimensions in International Security Part II*, Adelphi Papers 266 (London: International Institute for Strategic Studies, 1992), 14–24.

2 The theme of "millennial liberalism" is drawn from Bradley S. Klein and Frank Unger, "Die politik der USA gegenüber Militärdiktaturen in der 'Dritten Welt'," in Reiner Steinweg, ed., *Militärregime und Entwicklungspolitik* (Frankfurt: Suhrkamp, 1989), 392–421.

3 Adam Smith, *The Wealth of Nations* (New York: Random House, 1937), Bk. V, ch. 1, pt. 1, 653.

4 Ibid., Bk. IV, ch. 4, 431.

5 Seymour Martin Lipset, *The First New Nation* (New York: W.W. Norton, 1979), draws upon a liberal, consensualist view to explain the domestic politics of American exceptionalism. His institutionalist perspective complements Louis Hartz, *The Liberal Tradition in America* (New York: Harcourt, Brace, 1955), whose focus is on the pervasive liberal theories of the early American republic. That the school of American exceptionalism need not lead to similarly liberal interpretations of American diplomatic culture can be gleaned through comparing the conservatism of Felix Gilbert, *To the Farewell Address: Ideas of Early American Foreign Policy* (Princeton: Princeton University Press, 1961) with the radical critique of "Open Door" liberal imperialism presented by William Appelman Williams, *The Tragedy of American Diplomacy* (New York: Dell, 1962); and *Empire as a Way of Life* (New York: Oxford University Press, 1980).

6 "Washington's Final Manuscript of the Farewell Address," in Gilbert, *To the Farewell Address*, 145.

7 John Jay, "Federalist No. 4," in Alexander Hamilton, James Madison and John Jay, *The Federalist Papers* (New York: New American Library, 1961), 46.

8 Alexander Hamilton, "Federalist No. 6," in *The Federalist Papers*, 57.

9 Alexander Hamilton, "Federalist No. 11," in *The Federalist Papers*, 89.

10 Mahan, quoted in an essay that memorializes his thought and its influence upon US policy, Margaret Tuttle Sprout, "Mahan: Evangelist of Sea Power," in Edward Mead Earle, ed., *Makers of Modern Strategy: From Machiavelli to Hitler* (Princeton: Princeton University Press, 1944), 434. The argument is replayed, almost in the same words, in the mid-1950s critiques of Dulles' strategy of massive retaliation. A useful counterweight to Sprout's hagiographic essay is Philip A. Crowl, "Alfred Thayer Mahan: The Naval Historian," in Peter Paret, ed., *Makers of Modern Strategy: From Machiavelli to the Nuclear Age* (Princeton: Princeton University Press, 1986), 444–77. The difference in subtitles of these two essays reflects their marked variance in disposition toward Mahan. Crowl argues that Mahan's military historiography greatly overrates the naval factor in military affairs. Moreover, Mahan focused on direct combat at open sea and neglected the deployment of marines, overlooked artillery bombardment of enemy coastal forts, and was silent on the question of combined arms operations. Writes Crowl (p. 461): "Power-projection from the sea, a naval mission of growing significance in the twentieth century, was thus most disregarded by Mahan."

11 Capt. Alfred Thayer Mahan, *The Influence of Sea Power Upon History, 1660–1783* (Boston: Little, Brown, and Co., 1895), 87.

12 Ibid., 11.

13 Mahan's implicit critique of the idea of decisive naval engagements and his shift toward a more general history of sea power as part of world history is paralleled three quarters of a century later by John Keegan, *The Face of Battle* (New York: Viking Press, 1975), who explicitly repudiates the idea of "decisive battles" and conventional battlefield military narrative for an

account more rooted in attention to the actual physical, psychological and organizational conditions under which men fight – and flee – in fear. Keegan, however, avoids the nationalistically oriented, mercantilist model adopted by Mahan and focuses instead on the experience of battle. Whereas Mahan valorizes competition among states, Keegan highlights human adaptiveness to – and avoidance of – organized armed conflict.

14 Mahan, *The Influence of Sea Power Upon History, 1660–1783*, v–vi.

15 Mahan, quoted in Crowl, "Alfred Thayer Mahan: The Naval Historian," 451.

16 Mahan, *The Influence of Sea Power Upon History, 1660–1783*, 71.

17 Max Weber, "Der Nationalstaat und die Volkswirthschaft (1895)," in *Gesammelte politische Schriften*, 4th edn (Tubingen: J.C.B. Mohr, 1980), 1–25. Also see Robert W. Cox, "Social Forces, States and World Orders: Beyond International Relations Theory," *Millennium*, 10:2, Summer 1981, 126–155; and Wolfgang J. Mommsen, *Max Weber und die deutsche Politik, 1890–1920*, 2nd edn (Tubingen: J.C.B. Mohr, 1974), 73–96.

18 Mahan, *The Influence of Sea Power Upon History, 1660–1783*, 25–89.

19 Capt. Alfred Thayer Mahan, *Retrospect and Prospect: Studies in International Relations, Naval and Political* (Boston: Little, Brown, and Co., 1902), 139–40.

20 Capt. Alfred Thayer Mahan, *The Interests of America in Sea Power, Present and Future* (Boston: Little, Brown, and Co., 1897), 128. On Mahan's appropriation of Jomini's earlier arguments for land warfare, see Crowl, "Alfred Thayer Mahan: The Naval Historian," 455–7. The arguments which Mahan adapts are to be found in Baron Antoine Henri Jomini, *The Art of War*, trans. Capt. G.H. Mendell and Lieut. W.P. Craighill (Philadelphia: J.B. Lippincott and Co., 1862).

21 Mahan, *The Influence of Sea Power Upon History, 1660–1783*, 83.

22 Woodrow Wilson, "An Address to a Joint Session of Congress, January 8, 1918," in Arthur S. Link, ed., *The Papers of Woodrow Wilson*, vol. 45 (Princeton: Princeton University Press, 1984), 534–39.

23 It was, of course, Machiavelli who first theorized the inherent dilemma of the republic in having to impose itself violently in order to construct social order. For the clearest statement of this dilemma, see Sheldon Wolin, *Politics and Vision* (Boston: Little, Brown and Co., 1960), 195–238. Machiavelli's relevance to world politics has been subordinated because of the tendency to misread his works as solely the affirmation of an unbound *Realpolitik*. A useful corrective to this can be found in R.B.J. Walker, "*The Prince* and 'The Pauper': Tradition, Modernity, and Practice in the Theory of International Relations," in James Der Derian and Michael J. Shapiro, eds., *International/Intertextual Relations: Postmodern Readings of World Politics* (Lexington: Lexington Books, 1989), 25–48.

24 Klein and Unger, "Die politik der USA gegenber Militärdiktaturen in der 'Dritten Welt'," 395.

25 V.G. Kiernan, *America: The New Imperialism, From White Settlement to World Hegemony* (London: Zed Press, 1980), makes a powerful argument for the link between US policy toward Native Americans and the country's subsequent emergence as a global hegemon. Kiernan pays close attention to the violent extension of the American frontier. He finds, for instance, that the

cultural denigration of American Indians is replayed in global terms of an anti-Communist "Red Scare."

26 *US Congressional Record*, June 23, 1969, 16840–43; and September 10, 1969, 25063. Using different counting rules, and covering a more recent period, Barry M. Blechman and Stephen S. Kaplan, *Force Without War* (Washington, DC: The Brookings Institution, 1978), 547–53, list 215 incidents between January 1, 1946 and December 31, 1975 when the United States used armed forces as a political instrument.

27 The figure one half million is indicated by Ruth Leger Sivard, *World Military and Social Expenditures, 1991* (Washington, DC: World Priorities, 1991), 24. Harold Crouch, *The Army and Politics in Indonesia* (Ithaca: Cornell University Press, 1978), 155, reports that in the immediate aftermath of the failed coup and ensuing massacre, a government fact-finding commission estimated 78,000 dead, while an army-sponsored survey conducted by students from Bandung and Jakarta arrived at a figure of one million. "Although there is no way of knowing, the most commonly accepted estimate was between 250,000 and 500,000."

28 Istvan Kende, "Twenty-Five Years of Local Wars," *Journal of Peace Research*, 8:1, 1971, 3–22.

29 Andrew Shonfield, *Modern Capitalism: The Changing Balance of Public and Private Power* (New York: Oxford University Press, 1969). Karl Polyani's discovery, that historically speaking, the market system was planned, revealed an inherent tension in liberalism, between its self-proclaimed ideology and its requirements as a social practice. See Karl Polyani, *The Great Transformation* (Boston: Beacon Press, 1957). As E.H. Carr reminds students of world politics in *The Twenty Years' Crisis, 1919–1939*, 2nd edn (New York: Macmillan, 1946), liberal universalism always hides behind the mask of free markets in an attempt to obscure its own generative structure of power. A sociology of knowledge analysis is needed to reveal this lost moment within liberal political economy.

30 David Harvey, *The Condition of Postmodernity* (Oxford: Basil Blackwell, 1990), 68.

31 George F. Kennan, "PPS 23 – Review of Current Trends: US Foreign Policy, February 24, 1948," in Thomas W. Etzold and John Lewis Gaddis, eds., *Containment: Documents on American Policy and Strategy, 1945–1950* (New York: Columbia University Press, 1978), 100.

32 George F. Kennan, "Moscow Embassy Telegram #511: 'The Long Telegram,' February 22, 1946," in Etzold and Gaddis, eds., *Containment*, 63.

33 W.W. Rostow, *The Stages of Economic Growth: A Non-Communist Manifesto* (Cambridge: Cambridge University Press, 1960), 162; and W.W. Rostow, "Guerrilla Warfare in the Underdeveloped Areas," *U.S. Department of State Bulletin*, August 7, 1961, 235.

34 John Ellis, *The Social History of the Machine Gun* (New York: Pantheon, 1973). This paragraph draws together themes from a variety of sources. On the relationship between modernization and urban architecture, see Marshall Berman, *All That Is Solid Melts Into Air: The Experience of Modernity* (New York: Simon and Schuster, 1982); Harvey, *The Condition of Postmodernity*, 3–118; Tony Hiss, *The Experience of Place* (New York: Knopf, 1990); Jane

Jacobs, *The Death and Life of Great American Cities* (New York: Random House, 1961); Michael Sorkin, ed., *Variations on a Theme Park: The New American City and the End of Public Space* (New York: The Noonday Press, 1992); Paul Virilio, *Speed and Politics: An Essay on Dromology*, trans. Mark Polizzotti (New York: Semiotext(e), 1986); and Paul Virilio and Sylvere Lotringer, *Pure War*, trans. Mark Polizzotti (New York: Semiotext(e), 1983); Berman details the significance of Haussmann. Note, however, the comment made by David Harvey, *The Condition of Postmodernity*, 39, that "[w]ith respect to architecture, for example, C. Jencks dates the symbolic end of modernism and the passage to postmodernism as 3.32 p.m. on 15 July 1972, when the Pruitt-Igoe housing development in St. Louis (a prize-winning version of LeCorbusier's 'machine for modern living') was dynamited as an uninhabitable environment for the low-income people it housed."

35 Rostow, *Stages of Economic Growth*, 4.

36 Ibid., 6.

37 Daniel Bell, *The End of Ideology* (Glencoe: Free Press, 1960); Robert E. Lane, "The Politics of Consensus in an Age of Affluence," *American Political Science Review*, 49:4, December 1965, 874–95; James P. Young, ed., *Consensus and Conflict: Readings in American Politics* (New York: Dodd, Mead and Co., 1972).

38 Michael Howard, "Weapons and Peace," in *The Causes of Wars and Other Essays*, 2nd edn (Cambridge: Harvard University Press, 1984), 268, 271.

39 The most relentless critique of Rostow's assumptions argues that economic growth in the overdeveloped West could only have taken place because of the net outflow of fossil fuels from the underdeveloped Third World. See Malcolm Caldwell, *The Wealth of Some Nations* (London: Zed Press, 1977).

40 Samuel P. Huntington, *Political Order in Changing Societies* (New Haven, Yale University Press, 1968).

41 Richard J. Barnet, *Intervention and Revolution: The United States in the Third World* (Cleveland: World Publishing, 1968); Noam Chomsky and Edward S. Herman, *The Washington Connection and Third World Fascism* (Boston: South End Press, 1979); Michael T. Klare, *American Arms Supermarket* (Austin: University of Texas Press, 1984); Michael T. Klare and Peter Kornbluh, eds., *Low-Intensity Warfare* (New York: Pantheon, 1988); Miles Wolpin, *Military Aid and Counterrevolution in the Third World* (Lexington: D.C. Heath, 1973). For an interesting counterpoint to these overwhelmingly critical works, see the only slightly tongue-in-cheek entitled policy study by Daniel Pipes and Adam Garfinkle, eds., *Friendly Tyrants: An American Dilemma* (New York: St. Martin's Press, 1991).

42 Testimony of Secretary of Defense Clark M. Clifford, *Foreign Assistance Act of 1968, Part 2: Hearings Before the Committee on Foreign Relations*, US Senate, 90th Congress, 2nd Session, March and May 1968, 434.

43 See two essays by Timothy W. Luke: "'What's Wrong with Deterrence?': A Semiotic Interpretation of National Security Policy," in Der Derian and Shapiro, *International/Intertextual Relations*, 207–30; and "The Discipline of Security Studies and the Codes of Containment: Learning from Kuwait," *Alternatives*, 16:3, Summer 1991, 315–44.

44 Mary Kaldor, *The Baroque Arsenal* (New York: Hill and Wang, 1981); Robin Luckham, "Armament Culture," *Alternatives*, 10:1, Winter 1984, 1–44.
45 Richard M. Nixon, *United States Foreign Policy for the 1970's: A New Strategy for Peace. A Report by the President of the United States to the Congress, February 18, 1970* (Washington, DC: United States Information Service, 1970), 1. This document represents the first of many subsequent obituaries commemorating the Cold War.
46 Ibid., 5.
47 Ibid., 96.
48 *Changing Perspectives on US Arms. Transfer Policy: Report Prepared for the Subcommittee on International Security and Scientific Affairs of the Committee on Foreign Affairs, US House of Representatives, by the Congressional Research Service, Library of Congress,* 97th Congress, 1st Session, September 25, 1981 (Washington, DC: US Government Printing Office, 1981), 71.
49 *Foreign Military Sales, Foreign Military Construction Sales and Military Assistance Facts, as of September 30, 1985* (Washington, DC: Defense Security Assistance Agency, 1986), 10–11, 51–2.
50 Statement of Hon. Lucy Wilson Benson, Under Secretary for Security Assistance, Science and Technology, *Fiscal Year 1980 International Security Assistance Authorization, Hearings before the Committee on Foreign Relations,* 96th Congress, 1st Session, February 28, 1979, 12–13.

5 Deterrence as a social practice

1 James Schlesinger, "Reykjavik and Revelations: A Turn of the Tide?" *Foreign Affairs*, 65:3, 1987, 430.
2 Charles Baudelaire, "The Painter of Modern Life" (1863), in *The Painter of Modern Life and Other Essays*, ed. and trans. Jonathan Payne (London: Phaidon Press, 1964), 13.
3 Karl Marx and Friedrich Engels, "Manifesto of the Communist Party," in *The Marx-Engels Reader*, 2nd edn, ed. Robert C. Tucker (New York: W.W. Norton, 1978), 476. Marshall Berman, *All That Is Solid Melts Into Air: The Experience of Modernity* (New York: Simon and Schuster, 1982) shows how transformations in urban architecture embody changing attitudes toward the modern and post-modern.
4 Paul Bracken, *The Command and Control of Nuclear Forces* (New Haven: Yale University Press, 1983), 116; Catherine M. Kelleher, *Germany and the Politics of Nuclear Weapons* (New York: Columbia University Press, 1975); and Rudolf Steinke, "Introduction," in R. Steinke and M. Vale, eds., *Germany Debates Defense: The NATO Alliance at the Crossroads* (Armonk: M.E. Sharpe, 1983), ix–xxxii.
5 See Adm. Hyman R. Rickover, "Economics of Defense Policy," *Hearings Before the Joint Economic Committee of the United States*, 97th Congress, 2nd Session, January 28, 1982, 61–2. Also see Dwight Eisenhower, "President Eisenhower's Farewell to the Nation," *Department of State Bulletin*, February 6, 1961, 179–82; Daniel Ellsberg, "A Call to Mutiny," in E.P. Thompson and D. Smith, eds., *Protest and Survive* (New York: Monthly Review Press, 1981), i–xxviii; H.T. Nash, "The Bureaucratization of Homicide," in Thompson

and Smith (eds.), *Protest and Survive*, 149–65; Roger Molander, "How I Learned to Start Worrying and Hate the Bomb," *The Washington Post*, March 21, 1982; Robert McNamara, *Blundering into Disaster* (New York: Pantheon, 1985); Herbert Mitgang, "Profiles (Gene Robert La Rocque)," *The New Yorker*, October 6, 1986, 88–103; and McGeorge Bundy, *Danger and Survival: Choices About the Bomb in the First Fifty Years* (New York: Vintage Books, 1988).

6 Henry Kissinger, *Years of Upheaval* (Boston: Little, Brown and Co., 1982), 1,175.

7 Recently released transcripts of debates conducted by policy-makers during the Cuban Missile Crisis reveal the extent of uncertainty and anxiety they experienced, as well as the importance of conventional rather than nuclear forces in resolving the problem. See Marc Trachtenberg, "The Influence of Nuclear Weapons on the Cuban Missile Crisis," *International Security*, 10:1, Summer 1985, 137–63; "White House Tapes and Minutes of the Cuban Missile Crisis: ExCom Meetings October 1962," *International Security*, 10:1, Summer, 164–203; David A. Welch and James G. Blight, "The Eleventh Hour of the Cuban Missile Crisis: An Introduction to the ExComm Transcripts," *International Security*, 12:3, Winter 1987/8, 5–29; "October 27, 1962: Transcripts of the Meetings of the ExComm," *International Security*, 12:3, Winter 1987/88, 30–92; James G. Blight and David A. Welch, *On the Brink: Americans and Soviets Reexamine the Cuban Missile Crisis*, 2nd edn (New York: The Noonday Press, 1990).

8 Maj. Alexander P. de Seversky, *Victory through Air Power* (New York: Simon and Schuster, 1942), 352.

9 Ibid., 7.

10 Michael MccGwire, "Deterrence: The Problem – Not the Solution," *International Affairs*, 62:1, Winter 1985/6, 55–6.

11 William L. Borden, *There Will Be No Time: The Revolution in Strategy* (New York, Macmillan, 1946), 163.

12 Mary Kaldor, *The Imaginary War* (Oxford: Basil Blackwell, 1990); Robert Jervis, *The Meaning of the Nuclear Revolution* (Ithaca: Cornell University Press, 1989), esp. ch. 6, "The Symbolic Nature of Nuclear Politics," 176–225, comes amazingly close to a semiotic exchange relation theory of nuclear discourse. For a theoretically elaborated account of deterrence from such a perspective, see Timothy W. Luke, "'What's Wrong with Deterrence?': A Semiotic Interpretation of National Security Policy," in James Der Derian and Michael J. Shapiro, eds., *International/Intertextual Relations* (Lexington: Lexington Books, 1989), 207–29.

13 Stanley Hoffman, "An American Social Science: International Relations," *Daedalus*, 106:3, Summer 1977, 41–60; Fred Kaplan, *The Wizards of Armageddon* (New York: Simon & Schuster, 1983); Bradley S. Klein, "Hegemony and Strategic Culture: American Power Projection and Alliance Defence Politics," *Review of International Studies*, 14:2, Spring 1988, 133–48. The following three paragraphs are drawn from my essay, *Strategic Discourse and Its Alternatives*, Occasional Paper #3 (New York: John Jay College of Criminal Justice, Center on Violence and Human Survival, 1987), 7–8.

14 Kaplan, *The Wizards of Armageddon*, 52–57, 86–91. For a detailed account of

the shift from operations research to systems analysis, see I.B. Holly, Jr., "The Evolution of Operations Research and Its Impact on the Military Establishment: the Air Force Experience," in Lt. Col. Monte D. Wright and Lawrence J. Paszek, eds., *Science, Technology, and Warfare* (Washington, DC: Office of Air Force History, 1971), 89–109.

15 Albert Wohlstetter, "The Delicate Balance of Terror," *Foreign Affairs*, 37:2, January 1959, 211–34, makes no mention of what the USSR might be interested in achieving through a first-strike.

16 Lawrence Freedman, *US Intelligence and the Soviet Strategic Threat*, 2nd edn (Princeton: Princeton University Press, 1986), 66–7; Kaplan, *The Wizards of Armageddon*, 155–61.

17 "NSC 68: United States Objectives and Programs for National Security, April 14, 1950," in Thomas H. Etzold and John Lewis Gaddis, eds., *Containment: Documents on American Policy and Strategy 1945–1950* (New York: Columbia University Press, 1978), 386.

18 Ibid., 387.

19 Ibid., 391.

20 Ibid., 404.

21 Kennan's criticisms of NSC-68 are fleetingly referred to in Thomas H. Etzold and John Lewis Gaddis, "NSC-68: The Strategic Reassessment of 1950," in Etzold and Gaddis, eds., *Containment*, 384. Neither Kennan's memoirs nor his essays at the time written about US-Soviet relations even refer to the document. See George F. Kennan, *Memoirs, 1925–1950* (Boston: Atlantic-Little, Brown, 1967); *Memoirs, 1950–1963* (Boston: Atlantic-Little, Brown, 1972); *The Nuclear Delusion: Soviet-American Relations in the Atomic Age* (New York: Pantheon Books, 1983). Nor does the most detailed account of Kennan's writings of the time, Anders Stephanson, *Kennan and the Art of Foreign Policy* (Cambridge: Harvard University Press, 1989).

22 "NSC-68," 398.

23 Ibid., 400.

24 Ibid., 399.

25 Ibid., 400.

26 The most perceptive account of how the model of totalitarianism provides the interpretive code for Cold War strategy can be found in Herbert J. Spiro and Benjamin R. Barber, "Counter-Ideological Uses of 'Totalitarianism'," *Politics and Society*, 1:1, Fall 1970, 3–21.

27 David Campbell, "Global Inscription: How Foreign Policy Constitutes the United States," *Alternatives*, 15:3, Summer 1990, 263–86; David Campbell, *Writing Security* (Minneapolis: University of Minnesota Press, 1992); Kaplan, *The Wizards of Armageddon*; Charles E. Nathanson, "The Social Construction of the Soviet Threat: A Study in the Politics of Representation," *Alternatives*, 13:4, October 1988, 443–83; and Jerry Sanders, *Peddlers of Crisis* (Boston: South End Press, 1983).

28 David C. Skaggs, "Between the Hawks and the Doves: Alistair Buchan and the Institute for Strategic Studies," *Conflict* 7:1, 1987, 79–102; and Michael Howard, "IISS-The First Thirty Years: A General Overview,' in *The Changing Strategic Landscape, Part I*, Adelphi Papers 235 (London: International Institute for Strategic Studies, 1989), 10–19.

29 William Kaufmann, ed., *Military Policy and National Security* (Princeton: Princeton University Press, 1956); Paul Nitze, "Atoms, Strategy and Policy," *Foreign Affairs*, 34:2, January 1956, 187–98; Henry A. Kissinger, *Nuclear Weapons and Foreign Policy* (New York: Harper and Brothers, 1957); and Maxwell Taylor, *The Uncertain Trumpet* (New York: Harper and Row, 1960).

30 Raymond Aron, *The Great Debate: Theories of Nuclear Strategy*, trans. Ernest Pawel (New York: Doubleday, 1965); Lawrence Freedman, *The Evolution of Nuclear Strategy*, 2nd edn (New York: St. Martin's Press, 1989), 313–24; and Diana Johnstone, *The Politics of Euromissiles: Europe's Role in America's World* (London: Verso, 1984), 84–135;

31 John Lewis Gaddis, *The United States and the Origins of the Cold War, 1941–1947* (New York: Columbia University Press, 1972); and *Strategies of Containment* (New York, Oxford University Press, 1982).

32 Leon Sigal, *Nuclear Forces in Europe* (Washington, DC: Brookings Institution, 1984), 164.

33 Robert S. McNamara, "Defense Arrangements of the North Atlantic Community," *US Department of State Bulletin*, July 9, 1962, 64–9; and David N. Schwartz, *NATO's Nuclear Dilemmas* (Washington, DC: Brookings Institution, 1983).

34 *NATO: BASIC DOCUMENTS* (Brussels: NATO Information Service, 1981), 98–100; and Desmond Ball, "U.S. Strategic Forces: How Would They Be Used?," *International Security*, 7:3, Winter 1982/3), 31–60.

35 The Commission on Integrated Long-Term Strategy, *Discriminate Deterrence* (Washington, DC: US Government Printing Office, 1988), 27.

36 Bradley S. Klein, "Beyond the Western Alliance: The Politics of Post-Atlanticism," in Stephen Gill, ed., *Atlantic Relations: Beyond the Reagan Era* (Brighton: Harvester Wheatsheaf, 1989), 196–211.

37 William K. Domke, Richard C. Eichenberg and Catherine M. Kelleher, "Consensus Lost?: Domestic Politics and the 'Crisis' in NATO," *World Politics*, 39:3, April 1987, 382–407; Richard Eichenberg, *Public Opinion and National Security in Western Europe* (Ithaca: Cornell University Press, 1989); G. Flynn and H. Rattinger, eds., *The Public and Atlantic Defense* (Totowa, NJ: Rowman and Allanheld, 1985); and Thomas Rochon, *Mobilizing for Peace: The Antinuclear Movements in Western Europe* (Princeton: Princeton University Press, 1988).

6 The West of all possible worlds?

1 Barbara Einhorn, "'New Enemy Images for Old': The 'Boys' Debate' Around Timothy Garton Ash's *We The People*," in Mary Kaldor, ed., *Europe From Below: An East-West Dialogue* (London and New York: Verso, 1991), 130.

2 Robin Wright and Doyle McManus, *Flashpoints: Promise and Peril in a New World* (New York: Alfred A. Knopf, 1991), 5.

3 Ibid., 6.

4 The rest of this paragraph draws heavily from Bradley S. Klein, "After Strategy: The Search for a Post-Modern Politics of Peace," *Alternatives*, 13:3, July 1988, 296.

NOTES TO PAGES 125–130

5 John Lewis Gaddis, "The Strategy of Containment," in Thomas H. Etzold and John L. Gaddis, eds., *Containment: Documents on American Policy and Strategy, 1945–1950* (New York: Columbia University Press, 1978), 25–37.

6 R. Luckham, "Security and Disarmament in Africa," *Alternatives*, 9:2, April 1983, 203–228.

7 Charles Krauthammer, "Universal Dominion: Toward a Unipolar World," *National Interest*, 18, Winter 1989–90, 49, writes with the candor befitting a syndicated columnist: "I suggest we go all the way and stop at nothing short of world dominion." Also see Charles Krauthammer, "The Unipolar Moment," *Foreign Affairs*, 70:1, 1991, 23–33. Col. Harry G. Summers, Jr. (ret.), *On Strategy II: A Critical Analysis of the Gulf War* (New York: Dell, 1992), 180–214, concludes that the US in now freed to assume unilateral responsibility on a world scale. For similarly triumphant accounts that are measurably less sanguine when it comes to conclusions about American capabilities and missions, see John Lewis Gaddis, "Coping with Victory," *Atlantic Monthly*, 264, October 1989, 49–60; and "Toward the Post-Cold War World," *Foreign Affairs*, 70:2, Spring 1991, 102–22.

8 Anders Stephanson, *Kennan and the Art of Foreign Policy* (Cambridge: Harvard University Press, 1989).

9 Fred Halliday, "The Cold War as Inter-Systemic Conflict – Initial Theses," in Mike Bowker and Robin Brown, eds., *From Cold War to Collapse: Theory and World Politics in the 1980s* (Cambridge: Cambridge University Press, 1993), 21–34; "The Ends of Cold War," *New Left Review*, 180, March–April 1990, 5–23; and *The Making of the Second Cold War*, rev. edn (London, Verso, 1986). Mary Kaldor, *The Imaginary War: Understanding the East–West Conflict* (Oxford: Basil Blackwell, 1990), argues that the Cold War was characterized not by systemic conflict but by the systemic complementarity of Atlanticism and Post-Stalinism in which simulated rivalry – the imaginary war – was mutually functional for social integration.

10 I take up here indirectly the argument about "epistemic realism" made by David Campbell, *Writing Security: United States Foreign Policy and the Politics of Identity* (Minneapolis: University of Minnesota Press, 1992), 21–23. He explores how, despite their partisan differences, orthodox, revisionist, and critical accounts of the Cold War and its demise share this common logic of empiricist explanation by which the material world exhausts the bounds of the describable. What is needed, in effect, is a politics of identity regarding the interpretive codes by which meaning is produced and distributed as a political resource.

11 David Albright and Mark Hibbs, "Iraq and the Bomb: Were They Even Close?," *Bulletin of the Atomic Scientists*, 47:3, April 1991, 16–25, refute claims that Iraq was closing in on development of a workable nuclear weapon.

12 C. Wright Mills, *The Causes of World War Three* (New York: Simon and Schuster, 1958).

13 Dieter Senghaas, *Abschreckung und Frieden: Studien zur Kritik organisierte Friedlösigkeit*, 3rd edn (Frankfurt: Europäische Verlagsanstalt, 1981). The first edition was 1969.

14 E.P. Thompson, "Notes on Exterminism, the Last Stage of Civilization," in E.P. Thompson et al. *Exterminism and Cold War* (London: Verso, 1982), 1–33.

15 Rudolf Bahro, "A New Approach for the Peace Movement in Germany," in Thompson et al. *Exterminism and Cold War*, 98–106.

16 I owe the phrase "Gorbachev as a critical strategic theorist" to Alex Wendt.

17 David Holloway, "State, Society and the Military Under Gorbachev," *International Security*, 14:3, 1989/90, 5–24; Michael MccGwire, *Perestroika and Soviet National Security* (Washington, DC: The Brookings Institution, 1991); and Stephen Meyer, "The Sources and Prospects of Gorbachev's New Political Thinking on Security," *International Security*, 13:2, Fall 1988, 124–63. Mike Bowker, "Explaining Soviet Foreign Policy in the 1980s," in Bowker and Brown, eds., *From Cold War to Collapse*, 82–114, attributes Gorbachev's dramatic across the board reforms in foreign and military policy to domestic pressure from Soviet elites rather than to measures undertaken externally by the West.

18 Pertti Joenniemi, "The Social Constitution of Gorbachev: From an Intruder to a Communal Figure?" Paper prepared for the Annual Meeting of the International Studies Association. London, 1989; *Changes in the European Security Environment: Hearings Before the Committee on Armed Services*, US Senate, 102nd Congress, 1st Session, February 26–7, March 7, 1991.

19 For the basic elements of alternative defense, see Alternative Defence Commission, *Defence Without the Bomb* (New York: Taylor and Francis, 1983); Anders Boserup and Robert Neild, eds., *The Foundations of Defensive Defence* (London: Macmillan, 1990); Gene Sharp, *Making Europe Unconquerable* (Cambridge: Ballinger, 1985); "A New European Defense," special issue of *Bulletin of the Atomic Scientists*, 44:7, September 1988; and Carl Friedrich von Weizscker, ed. *Die Praxis der defensiven Verteidigung* (Hameln: Sponholtz, 1984).

20 Tair Tairov, "From New Thinking to a Civic Peace," in Mary Kaldor, ed., *Europe from Below: An East-West Dialogue* (London: Verso, 1991), 43–8.

21 Zbigniew Brzezinski, "Post-Communist Nationalism," *Foreign Affairs*, 68:5, Winter 1989/90, 1–25; and Jerry Hough, "Gorbachev's Politics," *Foreign Affairs*, 68:5, Winter 1989/90, 26–41.

22 Dorothy Nelkin and Michael Pollak, *The Atom Besieged: Antinuclear Politics in France and Germany* (Cambridge: MIT Press, 1981).

23 Barry Buzan, *People, States and Fear: An Agenda for International Security Studies in the Post-Cold War Era*, 2nd edn (Boulder, Co.: Lynne Rienner, 1991), cautiously raises a number of crucial issues regarding the issue of "whose" security and "what units of analysis" are appropriate to various spheres of security. But no sooner did Buzan open up these questions than he encased his answers within a "levels-of-analysis" framework reminiscent of Kenneth Waltz and J. David Singer. Far more illuminating of the webs and networks of security and modern life in which "man" is placed as the object of International Relations discourse are two essays by G.M. Dillon, "The Alliance of Security and Subjectivity," *Current Research on Peace and Violence*, 13:3, 1990–91, 101–24; and "Modernity, Discourse and Deterrence," *Current Research on Peace and Violence*, 12:2, 1989, 90–103. These debates, concerned to repoliticize strategic relations, parallel developments in political and social theory. See William E. Connolly, *Identity/Difference: Democratic Negotiations of Political Paradox* (Ithaca: Cornell University Press,

1991); Warren Magnusson and R.B.J. Walker, "De-Centring the State: Political Theory and Canadian Political Economy," *Studies in Political Economy*, 26, Summer 1988, 37–71; Edward W. Soja, *Postmodern Geographies: The Reassertion of Space in Critical Social Theory* (London: Verso, 1989); R.B.J. Walker, *One World/Many Worlds: Struggles for a Just World Peace* (Boulder, Co.: Lynne Rienner, 1988); and R.B.J. Walker, *Inside/Outside: International Relations as Political Theory* (Cambridge: Cambridge University Press, 1993).

24 Paul Kennedy, "A Declining Empire Goes to War," *The Wall Street Journal*, January 24, 1991, A-10. Also see Paul Kennedy, *The Rise and Fall of the Great Powers* (New York: Random House, 1987); and Joseph S. Nye, Jr., *Bound to Lead: The Changing Nature of American Power* (New York: Basic Books, 1991).

25 Joseph S. Nye, Jr., "Against 'Declinism'," *The New Republic*, October 15, 1990, 12–13; and Anthony H. Cordesman, "America's New Combat Culture," *New York Times*, February 28, 1991, A10.

26 "On Top of the World," *Economist*, March 9, 1991, 15.

27 "Excerpts From Pentagon's Plan: "Prevent the Re-Emergence of a New Rival'," *New York Times*, March 8, 1992, 14.

28 "Pentagon Drops Goal of Blocking New Superpowers," *New York Times*, May 24, 1992, A1.

29 "Cuts Force Review of War Strategies," *New York Times*, 30 May 1993, 16.

30 V. Spike Peterson, ed., *Gendered States* (Boulder, Co.: Lynne Rienner, 1992); Vandana Shiva, *Staying Alive: Women, Ecology and Development* (London: Zed Press, 1988); and J. Ann Tickner, *Gender in International Relations: Feminist Perspectives on Achieving Global Security* (New York: Columbia University Press, 1992). It is particularly striking how none of the standard "after the Cold War" volumes deals in the least with issues of gender. See, for instance, Hogan, ed., *The End of the Cold War*; Charles W. Kegley, Jr. and Eugene R. Wittkopf, eds., *The Future of American Foreign Policy* (New York: St. Martin's Press, 1992); Michael T. Klare and Daniel C. Thomas, eds., *World Security: Trends and Challenges at Century's End* (New York: St. Martin's Press, 1991); and Sean M. Lynn-Jones, ed., *The Cold War and After: Prospects for Peace* (Cambridge: MIT Press, 1991). While cognizant of this gap, Marysia Zalewski, "Feminist Theory and International Relations," in Bowker and Brown, eds. *From Cold War to Collapse*, 115–44, engages in a theoretical survey of recent feminist perspectives without attempting a specific critique of their implications for debates about the end of the Cold War. One significant domain of post-Cold War policies receiving public attention is the proliferation of prostitution in the former East bloc Communist countries. See "Sex for Sale" (cover story), *Time*, June 21, 1993, 45–55.

31 Jacques Attali, *Millennium: Winners and Losers in the Coming World Order*, trans. Leila Conners and Nathan Gardels (New York: Random House, 1991).

32 William E. Connolly, *Political Theory and Modernity* (Oxford: Basil Blackwell, 1988); and R.B.J. Walker, "*The Prince* and 'The Pauper': Tradition, Modernity and Practice in the Theory of International Relations," in James Der Derian and Michael J. Shapiro, eds., *Intertextual/International Relations* (Lexington: Lexington Books, 1989), 25–48.

33 Charles L. Glaser, "Nuclear Policy Without an Adversary," *International Security*, 16:4, Spring 1992, 34–78.
34 Jessica Tuchman Mathews, "The Environment and International Security," in Klare and Thomas, eds., *World Security*, 362–80; Jessica Tuchman Mathews, "Preserving the Global Environment: Implications for US Policy," in Kegley and Wittkopf, eds., *The Future of American Foreign Policy*, 85–94; Norman Myers, "Environment and Security," *Foreign Policy*, 74, Spring 1989, 23–41; Ian Rowlands, "The Security Challenges of Global Environmental Change," *The Washington Quarterly*, 14:1, Winter 1991, 99–114; Theodore C. Sorenson, "Rethinking National Security: Democracy and Economic Independence," *Foreign Affairs*, 69:3, Summer 1990, 1–18; and S. Dalby, "Security, Modernity, Ecology: The Dilemmas of Post-Cold War Security Discourse," *Alternatives*, 17:1, Winter 1992, 95–134.
35 Richard A. Falk, "Theory, Realism, and World Security," in Michael T. Klare and Daniel C. Thomas, eds., *World Security: Trends and Challenges at Century's End* (New York: St. Martin's Press, 1991), 6–24.

BIBLIOGRAPHY

Albright, David and Mark Hibbs. "Iraq and the Bomb: Were They Even Close?," *Bulletin of the Atomic Scientists*, 47:2, March 1991, 16–25.

Alternative Defence Commission. *Defence Without the Bomb*. New York: Taylor and Francis, 1983.

Anderson, Benedict. *Imagined Communities: Reflections on the Origin and Spread of Nationalism*. London, Verso, 1983.

Anderson, Perry. *Lineages of the Absolutist State*. London: New Left Books, 1974. *Passages from Antiquity to Feudalism*. London: New Left Books, 1974.

Aron, Raymond. *Clausewitz: Philosopher of War*. New York: Simon & Schuster, 1986.

The Great Debate: Theories of Nuclear Strategy, trans. E. Pawel. New York: Doubleday, 1965.

Ash, Timothy Garton. *The Magic Lantern: The Revolution of '89 Witnessed in Warsaw, Budapest, Berlin and Prague*. New York, Random House, 1990.

Ashley, Richard K. "The Geopolitics of Geopolitical Space," *Alternatives*, 12:4, October 1987, 403–34.

"Living on Border Lines: Man, Poststructuralism, and War," in James Der Derian and Michael J. Shapiro, eds., *International/Intertextual Relations*. Lexington: Lexington Books, 1989, 259–321.

"The Poverty of Neo-Realism," *International Organization*, 38:2, Spring 1984, 225–86.

"Untying the Sovereign State: A Double Reading of the Anarchy Problematique," *Millennium*, 17:2, Summer 1988, 227–62.

Ashley, Richard K. and R.B.J. Walker. "Reading Dissidence/Writing the Discipline: Crisis and the Question of Sovereignty in International Studies," *International Studies Quarterly*, 34:3, September 1990, 367–416.

"Speaking the Language of Exile: Dissident Thought in International Studies," *International Studies Quarterly*, 34:3, September 1990, 259–68.

Attali, Jacques. *Millennium: Winners and Losers in the Coming World Order*, trans. Leila Conners and Nathan Gardels. New York, Random House, 1991.

Augelli, Enrico and Craig Murphy. *America's Quest for Supremacy and the Third World: A Gramscian Analysis*. London: Francis Pinter, 1988.

Bahro, Rudolf. "A New Approach for the Peace Movement in Germany," in E.P. Thompson, et al., *Exterminism and Cold War*. London: Verso, 1982, 98–106.

Ball, Desmond. "Development of the SIOP, 1960–1983," in Desmond Ball and

Jeffrey Richelson, eds., *Strategic Nuclear Targeting.* Ithaca: Cornell University Press, 1986.

"U.S. Strategic Forces: How Would They be Used?," *International Security,* 7:3, Winter 1982/83, 31–59.

Ball, Nicole. *Security and Economy in the Third World.* Princeton: Princeton University Press, 1988.

Barnet, Richard J. *Intervention and Revolution: The United States in the Third World.* Cleveland: World Publishing, 1968.

Baudelaire, Charles. *The Painter of Modern Life and Other Essays,* ed. and trans. Jonathan Payne. London: Phaidon Press, 1964.

Bell, Daniel. *The End of Ideology.* Glencoe: Free Press, 1960.

Berman, Marshall. *All That Is Solid Melts Into Air: The Experience of Modernity.* New York: Simon & Schuster, 1982.

Bernstein, Richard. *Beyond Objectivism and Relativism.* Philadelphia: University of Pennsylvania Press, 1983

The Restructuring of Social and Political Theory. New York: Harcourt Brace Jovanovich, 1976.

Blechman, Barry M. and Stephen S. Kaplan, *Force Without War: U.S. Armed Forces as a Political Instrument.* Washington, DC: Brookings Institution, 1978.

Blight, James G. and David A. Welch. *On the Brink: Americans and Soviets Reexamine the Cuban Missile Crisis,* 2nd edn. New York: The Noonday Press, 1990.

Bodley, John H. *Victims of Progress,* 3rd edn. Mountain View: Mayfield Publishing, 1990.

Booth, Ken. "Security and Emancipation," *Review of International Studies,* 17:4, October 1991, 313–26.

"Security in Anarchy: Utopian Realism in Theory and Practice," *International Affairs,* 67:3, July 1991, 527–45.

"Strategy," in A.J.R. Groom and M. Light, eds., *International Relations: A Handbook of Current Theory,* 2nd edn. London: Pinter, forthcoming.

Strategy and Ethnocentrism. New York: Holmes and Meier, 1979.

Booth, Ken, ed. *New Thinking About Strategy and International Security.* London: HarperCollins, 1991.

Borden, William L. *There Will Be No Time: The Revolution in Strategy.* New York: Macmillan, 1946.

Boserup, Anders and Robert Neild, eds. *The Foundations of Defensive Defence.* London: Macmillan, 1990.

Bowker, Mike. "Explaining Soviet Foreign Policy in the 1980s," in Mike Bowker and Robin Brown, eds., *From Cold War to Collapse: Theory and World Politics in the 1980s.* Cambridge: Cambridge University Press, 1993, 82–114.

Bracken, Paul. *The Command and Control of Nuclear Forces.* New Haven: Yale University Press, 1983.

Brodie, Bernard, ed. *The Absolute Weapon: Atomic Power and World Order.* New York: Harcourt, Brace and Company, for the Yale Institute of International Studies, 1946.

"The Continuing Relevance of *On War,*" in Carl von Clausewitz, *On War,* ed. and trans. Michael Howard and Peter Paret (Princeton: Princeton University Press, 1976, 45–58.

Strategy in the Missile Age. Princeton: Princeton University Press, 1959.

Brzezinski, Zbigniew. "Post-Communist Nationalism," *Foreign Affairs*, 68:5, Winter 1989/90, 1–25.

Bull, Hedley. *The Anarchical Society*. New York: Columbia University Press, 1977.

"The Grotian Conception of International Society," in Herbert Butterfield and Martin Wight, eds., *Diplomatic Investigations: Essays in the Theory of International Politics*. Cambridge: Harvard University Press, 1966, 51–73.

"International Theory: The Case for a Classical Approach," *World Politics*, 18:3, April 1966, 361–77.

"Strategic Studies and its Critics," *World Politics*, 20:4, July 1968, 593–605.

Bulletin of the Atomic Scientists, special issue on "A New European Defense," 44:7, September 1988.

Bundy, McGeorge. *Danger and Survival: Choices About the Bomb in the First Fifty Years*. New York: Vintage Books, 1988.

Butterfield, Herbert and Martin Wight, eds. *Diplomatic Investigations: Essays in the Theory of International Politics*. Cambridge: Harvard University Press, 1966.

Buzan, Barry. *An Introduction to Strategic Studies: Military Technology and International Relations*. London: Macmillan and the International Institute for Strategic Studies, 1987.

People, States and Fear: An Agenda for International Security Studies in the Post-Cold War Era, 2nd edn. Boulder, Co.: Lynne Rienner, 1991.

Caldwell, Malcolm. *The Wealth of Some Nations*. London: Zed Press, 1977.

Campbell, David, "Global Inscription: How Foreign Policy Constitutes the United States," *Alternatives*, 15:3, Summer 1990, 263–86.

Writing Security: United States Foreign Policy and the Politics of Identity. Minneapolis: University of Minnesota Press, 1992.

Carr, E.H. *The Twenty Years' Crisis, 1919–1939*, 2nd edn. London: Macmillan, 1946.

"Carter Said to Back a Plan for Limiting Any Nuclear War," *New York Times*, August 6, 1980, A1.

Carter, Ashton B. and David N. Schwartz, eds. *Ballistic Missile Defense*. Washington, DC: Brookings Institution, 1984.

Chomsky, Noam and Edward S. Herman, *The Washington Connection and Third World Fascism*. Boston: South End Press, 1979.

Cipolla, Carlo. *Guns, Sails and Empires: Technological Innovation and the Early Phases of European Expansion, 1400–1700*. New York: Minerva Press, 1965.

Clausewitz, Carl von. *The Campaign of 1812 in Russia*. London: John Murray, 1843.

On War, ed. and trans. Michael Howard and Peter Paret. Princeton: Princeton University Press, 1976.

Politische Schriften und Briefe, ed. H. Rothfels. Munich: Drei Masken Verlag, 1922.

Schriften, Aufsätze, Studien, Briefe, ed. W. Hahlweg. Göttingen: Vandenhoeck und Ruprecht, 1966.

Verstreute kleine Schriften, ed. W. Hahlweg. Osnabruck: Biblio Verlag, 1979.

171

War, Politics and Power, ed. Edward M. Collins. Chicago: Henry Regnery and Co., 1962.

Cohn, Carol, "Sex and Death in the Rational World of Defense Intellectuals," *Signs*, 12:4, Summer 1987, 687–718.

Commission on Integrated Long-Term Strategy. *Discriminate Deterrence*. Washington, DC: US Government Printing Office, 1988.

Committee on the Present Danger. *Can America Catch Up?*. Washington, DC: Committee on the Present Danger, 1984.

Connolly, William E. *Appearance and Reality in Politics*. Cambridge: Cambridge University Press, 1981.

Identity/Difference: Democratic Negotiations of Political Paradox. Ithaca: Cornell University Press, 1991.

Political Theory and Modernity. Oxford: Basil Blackwell, 1988.

Politics and Ambiguity. Madison: University of Wisconsin Press, 1987.

The Terms of Political Discourse, 2nd edn. Princeton: Princeton University Press, 1984.

Cordesman, Anthony H. "America's New Combat Culture," *New York Times*, February 28, 1991, A10.

Corvisier, André. *Armies and Societies in Europe, 1494–1789*, trans. Abigail T. Siddall. Bloomington: Indiana University Press, 1979.

Cox, Robert W. "Gramsci, Hegemony and International Relations: An Essay in Method," *Millennium*, 11:2, Summer 1982, 162–75.

"Social Forces, States and World Orders: Beyond International Relations Theory," *Millennium*, 10:2, Summer 1981, 126–55.

Crouch, Harold. *The Army and Politics in Indonesia*. Ithaca: Cornell University Press, 1978.

Crowl, P.A., "Alfred Thayer Mahan: The Naval Historian," in Peter Paret, ed., *Makers of Modern Strategy: From Machiavelli to the Nuclear Age*. Princeton: Princeton University Press, 1986, 444–77.

"Cuts Force Review of War Strategies," *New York Times*, 30 May 1993, 16.

Dalby, Simon. "Geopolitical Discourse: The Soviet Union as Other," *Alternatives*, 13:4, October 1988, 415–43.

"Security, Modernity, Ecology: The Dilemmas of Post-Cold War Security Discourse," *Alternatives*, 17:1, Winter 1992, 95–134.

David, Stephen R. "Why the Third World Matters," *International Security*, 14:1, Summer 1989, 50–85.

"Why the Third World Still Matters," *International Security*, 17:3, Winter 1992/93, 127–59.

De Landa, Manuel. *War in the Age of Intelligent Machinery*. New York: Zone Books, 1991.

Delbrück, Hans. *History of the Art of War in the Framework of Political History, Vol. 4: The Modern Era*, trans. Walter J. Renfroe, Jr. Westport, Conn.: Greenwood Press, 1985.

Der Derian, James. *Antidiplomacy: Spies, Terror, Speed, and War*. Oxford: Basil Blackwell, 1992.

"Introducing Philosophical Traditions," *Millennium*, 17:2, Summer 1988, 189–93.

On Diplomacy: A Genealogy of Western Estrangement. Oxford: Basil Blackwell, 1987.

"The (S)pace of International Relations: Simulation, Surveillance and Speed," *International Studies Quarterly*, 34:3, September, 295–310.

Der Derian, James and Michael J. Shapiro, eds. *Intertextual/International Relations: Postmodern Readings of World Politics*. Lexington: Lexington Books, 1989.

Derrida, Jacques. *Of Grammatology*, trans. Gayatri Chakravorty Spivak. Baltimore: Johns Hopkins University Press, 1976.

"Racism's Last Word," *Critical Inquiry*, 12:1, Autumn 1985, 290–99.

Desch, Michael. "Turning the Caribbean Flank: Sea Lane Vulnerability During a European War," *Survival*, 29:6, November/December 1987, 528–51.

Dill, Günter, ed. *Clausewitz in Perspektive*. Frankfurt: Ullstein Materialien, 1980.

Dillon, G.M., "The Alliance of Security and Subjectivity," *Current Research on Peace and Violence*, 13:3, 1990–91, 101–24.

"Modernity, Discourse and Deterrence," *Current Research on Peace and Violence*, 12:2, 1989, 90–104.

Domke, William K., Richard C. Eichenberg and Catherine M. Kelleher, "Consensus Lost?: Domestic Politics and the 'Crisis' in NATO," *World Politics*, 39:3, April 1987, 382–407.

Douhet, Giulio. *The Command of the Air*, trans. Dino Ferrari. New York: Coward-McCann, 1942.

Downing, Brian M. *The Military Revolution and Political Change: Origins of Democracy and Autocracy in Early Modern Europe*. Princeton: Princeton University Press, 1992.

Doyle, Michael. "Kant, Liberal Legacies, and Foreign Affairs," Parts 1 and 2, *Philosophy and Public Affairs*, 12:3, Summer 1983, 205–35, and 12:4, Fall 1983, 323–53

"Liberalism and World Politics," *American Political Science Review*, 80:4, December 1986, 1,151–69.

Dulles, John Foster. "Policy for Security and Peace," *Foreign Affairs*, 32:3, April 1954, 353–64.

"A Policy of Boldness," *Life*, May 19, 1952, 146–60.

Earle, Edward Mead, ed. *Makers of Modern Strategy: Military Thought from Machiavelli to Hitler*. Princeton: Princeton University Press, 1944.

Eichenberg, Richard. *Public Opinion and National Security in Western Europe*. Ithaca: Cornell University Press, 1989.

Einhorn, Barbara. "'New Enemy Images for Old': The 'Boys' Debate' Around Timothy Garton Ash's *We The People*," in Mary Kaldor, ed., *Europe From Below: An East–West Dialogue*. London and New York: Verso, 1991, 130–5.

Eisenhower, Dwight. "President Eisenhower's Farewell to the Nation," *Department of State Bulletin*, February 6, 1961, 179–82.

Ellis, John. *The Social History of the Machine Gun*. New York: Pantheon, 1973.

Ellsberg, Daniel. "A Call to Mutiny," in E.P. Thompson and D. Smith, eds., *Protest and Survive*. New York: Monthly Review Press, 1981, i–xxviii.

Elshtain, Jean B. *Women and War*. New York: Basic Books, 1987.

Enloe, Cynthia. *Bananas, Beaches and Bases: Making Feminist Sense of International Politics*. Berkeley: University of California Press, 1989.

Etzold, Thomas H. and John Lewis Gaddis, eds. *Containment: Documents on American Policy and Strategy, 1945–1950*. New York: Columbia University Press, 1978.

Evangelista, Matthew. "Stalin's Postwar Army Reappraised," *International Security*, 7:3, Winter 1982/83, 110–38.

"Excerpts From Pentagon's Plan: 'Prevent the Re-Emergence of a New Rival'," *New York Times*, March 8, 1992, 15.

Fallows, James. *National Defense*. New York: Random House, 1981.

Falk, Richard A. "Theory, Realism, and World Security," in Michael T. Klare and Daniel C. Thomas, eds., *World Security: Trends and Challenges at Century's End*. New York: St. Martin's Press, 1991, 6–24.

Ferro, Marc. *The Great War, 1914–1918*, trans. N. Simon. Boston: Routledge and Kegan Paul, 1973.

Fleisher, Martin. "A Passion for Politics: The Vital Core of the World of Machiavelli," in Martin Fleisher, ed., *Machiavelli and the Nature of Political Thought*. New York: Atheneum, 1972, 114–47.

Fliess, Peter. *Thucydides and the Politics of Bipolarity*. Baton Rouge: Louisiana State University Press, 1966.

Flynn, G. and H. Rattinger, eds. *The Public and Atlantic Defense*. Totowa, NJ: Rowman and Allanheld, 1985.

Foucault, Michel. *The Archaeology of Knowledge and the Discourse on Language*, trans. A.M. Sheridan Smith. New York: Harper Colophon, 1976.

The Birth of the Clinic, trans. A.M. Sheridan Smith. New York: Vintage Books, 1975.

Discipline and Punish, trans. Alan Sheridan. New York: Vintage Books, 1979.

The Foucault Reader, ed. Paul Rabinow. New York: Pantheon, 1984.

Language, Counter-Memory, Practice: Selected Essays and Interviews, ed. Donald F. Bouchard, trans. Donald F. Bouchard and Sherry Simon. Ithaca: Cornell University Press, 1977.

Madness and Civilization, trans. Richard Howard. New York: Vintage Books, 1973.

Power/Knowledge: Selected Interviews and Other Writings, 1972–1977, ed. Colin Gordon. New York: Pantheon, 1980.

"Practicing Criticism," in *Politics, Philosophy, Culture: Interviews and Other Writings 1977–1984*, ed. Lawrence Kritzman, trans. Alan Sheridan and others. New York: Routledge, 1988, 152–56.

Freedman, Lawrence. *The Evolution of Nuclear Strategy*, 2nd edn. New York: St. Martin's Press, 1989.

US Intelligence and The Soviet Strategic Threat, 2nd edn. Princeton: Princeton University Press, 1986.

Fukuyama, Francis. "Democratization and International Security," in *New Dimensions in International Security Part II*, Adelphi Papers 266. London: International Institute for Strategic Studies, 1992, 14–24.

"The End of History," *The National Interest*, 16, Summer 1989, 3–18.

Fussell, Paul. *The Great War and Modern Memory*. New York: Oxford University Press, 1975.

Wartime: Understanding and Behaviour in the Second World War. New York: Oxford University Press, 1989.

Gaddis, John Lewis. "Coping with Victory," *Atlantic Monthly*, 264, October 1989, 49–60.

"The Long Peace: Elements of Stability in the Postwar International System," *International Security*, 10:4, Spring 1986, 99–142.

Strategies of Containment. New York: Oxford University Press, 1982.

"Toward the Post-Cold War World," *Foreign Affairs*, 70:2, Spring 1991, 102–22.

The United States and the Origins of the Cold War, 1941–1947. New York: Columbia University Press, 1972.

The US and the End of the Cold War. New York, Oxford University Press, 1992.

Gallie, W.B. *Philosophers of Peace and War*. Cambridge: Cambridge University Press, 1978.

Galtung, Johan. "Violence, Peace, and Peace Research," *Journal of Peace Research*, 6:2, 1969, 167–91.

Garst, Daniel. "Thucydides and Neorealism," *International Studies Quarterly*, 33:1, March 1989, 3–27.

George, Alexander L. and Richard Smoke. *Deterrence in American Foreign Policy: Theory and Practice*. New York: Columbia University Press, 1974.

George, Jim. "International Relations and the Search for Thinking Space: Another View of the Third Debate," *International Studies Quarterly*, 33:3, September 1989, 269–79.

George, Jim and David Campbell. "Patterns of Dissent and the Celebration of Difference: Critical Social Theory and International Relations," *International Studies Quarterly*, 34:3, September 1990, 269–93.

Giddens, Anthony. *The Nation-State and Violence*. Cambridge: Polity Press, 1985.

Gilbert, Felix. *To the Farewell Address: Ideas of Early American Foreign Policy*. Princeton: Princeton University Press, 1961.

Gill, Stephen. *American Hegemony and the Trilateral Commission*. Cambridge: Cambridge University Press, 1990.

Gill, Stephen, ed. *Gramsci, Historical Materialism and International Relations*. Cambridge: Cambridge University Press, 1993.

Gilligan, Carol. *In a Different Voice*. Cambridge: Harvard University Press, 1982.

Gilpin, Robert. "The Richness of the Tradition of Political Realism," *International Organization*, 38:2, Spring 1984, 287–304.

War and Change in World Politics. Princeton: Princeton University Press, 1981.

Glaser, Charles L. "Nuclear Policy Without an Adversary," *International Security*, 16:4, Spring 1992, 34–78.

Graham, Mac, Richard Jolly and Chris Smith, eds. *Disarmament and World Development*, 2nd edn. Oxford: Pergamon, 1986.

Grant, Rebecca and Kathleen Newland, eds. *Gender and International Relations*. Bloomington: Indiana University Press, 1991.

Grass, Günter. *Two States-One Nation?*, trans. Krishna Winston and A.S. Wensinger. San Diego: Harcourt Brace Jovanovich, 1990.

Gray, Colin. *The Geopolitics of the Nuclear Era*. New York: Crane, Russak, 1977.

Nuclear Strategy and Strategic Planning. Philadelphia: Foreign Policy Research Institute, 1984.

Gray, Colin and Keith Payne, "Victory is Possible," *Foreign Policy*, 39, Summer 1980, 14–27.

Green, Philip. *Deadly Logic: The Theory of Nuclear Deterrence*. Columbus: Ohio State University Press, 1966.

Gulick, E.V. *Europe's Classical Balance of Power*. New York: W.W. Norton, 1967.

Hahlweg, Werner. "Einleitung," in Carl von Clausewitz, *Verstreute kleine Schriften*, ed. Werner Hahlweg. Osnabruck: Biblio Verlag, 1979, ix–xxv.

Halliday, Fred. "The Cold War as Inter-Systemic Conflict – Initial Theses," in Mike Bowker and Robin Brown, eds., *From Cold War to Collapse: Theory and World Politics in the 1980s*. Cambridge: Cambridge University Press, 1993, 21–34.

"The Ends of Cold War," *New Left Review*, 180, March–April 1990, 5–23.

The Making of the Second Cold War, rev. edn. London: Verso, 1986.

Hamilton, Alexander, James Madison and John Jay. *The Federalist Papers*. New York: New American Library, 1961.

Handel, Michael, ed. *Clausewitz and Modern Strategy*. London: Frank Cass, 1986.

Hartz, Louis. *The Liberal Tradition in America*. New York: Harcourt, Brace, 1955.

Harvard Nuclear Study Group. *Living with Nuclear Weapons*. New York: Bantam Books, 1983.

Harvey, David. *The Condition of Postmodernity*. Oxford: Basil Blackwell, 1990.

Herken, Greg. *The Winning Weapon: The Atomic Bomb in the Cold War, 1945–1950*. New York: Vintage, 1982.

Counsels of War, exp. edn. New York: Oxford University Press, 1987.

Herz, John H. "Idealist Internationalism and the Security Dilemma," *World Politics*, 2:2, January 1950, 157–80.

"Rise and Demise of the Territorial State," *World Politics*, 9:4, July 1957, 473–93.

"The Territorial State Revisited," *Polity*, 1:1, Fall 1968, 1–34.

Hintze, Otto. "Military Organization and the Organization of the State," in *The Historical Essays of Otto Hintze*, ed. Felix Gilbert. New York: Oxford University Press, 1975, 178–215.

Hiss, Tony. *The Experience of Place*. New York: Knopf, 1990.

Hodges, Andrew. *Alan Turing: The Enigma*. New York: Simon & Schuster, 1983.

Hoffman, Mark, "Critical Theory and the Inter-Paradigm Debate," *Millennium*, 16:2, Summer 1987, 231–49.

Hoffmann, Stanley. "An American Social Science: International Relations," *Daedalus* 106:3, Summer 1977, 41–60.

Hogan, Michael J., ed. *The End of the Cold War: Its Meaning and Implications*. Cambridge: Cambridge University Press, 1992.

Holloway, David. *The Soviet Union and the Arms Race*, 2nd edn. New Haven: Yale University Press, 1984.

"State, Society and the Military Under Gorbachev," *International Security*, 14:3, 1989/90, 5–24.

Holly, I.B., Jr. "The Evolution of Operations Research and Its Impact on the Military Establishment: the Air Force Experience," in Lt. Col. Monte D. Wright and Lawrence J. Paszek, eds., *Science, Technology, and Warfare*. Washington, DC: Office of Air Force History, 1971, 89–109.

Holsti, K.J. *The Dividing Discipline: Hegemony and Diversity in International Theory*. Boston: Allen and Unwin, 1987.

Horne, Alistair. *The Price of Glory: Verdun 1916*. Harmondsworth: Penguin, 1964.

Hough, Jerry. "Gorbachev's Politics," *Foreign Affairs*, 68:5, Winter 1989/90, 26–41.

Howard, Michael. *The Causes of Wars and Other Essays*, 2nd edn. Cambridge, Mass.: Harvard University Press, 1984.

Clausewitz. New York: Oxford University Press, 1983.

"IISS – The First Thirty Years: A General Overview," in *The Changing Strategic Landscape, Part I*. Adelphi Papers 235. London: International Institute for Strategic Studies, 1989, 10–19.

"The Influence of Clausewitz," Carl von Clausewitz, *On War*, ed. and trans. Michael Howard and Peter Paret. Princeton: Princeton University Press, 1976, 27–44.

War in European History. Oxford: Oxford University Press, 1976.

Huntington, Samuel P. *Political Order in Changing Societies*. New Haven: Yale University Press, 1968.

Jackson, Robert H. *Quasi-States: Sovereignty, International Relations and the Third World*. Cambridge: Cambridge University Press, 1990.

Jacobs, Jane. *The Death and Life of Great American Cities*. New York: Random House, 1961.

Jervis, Robert. "Cooperation Under the Security Dilemma," *World Politics*, 30:2, January 1978, 167–214.

The Illogic of American Nuclear Strategy. Ithaca: Cornell University Press, 1984.

The Meaning of the Nuclear Revolution: Statecraft and the Prospect of Armageddon. Ithaca: Cornell University Press, 1989.

Perception and Misperception in International Politics. Princeton: Princeton University Press, 1976.

"Security Regimes," in Stephen Krasner, ed., *International Regimes*. Ithaca: Cornell University Press, 1983, 173–94.

"Why Nuclear Superiority Doesn't Matter," *Political Science Quarterly*, 94:2, Summer 1979–80, 617–33.

Jervis, Robert, Richard Ned Lebow, and Janice Gross Stein. *Psychology and Deterrence*. Baltimore: Johns Hopkins University Press 1985.

Joenniemi, Pertti. "The Social Constitution of Gorbachev: From an Intruder to a Communal Figure?" Paper prepared for the Annual Meeting of the International Studies Association. London, 1989.

Johnstone, Diana. *The Politics of Euromissiles: Europe's Role in America's World*. London: Verso, 1984.

Jomini, Baron Antoine Henri. *The Art of War*, trans. Capt. G.H. Mendell and Lieut. W.P. Craighill. Philadelphia: J.B. Lippincott and Co., 1862.

Kahn, Herman. *On Thermonuclear War*. Princeton: Princeton University Press, 1960.

Thinking About the Unthinkable. New York: Horizon Press, 1962.

Kaldor, Mary. *The Baroque Arsenal*. New York: Hill and Wang, 1981.

The Disintegrating West. New York: Hill and Wang, 1978.

The Imaginary War: Understanding the East–West Conflict. Oxford: Basil Blackwell, 1990.

Kaldor, Mary, ed., *Europe from Below: An East–West Dialogue*. London: Verso, 1991.

Kaplan, Fred. *The Wizards of Armageddon*. New York: Simon & Schuster, 1983.

Kaufmann, William, ed. *Military Policy and National Security*. Princeton: Princeton University Press, 1956.

Keegan, John. *The Face of Battle*. New York: Viking Press, 1975.

Kegley, Charles W., Jr. and Eugene R. Wittkopf, eds. *The Future of American Foreign Policy*. New York: St. Martin's Press, 1992.

Kelleher, Catherine M. *Germany and the Politics of Nuclear Weapons*. New York: Columbia University Press, 1975.

Kemp, Capt. Kenneth. "The Moral Case for the Strategic Defense Initiative," in D. P. Lackey, ed., *Ethics and Strategic Defense*. Belmont: Wadsworth Publishing, 1989, 39–45.

Kende, Istvan. "Twenty-Five Years of Local Wars," *Journal of Peace Research*, 8:1, 1971, 3–22.

Kennan, George F. *Memoirs: 1925–1950*. Boston: Atlantic-Little, Brown, 1967.
Memoirs, 1950–1965. Boston: Atlantic-Little, Brown, 1972.
The Nuclear Delusion: Soviet-American Relations in the Atomic Age. New York: Pantheon Books, 1983.

Kennedy, Paul. "A Declining Empire Goes to War," *The Wall Street Journal*, January 24, 1991, A-10.
The Rise and Fall of the Great Powers. New York: Random House, 1987.

Keohane, Robert O. *After Hegemony*. Princeton: Princeton University Press, 1984.
"International Institutions: Two Approaches," *International Studies Quarterly*, 32:4, December 1988, 379–96.

Keohane, Robert O., ed. *Neorealism and its Critics*. New York, Columbia University Press, 1986.

Keohane, Robert O. and Joseph S. Nye, *Power and Interdependence*. Boston: Little, Brown, and Co., 1977.

Keohane, Robert O. and Joseph S. Nye, eds. *Transnational Relations and World Politics*. Cambridge, Mass.: Harvard University Press, 1972.

Kielinger, Thomas and Max Otte. "Germany: The Pressured Power," *Foreign Policy*, 91, Summer 1993, 44–62.

Kiernan, V.G. *America: The New Imperialism, From White Settlement to World Hegemony*. London: Zed Press, 1980.
State and Society in Europe, 1550–1600. New York: St. Martin's Press, 1980.

Kipphardt, Heinar. *In the Matter of J. Robert Oppenheimer*, trans. Ruth Speirs. New York: Hill and Wang, 1967.

Kissinger, Henry A. *Nuclear Weapons and Foreign Policy*. New York: Harper and Brothers, for the Council on Foreign Relations, 1957.
A World Restored: Metternich, Castlereagh and the Problems of Peace, 1812–1822. Boston: Houghton Mifflin, 1957.
Years of Upheaval. Boston: Little, Brown and Co., 1982.

Klare, Michael. *American Arms Supermarket*. Austin, Texas: University of Texas Press, 1984.

Klare, Michael T. and Peter Kornbluh, eds. *Low-Intensity Warfare*. New York: Pantheon, 1988.

Klare, Michael T. and Daniel C. Thomas, eds. *World Security: Trends and Challenges at Century's End*. New York: St. Martin's Press, 1991.

Klein, Bradley S. "After Strategy: The Search for a Post-Modern Politics of Peace," *Alternatives*, 13:3, July 1988, 293–318.
"Beyond the Western Alliance: The Politics of Post-Atlanticism," in Stephen

Gill, ed., *Atlantic Relations: Beyond the Reagan Era*. Brighton: Harvester Wheatsheaf, 1989, 196–211.

"Discourse Analysis: Teaching World Politics Through International Relations," in Lev S. Gonick and Edward Weisband, eds., *Teaching World Politics: Contending Pedagogies for a New World Order*. Boulder, Co.: Westview Press, 1992, 153–69.

"Hegemony and Strategic Culture,' *Review of International Studies*, 14:2, April 1988, 131–46.

"How the West was One: Representational Politics of NATO," *International Studies Quarterly*, 34:3, September 1990, 311–25.

Strategic Discourse and its Alternatives. Occasional Paper No. 3. New York: Center on Violence and Human Survival, City University of New York, 1987.

"Textual Strategies of the Military: Or, Have Your Read Any Good Defense Manuals Lately?," in James Der Derian and Michael J. Shapiro, eds. *International/Intertextual Relations*. Lexington: Lexington Books, 1989, 97–112.

Klein, Bradley S. and Frank Unger, "U.S. Politik gegenüber Militärdiktaturen der dritten Welt," in Reiner Steinweg, ed., *Militärregime und Entwicklungspolitik*. Frankfurt: Suhrkamp, 1989, 392–421.

Kolodziej, Edward A. "Renaissance in Security Studies? Caveat Lector!" *International Studies Quarterly*, 36:4, December 1992, 421–38.

Krasner, Stephen D., ed. *International Regimes*. Ithaca: Cornell University Press, 1983.

Krass, Allan. "Death and Transfiguration: Nuclear Arms Control in the 1980s and 1990s," in Michael T. Klare and Daniel C. Thomas, eds., *World Security*. New York: St. Martin's Press, 1991, 68–100.

"The Death of Deterrence.' Unpublished manuscript, 1982.

"The Evolution of Military Technology and Deterrence Strategy," in *World Armaments and Disarmament: SIPRI Yearbook 1981*. Solna: Stockholm International Peace Research Institute, 1981, 19–67.

Kratochwil, Friedrich. "Of Systems, Boundaries, and Territoriality: An Inquiry into the Formation of the State System," *World Politics*, 39:1, October 1986, 27–52.

Krauthammer, Charles. "The Unipolar Moment," *Foreign Affairs*, 70:1, 1990/1, 23–33.

"Universal Dominion: Toward a Unipolar World," *National Interest*, 18, Winter 1989–90, 46–9.

Krippendorff, Ekkehart. *Amerikanische Strategie*. Frankfurt: Suhrkamp, 1970.

Internationales System als Geschichte. Frankfurt: Campus Verlag, 1975.

Staat und Krieg: Die historische Logik politischer Unvernunft. Frankfurt: Suhrkamp, 1985.

"The Victims – a Research Failure," *Journal of Peace Research*, 18:1, 1981, 97–101.

Kuhn, Thomas S. *The Structure of Scientific Revolutions*, 2nd edn. Chicago: University of Chicago Press, 1970.

Kull, Steven. *Minds at War: Nuclear Reality and the Inner Conflicts of Defense Policymakers*. New York: Basic Books, 1988.

"Nuclear Nonsense," *Foreign Policy*, 58, Spring 1985, 28–52.

Laclau, Ernesto and Chantal Mouffe. *Hegemony and Socialist Strategy*, London: Verso, 1985.

Lakatos, Imre and Alan Musgrave, eds. *Criticism and the Growth of Knowledge*. Cambridge: Cambridge University Press, 1970.

Lane, Robert E. "The Politics of Consensus in an Age of Affluence," *American Political Science Review*, 49:4, December 1965, 874–95.

Lapid, Yosef. "The Third Debate: On the Prospects of International Theory in a Post-Positivist Era," *International Studies Quarterly*, 33:3, Spring 1989, 235–54.

Lawrence, Philip K. "Nuclear Strategy and Political Theory: A Critical Assessment," *Review of International Studies*, 11:2, April 1985, 105–21.

Preparing for Armageddon: A Critique of Western Strategy. Brighton: Wheatsheaf, 1988.

"Strategy, the State and the Weberian Legacy," *Review of International Studies*, 13:4, October 1987, 295–310.

Lipset, Seymour Martin. *The First New Nation*. New York: W.W. Norton, 1979.

Livingstone, Neil C. *The Cult of Counterterrorism*. Lexington: Lexington Books, 1990.

Long, Franklin, Donald Hafner, and Jeffrey Boutwell, eds. *Weapons in Space*. New York: W.W. Norton, 1986.

Luckham, Robin. "Armament Culture," *Alternatives*, 10:1, Summer 1984, 1–44.

"Security and Disarmament in Africa," *Alternatives*, 9:2, April 1983, 203–228.

Luke, Timothy W. "'What's Wrong with Deterrence?': A Semiotic Interpretation of National Security Policy," in James Der Derian and Michael J. Shapiro, eds., *International/Intertextual Relations*. Lexington: Lexington Books, 1989, 207–29.

"The Discipline of Security Studies and the Codes of Containment," *Alternatives*, 16:3, Summer 1991, 315–44.

Lynn-Jones, Sean M., ed. *The Cold War and After: Prospects for Peace*. Cambridge: MIT Press, 1991.

Lyotard, Jean-François. *The Postmodern Condition: A Report on Knowledge*, trans. Geoff Bennington and Brian Massumi. Minneapolis: University of Minnesota Press, 1984.

Machiavelli, Niccolo. *Machiavelli: the Chief Works and Others*. 3 vols. trans. and ed. Alan Gilbert. Durham: Duke University Press, 1965.

Magnusson, Warren and R.B.J. Walker. "De-Centring the State: Political Theory and Canadian Political Economy," *Studies in Political Economy*, 26, Summer 1988, 37–71.

Mahan, Capt. A. T. *The Influence of Sea Power Upon History 1660–1783*. Boston: Little, Brown, and Co., 1895.

The Interests of America in Sea Power, Present and Future. Boston: Little, Brown, and Co., 1897.

Retrospect and Prospect: Studies in International Relations, Naval and Political. Boston: Little, Brown, and Co., 1902.

Malcolmson, Robert W. *Beyond Nuclear Thinking*. Montreal and Kingston: McGill-Queen's University Press, 1990.

Mandelbaum, Michael. *The Nuclear Question: The United States and Nuclear Weapons, 1946–1976.* Cambridge: Cambridge University Press, 1979.

Mann, Michael. *The Sources of Social Power.* Cambridge: Cambridge University Press, 1986.

States, War, and Capitalism in Political Sociology. Oxford: Basil Blackwell, 1988.

Marx, Karl and Friedrich Engels. *The Marx–Engels Reader,* 2nd edn, ed. Robert C. Tucker. New York: W.W. Norton, 1978.

Mathews, Jessica Tuchman. "The Environment and International Security," in Michael T. Klare and Daniel C. Thomas, eds., *World Security: Trends and Challenges at Century's End.* New York: St. Martin's Press, 1991, 362–80.

"Preserving the Global Environment: Implications for U.S. Policy," in Charles W. Kegley and Eugene R. Wittkopf, eds., *The Future of American Foreign Policy.* New York: St. Martin's Press, 1992, 85–94.

Mattingly, Garrett. *Renaissance Diplomacy.* Boston: Houghton Mifflin, 1971.

MccGwire, Michael. "Deterrence. The Problem – Not the Solution," *International Affairs,* 62:1, Winter 1985/86, 55–70.

Perestroika and Soviet National Security. Washington, DC: The Brookings Institution, 1991.

McIsaac, David. "Voices from the Central Blue: The Air Power Theorists," in Peter Paret, ed., *Makers of Modern Strategy.* Princeton: Princeton University Press, 1986, 624–47.

McNamara, Robert S. *Blundering into Disaster.* New York: Pantheon, 1985.

"Defense Arrangements of the North Atlantic Community," *US Department of State Bulletin,* July 9, 1962, 64–9.

McNeill, William H. *The Pursuit of Power: Technology, Armed Force, and Society since A.D. 1000.* Chicago: The University of Chicago Press, 1982.

Mcpherson, C.B. *The Political Theory of Possessive Individualism: Hobbes to Locke.* New York: Clarendon Press, 1962.

Mearsheimer, John. "Back to the Future: Instability in Europe After the Cold War," *International Security,* 15:1, Summer 1990, 5–56.

Conventional Deterrence. Ithaca: Cornell University Press, 1983.

"Correspondence: Back to the Future, Part III: Realism and the Realities of European Security," *International Security,* 15:3, Winter 1990/1, 220–21.

"Why We Will Soon Miss the Cold War," *The Atlantic Monthly,* August 1990, 35–50.

Mendlovitz, Saul H. and R.B.J. Walker, eds. *Towards a Just World Peace: Perspectives From Social Movements.* London: Butterworths, 1987.

Meyer, Stephen. "The Sources and Prospects of Gorbachev's New Political Thinking on Security," *International Security,* 13:2, Fall 1988, 124–63.

Mills, C. Wright. *The Causes of World War Three.* New York: Simon & Schuster, 1958.

Mitgang, Herbert. "Profiles (Gene Robert La Rocque)," *The New Yorker,* October 6, 1986, 88–103.

Molander, Roger. "How I Learned to Start Worrying and Hate the Bomb," *The Washington Post,* March 21, 1982.

Mommsen, Wolfgang J. *Max Weber und die deutsche Politik, 1890–1920,* 2nd edn. Tubingen: J.C.B. Mohr, 1974.

Moore, Barrington, Jr. *Social Origins of Dictatorship and Democracy*. Boston: Beacon Press, 1966.

Morgenthau, Hans. "The Fallacy of Thinking Conventionally About Nuclear Weapons," in D. Carlton and C. Schaerf, eds., *Arms Control and Technological Innovation*. New York: Wiley, 1976, 256–64.

Politics Among Nations, 5th edn. New York: Alfred A. Knopf, 1973.

Mueller, John. "The Essential Irrelevance of Nuclear Weapons," *International Security*, 13:2, Fall 1988, 55–79.

"Quiet Cataclysm: Some Thoughts on World War III," in Michael J. Hogan, ed., *The End of the Cold War*. Cambridge: Cambridge University Press, 1992, 39–52.

Myers, Norman. "Environment and Security," *Foreign Policy*, 74, Spring 1989, 23–41.

Nathanson, Charles E. "The Social Construction of the Soviet Threat: A Study in the Politics of Representation," *Alternatives*, 13:4, October 1988, 443–84.

NATO: Basic Documents. Brussels, NATO Information Service, 1981.

Nash, H.T. "The Bureaucratization of Homicide," in E.P. Thompson and Dan Smith, eds., *Protest and Survive*. New York: Monthly Review Press, 1981, 149–65.

Neckermann, Peter. "What Went Wrong: Germany After the Unification?," *East European Quarterly*, 26:4, January 1993, 447–69.

Nef, John U. *War and Human Progress: An Essay on the Rise of Industrial Civilization*. New York: W.W. Norton, 1963.

Nelkin, Dorothy and Michael Pollack. *The Atom Beseiged: Antinuclear Movements in France and West Germany*. Cambridge: MIT Press, 1981.

Nitze, Paul. "Atoms, Strategy and Policy," *Foreign Affairs*, 34:2, January 1956, 187–98.

"Deterring Our Deterrent," *Foreign Policy*, 25, Winter 1976–77, 195–210.

Nixon, Richard M. *United States Foreign Policy for the 1970s: A New Strategy for Peace*. Washington, DC: United States Information Service, 1970.

"NSC-68, United States Objectives and Programs for National Security, April 14, 1950," in Thomas W. Etzold and John Lewis Gaddis, eds., *Containment: Documents on American Strategy and Foreign Policy, 1945–50*. New York: Columbia University Press, 1978, 385–442.

Nye, Joseph S. Jr. "Against 'Declinism'," *The New Republic*, October 15, 1990, 12–13.

Bound to Lead: The Changing Nature of American Power. New York: Basic Books, 1991.

Nye, Joseph S., Jr. and Sean M. Lynn-Jones. "International Security Studies: A Report of a Conference on the State of the Field," *International Security*, 12:4, Spring 1988, 5–27

"October 27, 1962: Transcripts of the Meetings of the ExComm," *International Security*, 12:3, Winter 1987/8, 30–92.

"On Top of the World," *Economist*, March 9, 1991, 15.

Orwell, George. *A Collection of Essays*. San Diego: Harcourt Brace Jovanovich, 1953.

Packenham, R.A. *Liberal America and the Third World*. Princeton: Princeton University Press, 1973.

Paret, Peter. "Clausewitz," in Peter Paret, ed., *Makers of Modern Strategy: From Machiavelli to the Nuclear Age.* Princeton: Princeton University Press, 1986, 186–213.

Clausewitz and the State. Oxford: Oxford University Press, 1976.

Parker, Geoffrey. *The Military Revolution.* Cambridge: Cambridge University Press, 1988.

"Pentagon Drops Goal of Blocking New Superpowers," *New York Times,* May 24, 1992, A1.

Peterson, V. Spike, ed. *Gendered States: Feminist (Re)Visions of International Relations Theory.* Boulder, Co.: Lynne Rienner, 1992.

Pierre, Andrew J. *The Global Politics of Arms Sales.* Princeton: Princeton University Press, 1982.

Pipes, Daniel and Adam Garfinkle, eds. *Friendly Tyrants: An American Dilemma* New York: St. Martin's Press, 1991.

Pitkin, Hannah Fenichel. *Fortuna is a Woman: Gender and Politics in the Thought of Machiavelli.* Berkeley: University of California Press, 1984.

Pocock, J.G.A. *The Machiavellian Moment.* Princeton: Princeton University Press, 1975.

Polanyi, Karl. *The Great Transformation.* Boston: Beacon Press, 1957.

Poggi, Gianfranco. *The Development of the Modern State: A Sociological Introduction.* Stanford: Stanford University Press, 1978.

Postol, Theodore A. "Lessons of the Gulf War Experiment with Patriot," *International Security,* 16:3, Winter 1991/2, 119–71.

"Quick Outcome Is Not Expected On Fate of MX," *New York Times,* December 6, 1982, A1.

Rapoport, Anatol. "Introduction," in Carl von Clausewitz, *On War,* ed. Anatol Rapoport, trans. Col. J.J. Graham. Harmondsworth: Penguin, 1968, 11–80.

Ravetz, Jerome R. *Scientific Knowledge and its Social Problems.* New York: Oxford University Press, 1971.

Robbins, Keith. *The First World War.* Oxford: Oxford University Press, 1984.

Rochon, Thomas. *Mobilizing for Peace: The Antinuclear Movements in Western Europe.* Princeton, Princeton University Press, 1988.

Rorty, Richard. *Philosophy and the Mirror of Nature.* Princeton: Princeton University Press, 1980.

Rosenau, James N., ed. *International Politics and Foreign Policy,* rev. edn. New York: Free Press, 1969.

Rostow, W.W. *The Stages of Economic Growth: A Non-Communist Manifesto.* Cambridge: Cambridge University Press, 1960.

"Guerrilla Warfare in the Underdeveloped Areas," *US Department of State Bulletin,* August 7, 1961, 233–8.

Rothfels, Hans. "Clausewitz," in Edward Mead Earle, ed., *Makers of Modern Strategy: Military Thought From Machiavelli to Hitler.* Princeton: Princeton University Press, 1944, 93–113

Rowlands, Ian. "The Security Challenges of Global Environmental Change," *The Washington Quarterly,* 14:1, Winter 1991, 99–114.

Ruggie, John Gerard. "Territoriality and Beyond: Problematizing Modernity in International Relations," *International Organization,* 47:1, Winter 1993, 139–74.

Said, Edward. *The World, the Text, and the Critic*. Cambridge, Mass.: Harvard University Press, 1983.

Sanders, Jerry. *Peddlers of Crisis*. Boston: South End Press, 1983.

Schlesinger, James. "Reykjavik and Revelations: A Turn of the Tide?" *Foreign Affairs*, 65:3, 1986, 423–46.

Schmidt, Helmut. *Verteidigung oder Vergeltung: ein deutscher Beitrag zur strategischen Problem der NATO*. Stuttgart: Seewald Verlag, 1961.

Strategie des Gleichgewichts: Deutsche Friedenspolitik und die Weltmächte. Stuttgart: Seewald Verlag, 1969.

A Grand Strategy for the West: The Anachronism of National Strategies in an Interdependent World. New Haven: Yale University Press, 1985.

Schwartz, David N. *NATO's Nuclear Dilemmas*. Washington, DC: Brookings Institution, 1983.

Senghaas, Dieter. *Abschreckung und Frieden*, 3rd edn. Frankfurt: Europäische Verlagsanstalt, 1981.

Seversky, Maj. Alexander de. *Victory through Air Power*. New York: Simon & Schuster, 1942.

"Sex for Sale" (cover story), *Time*, June 21, 1993, 45–55.

Shapiro, Michael J. *Language and Political Understanding*. New Haven: Yale University Press, 1981.

The Politics of Representation. Madison: University of Wisconsin Press, 1988.

Reading the Postmodern Polity. Minneapolis: University of Minnesota Press, 1992.

Shapiro, Michael J., ed. *Language and Politics*. New York: New York University Press, 1984.

Sharp, Gene. *Making Europe Unconquerable*. Cambridge: Ballinger, 1985.

Sherry, Michael S. *The Rise of American Air Power*. New Haven: Yale University Press, 1987.

Shlaes, Amity. *Germany: The Empire Within*. New York: Farrar, Straus and Giroux, 1991.

Shiva, Vandana. *Staying Alive: Women, Ecology and Development*. London: Zed Press, 1988.

Shonfield, Andrew. *Modern Capitalism: The Changing Balance of Public and Private Power*. New York: Oxford University Press, 1969.

Sigal, Leon V. *Nuclear Forces in Europe*. Washington, DC: Brookings Institution, 1984.

Sivard, Ruth Leger. *World Military and Social Expenditures, 1991*. Washington: DC, World Priorities, 1991.

Skaggs, David C. "Between the Hawks and the Doves: Alastair Buchan and the Institute for Strategic Studies," *Conflict*, 7:1, 1987, 79–102.

Skocpol, Theda. *States and Social Revolutions*. Cambridge: Cambridge University Press, 1979.

Smith, Adam. *The Wealth of Nations*. New York: Random House, 1937.

Snow, Donald M. *Distant Thunder: Third World Conflict and the New International Order*. New York: St. Martin's Press, 1993.

Snyder, Craig, ed. *The Strategic Defense Debate: Can "Star Wars" Makes Us Safe?*. Philadelphia: University of Pennsylvania Press, 1986.

Soja, Edward W. *Postmodern Geographies: The Reassertion of Space in Critical Social Theory*. London: Verso, 1989.

Sorenson, Theodore C. "Rethinking National Security: Democracy and Economic Independence," *Foreign Affairs*, 69:3, Summer 1990, 1–18.

Sorkin, Michael, ed. *Variations on a Theme Park: The New American City and the End of Public Space.* New York: The Noonday Press, 1992.

Spencer, Herbert. *Principles of Sociology*, ed. Stanislav Andrewski. London: Macmillan, 1969.

Spiro, Herbert J. and Benjamin R. Barber. "Counter-Ideological Uses of 'Totalitarianism'," *Politics and Society*, 1:1, Fall 1970, 3–21.

Sprout, Margaret Tuttle. "Mahan: Evangelist of Sea Power," in Edward Mead Earle, ed., *Makers of Modern Strategy: From Machiavelli to Hitler.* Princeton: Princeton University Press, 1944, 415–45.

Stammer, Otto, ed. *Max Weber und die Soziologie heute.* Tübingen, J.C.B. Mohr, 1964.

Steinke, Rudolf. "Introduction," in Rudolf Steinke and Michael Vale, eds., *Germany Debates Defense: The NATO Alliance at the Crossroads.* Armonk: M.E. Sharpe, 1983, ix–xxxii.

Stephanson, Anders. *Kennan and the Art of Foreign Policy.* Cambridge, Mass.: Harvard University Press, 1989.

Strachan, Hew. *European Armies and the Conduct of War.* London: George Allen and Unwin, 1983.

Summers, Jr., Col. H. G. *On Strategy II: A Critical Analysis of the Gulf War.* New York: Dell, 1992.

Sylvester, Christine. "The Emperor's Theories and Transformations: Looking at the Field Through Feminist Lenses," in Dennis Pirages and Christine Sylvester, eds., *Transformations in the Global Political Economy.* New York: St. Martin's Press, 1990, 230–53.

Tairov, Tair. "From New Thinking to a Civic Peace," in Mary Kaldor, ed., *Europe from Below: An East-West Dialogue.* London: Verso, 1991, 43–8.

Taylor, Maxwell. *The Uncertain Trumpet.* New York: Harper and Row, 1960.

Thomas, Caroline. *In Search of Security: The Third World in International Relations.* Boulder, Co.: Lynne Rienner, 1987.

Thompson, E.P., et al. *Exterminism and Cold War.* London: Verso, 1982.

Thucydides. *The Peloponnesian War*, trans. R. Warner. Harmondsworth: Penguin Books, 1972.

Tickner, J. Ann. *Gender in International Relations: Feminist Perspectives on Achieving Global Security.* New York: Columbia University Press, 1992..

Todorov, Tzvetan. *The Conquest of America*, trans. Richard Howard. New York: Harper and Row, 1984.

Toulmin, Stephen. *Foresight and Understanding.* Bloomington: Indiana University Press, 1961.

Trachtenberg, Marc. "The Influence of Nuclear Weapons on the Cuban Missile Crisis," *International Security*, 10:1, Summer 1985, 137–63.

Tucker, Jonathan B. "Strategic Command and Control: America's Achilles Heel?," *Technology Review*, 86:6, August/September 1983, 38–49.

US Congress. *Changes in the European Security Environment: Hearings Before the Committee on Armed Services.* US Senate, 102nd Congress, 1st Session, February 26–27, March 7, 1991.

Changing Perspectives on US Arms Transfer Policy: Report Prepared for the Subcommittee on International Security and Scientific Affairs of the Committee on Foreign Affairs, US House of Representatives, by the Congressional Research Service, Library of Congress. 97th Congress, 1st Session. Washington, DC: US Government Printing Office, 1981.

Fiscal Year 1980 International Security Assistance Authorization, Hearings Before the Committee on Foreign Relations, US Senate. 96th Congress, 1st Session, February 28, 1979.

Foreign Assistance Act of 1968, Part 2: Hearings Before the Committee on Foreign Relations, US Senate. 90th Congress, 2nd Session, March and May 1968.

Hearings Before the Joint Economic Committee of the United States. 97th Congress, 2nd Session, January 28, 1982.

US and USSR Strategic Policies: Hearing Before the Subcommittee on Arms Control, International Law and Organization of the Commitee on Foreign Relations, United States Senate. 93rd Congress, 2nd Session, March 4, 1974.

US Defense Security Assistance Agency. *Foreign Military Sales, Foreign Military Construction Sales and Military Assistance Facts, as of September 30, 1985.* Washington, DC: Defense Security Assistance Agency, 1986.

US Department of Defense. *Soviet Military Power.* Washington, DC: US Government Printing Office, 1981.

US Secretary of Defense Caspar W. Weinberger. *Annual Report to the Congress: Fiscal Year 1986.* Washington, DC: US Government Printing Office, 1986.

USSR Ministry of Defense. *Whence the Threat to Peace.* Moscow: Military Publishing House, 1982.

Viotti, Paul R. and Mark V. Kauppi. *International Relations Theory: Realism, Pluralism, Globalism.* New York: Macmillan, 1987.

Virilio, Paul. *Speed and Politic: An Essay on Dromology,* trans. Mark Polizzotti. New York: Semiotext(e), 1986.

War and Cinema: The Logistics of Perception, trans. Patrick Camiller. London: Verso, 1989.

Virilio, Paul and Sylvere Lotringer, *Pure War,* trans. Mark Polizzotti. New York: Semiotext(e), 1983.

Visvanathan, Shiv. "From the Annals of the Laboratory State," *Alternatives* 12:1, January 1987, 37–60.

Walker, R.B.J. "Contemporary Militarism and the Discourse of Dissent," in R.B.J. Walker, ed., *Culture, Ideology, and World Order.* Boulder, Co.: Westview Press, 1984, 302–22.

"History and Structure in the Theory of International Relations," *Millennium,* 18:2, Summer 1989, 163–83.

Inside/Outside: International Relations as Political Theory. Cambridge: Cambridge University Press, 1993.

One World/Many Worlds: Struggles for a Just World Peace. Boulder, Co.: Lynne Rienner, 1988.

"'The Prince' and 'The Pauper': Tradition, Modernity and Practice in the Theory of International Relations," in James Der Derian and Michael J. Shapiro, eds., *Intertextual/International Relations.* Lexington: Lexington Books, 1989, 25–48.

"Realism, Change, and International Political Theory," *International Studies Quarterly,* 31:2, March 1987, 65–86.

Wallerstein, Immanuel. *The Capitalist World-Economy: Essays.* Cambridge: Cambridge University Press, 1979.

The Modern World-System. New York: Academic Press, 1974.

The Politics of the World-Economy. Cambridge: Cambridge University Press, 1984.

Walt, Stephen M. "The Renaissance of Security Studies," *International Studies Quarterly,* 35:2, June 1991, 211–39.

Waltz, Kenneth. *Man, the State, and War: A Theoretical Analysis.* New York: Columbia University Press, 1959.

Theory of International Politics. Reading: Addison-Wesley, 1979.

Warner, Edward. "Douhet, Mitchell, Seversky: Theories of Air Warfare," in Edward Mead Earle, ed., *Makers of Modern Strategy.* Princeton: Princeton University Press, 1944, 485–503.

Watts, Barry. *The Foundations of U.S. Air Doctrine.* Washington, DC: Government Printing Office, 1984.

Weber, Max. "Der Nationalstaat und die Volkswirthschaft (1895)," in *Gesammelte politische Schriften,* 4th edn. Tubingen: J.C.B. Mohr, 1980, 1–25.

"Politics as a Vocation," in *From Max Weber: Essays in Sociology,* ed. and trans. Hans Gerth and C. Wright Mills. New York: The Free Press, 1946, 77–128.

Weizsäcker, Carl Friedrich von, ed. *Die Praxis der defensiven Verteidigung* Hameln: Sponholtz, 1984.

Welch, David A. and James G. Blight. "The Eleventh Hour of the Cuban Missile Crisis: An Introduction to the ExComm Transcripts," *International Security,* 12:3, Winter 1987/8, 5–29.

Wells, Samuel F., Jr. and Robert S. Litwak, ed. *Strategic Defenses and Soviet–American Relations.* Cambridge: Ballinger, 1987.

Wendt, Alexander. "Anarchy is What States Make of It: The Social Construction of Power Politics," *International Organization,* 46:2, Spring 1992, 391–425.

"White House Tapes and Minutes of the Cuban Missile Crisis: ExCom Meetings October 1962," *International Security,* 10:1, Summer, 164–203.

Wight, Martin. "Why is There No International Theory?," in Herbert Butterfield and Martin Wight, eds., *Diplomatic Investigations: Essays in the Theory of International Politics.* Cambridge: Harvard University Press, 1966, 17–34.

Williams, Michael C. "Rethinking the 'Logic' of Deterrence," *Alternatives,* 17:1, Winter 1992, 67–93.

"Neo-Realism and the Future of Strategy," *Review of International Studies,* 19:2, April 1993, 103–21.

Williams, William Appelman. *Empire as a Way of Life.* New York: Oxford University Press, 1980.

The Tragedy of American Diplomacy. New York: Dell, 1962.

Wilson, Woodrow. "An Address to a Joint Session of Congress, January 8, 1918," in *The Papers of Woodrow Wilson,* vol. 45, ed. Arthur S. Link. Princeton: Princeton University Press, 1984, 534–9.

Wohlstetter, Albert. "The Delicate Balance of Terror," *Foreign Affairs,* 37:2, January 1959, 221–34.

Wolf, Eric. *Europe and the People Without History.* Berkeley: University of California Press, 1982.

Wolin, Sheldon. *Politics and Vision.* Boston: Little, Brown, and Co., 1960.

Wolpin, Miles. *Military Aid and Counterrevolution in the Third World.* Lexington: D.C. Heath, 1973.

Wright, Robin and Doyle McManus. *Flashpoints: Promise and Peril in a New World Order*. New York: Alfred A. Knopf, 1991.

Wulf, Herbert. *Aufrüstung und Unterentwicklung*. Reinbek bei Hamburg: Rowohlt, 1983.

Young, James P., ed. *Consensus and Conflict: Readings in American Politics*. New York: Dodd, Mead, and Co., 1972.

Zalewski, Marysia. "Feminist Theory and International Relations," in Mike Bowker and Robin Brown, eds., *From Cold War to Collapse: Theory and World Politics in the 1980s*. Cambridge: Cambridge University Press, 1993, 115–44.

INDEX

absolute war
  in Clausewitz, 47–53
  Napoleonic warfare as, 52–53
  nuclear technology and, 48–49, 53, 59
Absolute Weapon, The (Brodie), 59–61
"action policy," 77–78
active vs. passive policies
  global commerce and, 85–86
  nuclear defenses and, 68–70
air power
  advent of, 56–59
  anti-aircraft defenses and, 69
  minimal deterrence position and, 64
  technologically driven strategy and, 109–11
Albright, David, 165n11
alliance systems, and strategic practice, 31–32, 131 *see also* Eastern alliance; Western alliance
American exceptionalism, 157n5
anarchy, and politics of strategy, 20, 115
Aquino, Corazon, 101
armaments industry, 13, 102–4
Aron, Raymond, 150n10
Ashley, Richard K., 5, 149n58
Augustine, Saint, 43

Bahro, Rudolf, 130
balance of power politics
  American involvement in, 84–85
  concept of, 25
  "Hundred Years' Peace" and, 29
  nuclear technology and, 128–30
  role of wars in, 45–47
  state as construct and, 19–20
  strategic violence and, 24–25, 26–27
balance of terror, 29, 30, 66
Ball, Desmond, 155n65, 156n68
Ball, Nicole, 143n2
Barber, Benjamin R., 163n26
Baudelaire, Charles, 106
Benson, Lucy Wilson, 104
Berman, Marshall, 159n34, 161n3
Bernstein, Richard, 148n55

Blechman, Barry M., 159n26
Blight, James G., 162n7
Bodin, Jean, 2, 17
"bomber gap," 114, 117
Booth, Ken, 76, 155n67
Borden, William L., 63, 111–12
Bowker, Mike, 166n17
Brodie, Bernard, 49, 59–61, 68, 73, 150n10, 151n12
Bull, Hedley, 125, 142n12
Buzan, Barry, 20–22, 166n23

Caldwell, Malcolm, 160n39
Campbell, David, 142n13, 150n58, 165n10
capabilities vs. intentions, 115–17
capitalism, 83–84 *see also* Liberalism
Carr, E. H., 2, 8, 159n29
Carter adminstration, 103–4
Christian cosmology, collapse of, 17
Cipolla, Carlo, 147n34
citizen-army, 45
civil defense shelters, 68–69
civilians, in war, 56–57, 58–59
civil wars, 33
classical era, states systems in, 1–2, 40
classical realism *see* Realist tradition
Clausewitz, Carl von, 47–54, 57, 58, 59, 62, 101, 128, 150n10, 151n11, 151n14, 152n20
Clifford, Clark M., 100
Clinton, Bill, 136
Cohn, Carol, 147n43
Cold War
  classical realist view of, 125–27
  as contest among social systems, 104–5, 127
  critical accounts of, 165n10
  minimal deterrence position and, 63–64
  Third World modernization and, 100–101
  see also Nuclear deterrence strategy
Cold War, end of
  celebratory triumphalism and, 4–5, 123–24

Cold War, end of (*cont.*)
  global changes from, 31–33, 134–35, 137
  potential meaning of, 133–40
  social sciences and, 33–38
  "use" of nuclear weapons and, 111–12
  see also Post-Cold War world
colonialism, 14–15
common sense, 29
Communism, 93, 105, 115, 127 *see also* Soviet Union
Connolly, William E., 146n26, 166n23
containment policies, 125
contestability, 20, 25–26
Continental security problem
  end of Cold War and, 130–33
  minimal deterrence strategy and, 65–66, 68, 72–73, 118, 119
  NATO strategy and, 118–22
  see also Western Alliance
Cortez, Hernando, 15
"countermemorializing," 5, 28–29
Cox, Robert W., 35, 87
creative destruction, 106–7
credibility, and NATO strategy, 72–73, 108, 118
critical theory, 1, 7, 35–37 *see also* Frankfurt School
Crouch, Harold, 159n27
Crowl, Philip A., 157n10, 158n20
Cuban Missile Crisis, 162n7
cultural constructs, 2–3, 10–11, 16–17, 125, 136–37 *see also* key concepts
cultural identity *see* Western cultural identity

"declaratory policy," 77–78
deconstructionist approaches *see* Poststructural approaches
defense
  active, 69–70
  as futile, 59, 60–61, 68, 74
  global trade and, 85–89
  passive, 68–69
  Six Day War and, 154n51
  strength of position of, 50–51, 55–56, 57
De Gaulle, Charles, 118
De Landa, Manuel, 153n55
Delbrx Gck, Hans, 50, 151n15
democracy
  Cold War rhetoric and, 115
  end of Cold War and, 123–24, 132
  violent defense of liberal order and, 89–91
democratization, 31–33, 131
"demonstration effect," 25, 98
Derrida, Jacques, 142n13
Desch, Michael, 147n41
Dill, Günter, 150n10

Dillon, G. M., 166n23
"disciplines," and principles of inclusion, 23
discourse analysis, 7, 36–37, 149n55
  practices in Strategic Studies and, 5–6, 65–66, 112–18, 137, 139–40
Discriminate Deterrence (Commission on Integrated Long-Term Strategy), 120
Doty, Paul, 154n61
Douhet, Giulio, 56–59, 64
Downing, Brian M., 150n4
Dulles, John Foster, 64–66, 77, 118, 157n10

Eastern alliance
  democratization and, 31–33, 131
  East–West power and, 128
  NATO strategy and, 72–73, 108, 118
  see also Soviet Union
Einhorn, Barbara, 123
Eisenhower, Dwight D., 65, 118
Ellis, John, 153n35, 159n34
empiricist tradition, 25–26, 75–77, 134 *see also* Realist tradition
"end of history," 30, 123, 135
engendered discourse, 16–17, 65–66, 137
Enlightenment, the, 41, 123
Etzold, Thomas H., 163n21
European Recovery Plan (ERP), 92–93
"existential deterrence," 70

Fallows, James, 152n22
Federalist Papers, The, 84, 85
feminist studies, 137, 167n30
Ferro, Marc, 153n35
first-strike capability, 68, 70, 72, 152n22
"first-use" orientation, 68
Fleisher, Martin, 145n13
flexible response strategy, 120
Fliess, Peter, 145n17
Foreign Military Sales (FMS), 100, 103
"fortuna," 18, 43, 45
Foucault, Michel, 6, 142n9, 146n28, 148n49, 149n55
foundationalism, 36–37, 40 *see also* key concepts
"Fourteen Points" (Wilson), 90
France, 118–19
Frankfurt School, 35, 36 *see also* critical theory
Frederick the Great (king of Prussia), 45, 46
"friction"
  absolute vs. real war and, 51
  air power and, 56, 57
  concept of, 50, 51, 152n22
Fukuyama, Francis, 30, 123
Fussell, Paul, 142n14

Gaddis, John Lewis, 163n21, 165n7

Gaither Report, 69
Gallie, W. B., 151n11
Garfinkle, Adam, 160n41
Garst, Daniel, 150n2
Gemeinschaft vs. *Gesellschaft*, 94
George, Jim, 149n58
German historicist tradition, 41–42,
  145n22
Germany
  postwar division of, 118–19
  unification of, 32–33
Gilbert, Felix, 157n5
Gilpin, Robert, 2, 141n6
global conflict
  commerce and, 83–85
  contemporary power relations and, 22
  end of Cold War and, 33
  see also War
global economic relations
  end of Cold War and, 137
  strategic violence and, 14–16, 90–105
  US link between trade and strategy
    and, 83–89
Gorbachev, Mikhail, 33, 130–31, 166n17
Graham, Mac, 143n2
Grass, Günter, 148n51
Gray, Colin, 49, 63, 73–74, 154n53
Great Britain, 85
great powers
  balance of power perspective and, 25,
    26
  postwar peace and, 30–31
  see also superpowers
Green, Philip, 142n12

Habermas, Jürgen, 1, 35
Hahlweg, Werner, 151n10
Haig, Alexander, 108
Hamilton, Alexander, 85
Handel, Michael, 150n10
Harvard Nuclear Study Group, 70,
  154n61
Harvey, David, 92, 159n34, 160n34
Haussmann, Georges, 95, 160n34
Hegel, Georg Wilhelm Friedrich, 2, 53
hegemony, and International Relations,
  11–12, 134 *see also* great powers;
    superpowers
Herz, John H., 62–63, 145n22, 154n51
Hibbs, Mark, 165n11
Hintze, Otto, 9, 41–42
Hiss, Tony, 159n34
Hobbes, Thomas, 17, 84, 90, 138
Hodges, Andrew, 146n28
Hogan, Michael J., 167n30
Holly, I. B., Jr., 162n14
Holsti, K. J., 149n56
"Home front," 56–57, 58

Howard, Michael, 19, 98–99, 125, 150n10,
  153n35
"Hundred Years' Peace," 29, 148n47
Huntington, Samuel P., 99–100, 102, 103
Hussein, Saddam, 6, 28, 129

identity *see* Western cultural identity
IISS *see* International Institute for
    Strategic Studies (IISS)
Indonesia, 91
industrialization, 54–55 *see also*
    modernization
*Influence of Sea Power Upon History,
  1660–1783, The* (Mahan), 87–89
INF Treaty, 131
Institute for Strategic Studies (London),
    118
intelligence capabilities, 25–26, 116–17
interdependence model, 134
internal vs. external distinction, 21, 24
  modernization and, 97, 98–99
  see also otherness; Unity of identity
    assumption
International Institute for Strategic
    Studies (IISS), 118
International Political Economy, basic
    categories of, 3–4
International Relations (discipline)
  constructs of, in post-Cold War era,
    136–37
  end of Cold War and, 34–38, 134
  paradigms and, 11–12, 35–37, 134
  place of Strategic Studies in, 21–22, 113
  relation to philosophical traditions,
    8–12
  social theory and, 1–3, 28
  theory in, 2, 28
  "Third Debate" in, 3–4
  see also Strategic Studies
invulnerability, 60–61, 69

Jacobs, Jane, 159n34
Jay, John, 85
Jencks, C., 160n34
Jervis, Robert, 49, 60, 70, 76–77, 145n22,
  155n67, 162n12
Jolly, Richard, 143n2
Jomini, Antoine Henri, 88, 158n20
justice, 21

Kahn, Herman, 49, 63
Kaldor, Mary, 143n2, 165n9
Kant, Immanuel, 47, 48, 52, 53
Kantian epistemology, 47, 48, 52, 53
Kaplan, Fred, 155n62
Kaplan, Stephen S., 159n26
Kaufman, William, 63
Kauppi, Mark V., 149n56

Kautilya, 40
Keegan, John, 153n55, 157n13
Kegley, Charles W., Jr., 167n30
Kennan, George F., 92–93, 115, 124,
    125–27, 163n21
Kennedy, John F., 102
Keohane, Robert O., 36, 142n12, 149n56,
    149n58
key concepts
    contestability of, 20
    meaning of, 10–11, 20, 138
    as product of social forces, 22
    textual strategy and, 23
    as unexamined, 28
    see also cultural constructs; discourse
        analysis; State, the
Keynesian economics, 92
Kielinger, Thomas, 148n51
Kiernan, V. G., 158n25
Kipphardt, Heinar, 146n28
Kissinger, Henry A., 63, 108
Klare, Michael T., 148n54, 167n30
Kolodziej, Edward A., 153n45
Krass, Allan, 153n49
Krauthammer, Charles, 136, 165n7
Krippendorff, Ekkehart, 14, 144n6, 147n34
Kuhn, Thomas S., 148n55
Kull, Steven, 76, 77, 155n67

Lakatos, Imre, 148n55
Latin America, 91
Le Corbusier, 160n34
liberalism
    Janus-face of, 90–91
    link between strategy and commerce in
        US and, 83–89, 159n29
    militarization and, 81–82
    strategic violence and, 14–16, 90–105
linguistic turn, in social science, 36–37
Lipset, Seymour Martin, 157n5
Locke, John, 17, 84, 90
Lotringer, Sylvere, 160n34
Luke, Timothy W., 162n12
Lynn-Jones, Sean M., 142n12, 167n30

Machiavelli, Niccolò, 18, 42, 43–45, 46, 47,
    51, 158n23
McManus, Doyle, 123–24
McNamara, Robert S., 60, 63, 73
McNeill, William H., 147n34, 153n35
Magnusson, Warren, 167n23
Mahan, Alfred Thayer, 9, 86–89, 157n10,
    157n13, 158n20
Malcolmson, Robert W., 156n70
"man," as construct, 16–17
MAP see Military Assistance Program
    (MAP)
marginalization

of issues, 34–35
of the non-Western, 28
Marx, Karl, 96, 106
Marxist tradition, 8–9
Mattingly, Garrett, 145n17
Mearsheimer, John, 19, 33, 145n16
memorializing accounts, 28, 36
mercantilism, 46–47
mercenary armies, 45–47
metanarratives see key concepts
militarism
    bureaucratic institutions and, 46–47
    citizen-army and, 45
    economic security and, 84, 85
    mercenary armies and, 45–47
    social function of military power and,
        86–89, 101–2
    structure of the state and, 41–42
militarization
    as dimension of daily life, 15–16
    liberalism and, 81–82
    modernization and, 4, 99–105
    naturalization of, 57–58, 70
    peace research and, 13, 14–16
    role of US strategy in, 81
    technological imperative and, 21–22,
        109–10
    see also nuclear deterrence strategy
Military Assistance Program (MAP), 100,
    103
military technology
    friction and, 152n22
    refinements in, 66–67
    total war and, 54–59
    see also air power; nuclear technology
Mills, C. Wright, 129
minimal deterrence strategy, 60–63
    compared with maximalist orientation,
        78–79
    France and, 119
    maximalist critiques of, 63–74
    size of nuclear arsenal and, 62, 70–72
    targeting strategy and, 71, 72–73
"missile gap," 114, 117
modernity, 94, 106, 112
modernization
    casualties of, 14–15, 28–29, 91
    end of Cold War and, 111–12, 123
    Janus-face of liberal project and, 92–105
    militarization and, 4, 100–105
    pre-modern societies and, 28–29, 95–98
    role of the state in, 17
    stages of growth in, 95–99
Monroe Doctrine, 91
morale, 58–59
Morgenthau, Hans, 2, 42, 125
Mueller, John, 144n6
Musgrave, Alan, 148n55

"Mutual Assured Destruction," 60, 153n47

Napoleon Bonaparte, 46, 52–53, 54, 55
Napoleonic warfare, 47, 48, 49, 52–53, 57
national interest, and modern societies, 2–3
native Americans, 91, 158n25
NATO *see* Western Alliance
naval power, 85–89, 157n13
Neckermann, Peter, 148n51
Nef, John U., 147n34, 152n35
neorealism *see* structural realism
New International Economic Order, 33–34, 137
Nitze, Paul, 49, 63, 77, 124, 127
Nixon, Richard M., 102–3, 161n45
"Nixon Doctrine," 102–3
"no-first-use" principle, 60, 68
Noriega, Manuel, 6
"NSC 68:United States Objectives and Programs for National Security, April 4, 1950," 114–17, 163n21
nuclear arsenal
    purpose for, 108–9, 111–12
    size of, in minimal deterrence strategy, 62, 70–72
    systems analysis approach and, 113–18
nuclear club, 129
nuclear deterrence strategy
    Clausewitz and, 53
    extended, 78, 102
    as guarantor of peace, 21–22, 29–31
    as instrument of world order, 21–22, 29–31, 38
    maximalist orientation in, 63–74, 78, 79
    minimalist orientation in, 60–63, 77–79
    multi-dimensionality of, 156n68
    nuclear war as absolute and, 49
    philosophical dilemma of, 156n70
    power of, 5, 140
    rationality of, 21–22
    as social practice, 4, 78, 101–2, 106–9, 112
    Soviet policy under Gorbachev and, 130
    structural perspective on, 127
    synthesis of views in, 74–80
    see also militarization; minimal deterrence strategy
nuclear revolution
    Brodie's characterization of, 59–61
    claims about, 2, 76–77
    maximalist strategy and, 73–74
    minimal deterrence posture and, 61–63, 70
    rationality and, 76–77
nuclear technology
    ambivalent character of, 107
    arsenal strength and, 62, 70–72

as determinant in balance of power, 128–30
France and, 119
modernity and, 112
real vs. absolute war and, 48–49, 53, 59
Strategic Studies as product of, 21–22, 113
nuclear war-fighting strategies, 67–74, 111–12
Nye, Joseph S., Jr., 142n12, 149n56

On War (Clausewitz), 48–53
operations research, 58, 113
Oppenheimer, J. Robert, 146n28
organizing principles *see* key concepts
Orwell, George, 14, 143n5
otherness
    end of Cold War and, 132, 133
    strategic violence and, 5–6
    USSR constituted in terms of, 117, 126, 129
    see also internal vs. external distinction; unity of identity assumption
Otte, Max, 148n51

Pakistan, 103
paradigms, in International Relations, 11–12, 34–37, 134, 138–39, 148n55
Paret, Peter, 151n10
passive defenses, 68–69
patriarchy, 16–17, 137
patriotism, vs. militarism, 44–45
Payne, Keith, 73–74
peace
    as characteristic of capitalism, 83–84
    deterrence as guarantor of, 21–22, 29–31
    distinction between war and, 30–31
    Third World countries and, 30
    see also War and peace issues
"peace dividend," 33, 135
peace movements, 31, 132–33
peace research, 13, 14–16
Peloponnesian War, 42–43
Persian Gulf War, 135, 152n22
phallocentrism, 65–66, 137
Pierre, Andrew J., 143n2
Pipes, Daniel, 160n41
Pitkin, Hannah Fenichel, 145n13
pluralism, 35
Pocock, J. G. A., 145n13
"point defenses," 69
political vs. strategic realm, 22, 49–50
Polyani, Karl, 148n47, 159n29
population loss, and modernization, 14–15, 28–29, 91
post-Cold War world
    empiricist tradition and, 134

post-Cold War world (*cont.*)
  feminist perspectives and, 167n30
  realist constructs and, 2–3, 125, 136–37
  security in, 121, 133, 138–39
  the state in, 2–3, 125
  strategic practice in, 121–22, 135–36
  superpowers in, 135–36
  see also Cold War, end of
postmodernism, 134, 160n34
Postol, Theodore A., 152n22
poststructural approaches, 7, 9–11
postwar world order *see* world order
power
  brutality in achievement of, 28
  dimensions of, 11
  enabling nature of, 6–7
  nuclear articulation of, 128–30
  realist centering of, 8
  see also air power; balance of power
    politics; hegemony; sea power
public opinion
  NATO and, 120–21
  strategic practice and, 31–33, 107–8, 136

Qaddafi, Muammar, 6, 28

radical tradition, 11 *see also* Marxist
    tradition
Rapoport, Anatol, 151n10
rationality, 76–77, 97
Reagan, Ronald, 74, 108
realist tradition
  vs. Cold Warriorism, 126
  dilemma for statesmanship in, 43
  end of Cold War and, 137–38
  "epistemic realism" and, 165n10
  European, 2, 125–26
  geneology of, 42–47
  hegemony and, 11
  International Relations and, 8, 34–35,
    134
  power relations and, 8, 22
  sea power and, 87–88
  the state and, 18–22, 23
  see also empiricist tradition; states
    system; structural realism
Realpolitik, 2, 19, 43, 125 *see also* realist
    tradition
"reflectivist" approaches, 29, 36, 149n58
  see also critical theory
research institutes, 113
retaliation
  credibility of threat of, 72–73
  minimal deterrence position and, 64,
    65–66, 67–68, 69–72, 153n47
  in nuclear era, 60, 61, 62
Rickover, H. G., 108
Robbins, Keith, 153n35

Roosevelt, Theodore, 89
Rorty, Richard, 150n59
Rostow, W. W., 25, 93–99, 100, 102, 103,
    160n39
Rothfels, Hans, 151n10
Rousseau, Jean Jacques, 90
Ruggie, John Gerard, 142n12

Said, Edward, 142n13
Schlaes, Amity, 148n51
Schlesinger, James R., 106, 155n65
Schlieffen Plan, 54–55
sea power, 85–89, 157n13
second-strike capability, 70–71, 72
security
  economic power and, 84
  historicist vs. structural realist views of,
    145n22
  levels of analysis and, 20
  meaning of, 20, 30, 34, 136
  national, and modern societies, 2–3,
    138–39
  in post-Cold War era, 121, 133, 138–39
  technological promise of, 109–12
  see also continental security problem;
    invulnerability
"security dilemma," 20–22
"security partnerships," 91
Senghaas, Dieter, 129–30, 151n10
Seversky, Alexander P. de, 109–10
Shapiro, Michael J., 142n9, 147n41, 149n55
Sigal, Leon V., 119
Singer, J. David, 166n23
Sivard, Ruth Leger, 159n27
Smith, Adam, 83–84, 85
Smith, Chris, 143n2
Snow, Donald M., 143n3
social sciences, critical developments in,
    33, 34–38
social systems
  Cold War as contest among, 127
  strategic debate and, 115, 129–30
  see also communism; democracy;
    liberalism
social theory, 1–3, 28
sociological tradition, 3
Soja, Edward W., 167n23
Sorkin, Michael, 160n34
sovereignty, 6–7, 17–18 *see also* State, the
Soviet Union
  end of Cold War and, 33, 127
  Kennan's position and, 93, 126–27
  "NSC 68" characterization of, 114–17
  policy under Gorbachev in, 130–33
  superpower status of, 128–29
specific intellectual, concept of, 146n28
Spencer, Herbert, 42, 83, 150n7
Spiro, Herbert J., 163n26

Sprout, Margaret Tuttle, 157n10
State, the
  city-state to nation-state and, 39–47
  as construct, 2–3, 16–22
  domestic unity of, 24
  formation of, 18–19, 37–38
  internal vs. external order and, 21, 24
  military structure and, 41–42
  in post-Cold War world order, 2–3, 125
  postwar obsolescence of, 62–63
  realist view of, 8, 9, 18–19
  states systems and, 19–22, 40
  structure of, 24, 41
  as unit in strategic analysis, 24, 37, 40,
    136–37
  violence as constitutive of, 6–7, 37–38
  see also key concepts; sovereignty
state-building, 18–19, 112
statesmanship, 43–45
states system
  appearance of, 19–22, 23, 40, 45–47
  rationale of nuclear deterrence and,
    21–22
  universality of, 40–41
  see also world order
Stephanson, Anders, 163n21
"strategicalization," 27, 58–59, 127
strategic practice
  democratization and, 31–33
  link between commerce and, in US,
    83–89
  for Machiavelli, 44–45
  multi-dimensionality of, 156n68
  nuclear war-fighting strategies and,
    63–74, 111–12
  organizing principles of, 10
  politicization of, 111–12, 130–33
  in post-Cold War era, 121–22, 135–36
Strategic Studies (discipline)
  as component of Western world order,
    39–41, 124–25
  data on nuclear war and, 75–76
  discursive practices in, 5–6, 65–66,
    112–18, 137, 139–40
  end of Cold War and, 34–38, 132–33
  genesis of, 59, 112–13
  as historical achievement, 27, 124
  historicization of, 37–38
  neglect of social theory in, 1–2, 22, 28
  perceptions in strategic relations and,
    76–77
  relation to philosophical traditions,
    8–12
  role of violence and, 91
structuralism see critical theory
structural realism, 3, 11, 23–27, 35, 134,
  145n22
Summers, Harry G., Jr., 165n7

Sun Tzu, 40
superpowers, 128–30, 136 see also Soviet
  Union; United States
systems analysis, 113–18

targeting strategy, 71, 72–74
"technological imperative," 21–22, 109–10
terrorism, 26, 28
think tanks, 113
Third World
  concerns of Strategic Studies and, 13–14
  modernization and, 93–94, 95–105, 135
  promise of modernization and, 100, 135
  respatialization of, 133
  US military intervention and, 91, 100
Thirty Years' War, 46
Thomas, Daniel C., 148n54, 167n30
Thompson, E. P., 130
Thucydides, 19, 40, 42–43, 145n17, 150n2
Todorov, Tzvetan, 147n41
Toulmin, Stephen, 148n55
Trachtenberg, Marc, 162n7
traditional societies, and modernization,
  28–29, 95–99 see also Third World
transnational regimes, 92, 123, 134
Truman Doctrine, 101, 102
Turing, Alan, 146n28

uncertainty, 25–26, 126, 162n7
Unger, Frank, 156n2
"unipolar moment," 136
United Nations, 136
United States
  declaratory vs. action policy in, 77–78
  domestic issues in, 135
  Janus-character of foreign policy in,
    90–105
  link between strategy and trade in, 83–89
  military assistance to Third World
    states and, 91, 100–101, 102–4
  post-Cold War power of, 135–36
US Congressional Record, 91
unity of identity assumption, 115, 127–28
  see also internal vs. external
    distinction; otherness
universality of states system, 40–41
Urban design, 94–95
USSR see Soviet Union

violence
  as constitutive of states, 6–7, 37–38
  in defense of liberal order, 89–91
  domestic use of, 24
  generative nature of, 5
  inappropriate forms of, 26
  real vs. absolute war and, 48
  regulative function of, 24–25
  world order and, 14–16, 37

Viotti, Paul R., 149n56
Virilio, Paul, 153n55, 160n34
virtue, 44–45, 46

Walker, R. B. J., 5, 141n1, 145n13, 146n22,
    146n31, 149n58, 158n23, 167n23
Wallerstein, Immanuel, 35
Walt, Stephen M., 59, 142n12, 153n45
Waltz, Kenneth, 20, 23–24, 27, 42, 166n23
war
    civilians in, 56–57, 58–59
    Clausewitzian principles of, 47–54, 79
    conflicts since World War II and, 15, 30
    distinction between peace and, 30–31,
        136
    lack of finality of, 51–52
    as political, for Machiavelli, 49–50
    as protracted, 50–51, 53–54
    real vs. absolute, 47–53
    role of, in balance of power politics,
        45–47, 53
    total, 54–59
    total vs. limited, 53, 54
    twentieth-century technology and, 53–59
    see also global conflict
war and peace issues, 1, 3, 13
war-fighting capacity
    naval, 86
    nuclear strategies and, 67–74, 111–12
Warsaw Pact see Eastern alliance
Washington, George, 84
Wealth of Nations, The (Smith), 83–84
Weber, Max, 18, 24, 42, 88, 94
Weinberger, Caspar W., 155n65
Welch, David A., 162n7
Wendt, Alexander, 146n33
Western Alliance
    dominance of US in, 101
    East-West power and, 128
    "first-use" orientation and, 68
    in late 1970s, 107–8
    in late 1980s, 31–32, 131–32
    NATO strategy and, 68, 118–22
    Strategic Studies in politics of, 118, 121

unity of identity in, 115, 120–21, 127–28
    see also Continental security problem
Western cultural identity
    end of Cold War and, 132, 133
    NATO strength and, 120
    nuclear strategy as constitutive of,
        107–8, 112
    presumption of unity of, 115, 127–28
    Strategic Studies and, 28, 39–41
    superiority of modern over traditional
        societies and, 95–98
    violence as constitutive of, 37–38, 97–98
Westphalia, Peace of, 45, 46
Williams, Michael C., 156n70
Williams, William Appelman, 157n5
Wilson, Woodrow, 89–90, 92
Wittkopf, Eugene R., 167n30
Wohlstetter, Albert, 63, 66, 71, 114, 154n62,
        163n15
Wolf, Eric, 15
Wolin, Sheldon, 144n13, 158n23
world order
    analytical approaches and, 4–5
    capitalism and, 83–84
    deterrence as guarantor of peace in,
        21–22
    end of Cold War and, 31–34
    liberal tradition and, 83–84
    master narrative of, 28
    modernist project in, 92–106
    obsolescence of the state in, 62–63
    peace in, and great powers, 30–31
    Strategic Studies as component of,
        124–25
    strategic violence and, 14–16, 25, 28–29
    see also Liberalism; Post-Cold War
        world; States system
world state, 21, 140
world systems theory, 35
World War I, 54–56
Wright, Robin, 123–24
Wulf, Herbert, 143n2

Yugoslavia, 33, 132

18 JOHN STOPFORD and SUSAN STRANGE
Rival states, rival firms
Competition for world market shares

17 TERRY NARDIN and DAVID R. MAPEL (eds.)
Traditions of international ethics

16 CHARLES F. DORAN
Systems in crisis
New imperatives of high politics at century's end

15 DEON GELDENHUYS
Isolated states: a comparative analysis

14 KALEVI J. HOLSTI
Peace and war: armed conflicts and international order 1648–1989

13 SAKI DOCKRILL
Britain's policy for West German rearmament 1950–1955

12 ROBERT J. JACKSON
Quasi-states: sovereignty, international relations and the Third World

11 JAMES BARBER and JOHN BARRATT
South Africa's foreign policy
The search for status and security 1945–1988

10 JAMES MAYALL
Nationalism and international society

9 WILLIAM BLOOM
Personal identity, national identity and international relations

8 ZEEV MAOZ
National choices and international processes

7 IAN CLARK
The hierarchy of states
Reform and resistance in the international order

6 HIDEMI SUGANAMI
The domestic analogy and world order proposals

5 STEPHEN GILL
American hegemony and the Trilateral Commission

4 MICHAEL C. PUGH
The ANZUS crisis, nuclear visiting and deterrence

3 MICHAEL NICHOLSON
Formal theories in international relations

2 FRIEDRICH V. KRATOCHWIL
   Rules, norms, and decisions
   On the conditions of practical and legal reasoning in international relations and domestic affairs

1 MYLES L. C. ROBERTSON
   Soviet policy towards Japan
   An analysis of trends in the 1970s and 1980s